THE LANGUAGE OF 1984

W. F. Bolton

THE LANGUAGE OF 1984

Orwell's English and Ours

The University of Tennessee Press
Knoxville

Published in the United States of America in 1984 by
The University of Tennessee Press, Knoxville 37996–0325

Typset by Inforum Ltd, Portsmouth

Library of Congress Cataloging in Publication Data

Bolton, W. F. (Whitney French), 1930–
    The language of 1984.

    Bibliography: p.
    Includes index.
    1. Orwell, George, 1903–1950—Language.
2. English language—20th century.   I. Title.
PR6029.R8Z588   1984   823′.912   83–21671

ISBN 0–87049–412–0

Printed in Great Britain by
Billing and Sons Ltd, Worcester

Contents

ඕඕඕඕඕඕ

Abbreviations

◈◈◈◈◈◈

Works of Orwell:

AF *Animal Farm* by George Orwell, copyright 1946 by Harcourt
    Brace Jovanovich Inc.; renewed 1974 by Sonia Orwell.
    Reprinted by permission of the publisher.

BD *Burmese Days*, copyright 1934 by George Orwell; renewed
    1962 by Sonia Pitt Rivers. Reprinted by permission of
    Harcourt Brace Jovanovich Inc.

CA *Coming Up For Air* by George Orwell, reprinted by
    permission of Harcourt Brace Jovanovich Inc.

CD *A Clergyman's Daughter* by George Orwell, reprinted by
    permission of Harcourt Brace Jovanovich Inc.

CE *The Collected Essays, Journalism and Letters of George
    Orwell, Volume 4*, copyright © 1968 by Sonia Brownell
    Orwell. Reprinted by permission of Harcourt Brace
    Jovanovich Inc.

HC *Homage to Catalonia* by George Orwell, copyright 1952 by
    Sonia Brownell Orwell. Reprinted by permission of Harcourt
    Brace Jovanovich Inc.

KA *Keep the Aspidistra Flying* by George Orwell, reprinted by
    permission of Harcourt Brace Jovanovich Inc.

NE *Nineteen Eighty-Four* by George Orwell, copyright 1949 by
    Harcourt Brace Jovanovich Inc.; renewed 1977 by Sonia
    Brownell Orwell. Reprinted by permission of the publisher.

PL *Down and Out in Paris and London*, copyright 1933 by
    George Orwell; renewed 1961 by Sonia Pitt Rivers.
    Reprinted by permission of Harcourt Brace Jovanovich Inc.

RW *The Road to Wigan Pier* by George Orwell, reprinted by
    permission of Harcourt Brace Jovanovich Inc.

Other Works:

DAE   *A Dictionary of American English on Historical Principles*,
ed. William Craigie and James R. Hulbert. 4 vols. Chicago:
University of Chicago Press, 1936 – 44.

HL   'The English Language: Deterioration in Usage', House of
Lords Debate 21 November 1979. *The Parliamentary
Debates*, Lords vol. 403, columns 124 – 96.

OED   *The Oxford English Dictionary*, ed. James A. H. Murray et
al. 11 vols. Clarendon Press, 1888 – 1933; Supplements
1972 – 82.

RCD   *The Random House College Dictionary*, ed. Laurence
Urdang and Stuart Berg Flexner. New York: Random
House, 1968.

SPE   Society for Pure English *Tracts* 1 – 66. Oxford: Clarendon
Press, 1919 – 48.

* marks an unattested word, either unrecorded or ungrammatical

Phonetic Symbols

🔒🔒🔒🔒🔒🔒

The following letters are used as phonetic symbols with their usual
English values: p, b, t, d, k, g, f, v, s, z, h, l, r, m, n, w. Other
symbols are used with the values indicated by the italicized letters in
the keywords which follow:

CONSONANTS

ʃ	*sh*ip		θ	*th*in
ʒ	plea*s*ure		ð	*th*en
tʃ	*ch*in		j	*y*es
dʒ	*j*u*dg*e		ç	German i*ch*
η	si*ng*			

VOWELS

i	s*i*t		ɑ:	f*a*ther
i:	s*ee*		ɔ	h*o*t
e	g*e*t		ɔ:	s*aw*
a	f*a*t		u	p*u*t
ə	fath*er*		u:	s*oo*n
ə:	b*ir*d		ʌ	b*u*t

DIPHTHONGS

ei	d*ay*		ɔi	b*oy*
ou	g*o*		iə	h*ere*
ai	f*ly*		ɛə	th*ere*
au	n*ow*		uə	g*ou*rd

Square brackets are used to enclose phonetic symbols. A colon after a
phonetic symbol indicates length.

Preface

〰〰〰〰〰〰

THIS BOOK focuses on changes in the English language since the Second World War, the English of the last generation. It takes account of changes in the vocabulary, forms, and pronunciation of English. It also looks at changes in attitudes towards the language, changes in its study, teaching, and even legislation and litigation about English.

The subject is much too large for any one book. No author could write it and no reader would read it. So this book limits its field by taking George Orwell as its starting point, concentrating on changes in English and the attitudes towards it as they diverge from his. In consequence the book has a double perspective: a telephoto close-up that studies Orwell's English in detail across the thirty-four years since his death, and a wide-angle panorama of English today in which he occupies the middle distance. The book, to continue the optical comparison, zooms from one perspective on its subject to the other. I found that the extensive literature about Orwell contained little of substance about his language theory and practice, so I had to clarify that subject before I could use it as the framework for a discussion of changes in English. The outcome is a book that sets out both a view of Orwell and a view of our present-day language.

The standpoint of this double perspective is, however, single: that of a linguist in 1984. My opinions about language result in part from my observation, but even more from the last thirty years of research and teaching about language. They hold, to summarize too briefly, that language is a process 'close to the essence of human thought';[1] that variety is the salient attribute of language; and that mistaken notions about variety commonly deform thoughts, words and deeds about language.

For those reasons, this book does not seek to continue Eric Partridge and John W. Clark's *British and American English since 1900* (1951), though it takes up the story almost exactly where they left off, and readers of their book will have a useful starting point for reading this one. Partridge and Clark concentrated more than I do on the forms of the language, and less on views about it. And they surveyed a language that had been little subject to the courts and Congress. This book also does not inquire whether Orwell's predictions about language have come true now that 1984 is here. Chapter Five includes the argument that Orwell did not intend *Nineteen Eighty-Four* as a prophecy. It is worth noting, as Orwell liked to say, that Nigel Calder's prophetic *The World in 1984* (1965) had sections on practically everything, including computers, but Calder did not feel that '1984' called for a prediction about language.

The year 1984 does bring, however, more admiring books and articles about Orwell. His admirers may be disappointed in this book for what they see as its unsympathetic view of him. But Orwell's achievement, I believe, was that of a social critic and a man of letters. He is not well-served, or best understood, by admiration of him as a prophet, a linguistic sage, an abstract thinker, or a tragic hero. On that score I may be allowed an autobiographical note. I am a child of 'the age of Orwell'; Orwell died during my second college year. When I began teaching a few years later, I assigned his essay 'Politics and the English Language' to my freshman composition students. The difficulty the students had with the essay, I supposed, resulted from my inexperience. Now less inexperienced, I have come to believe that the difficulty resulted from my inappropriate choice of the essay for freshmen, and my inappropriate approach to it. As Chapter Seven argues, the right students are more advanced, and the right approach takes a critical view of the essay's intellectual sources, Orwell's other writing, and our present knowledge about the subjects he treats.

That is the approach I attempt in this book. I have taken account of all Orwell's available writing: not simply the 'Politics' essay and *Nineteen Eighty-Four*, but also his books of fiction and non-fiction, his journalism and essays, and his letters. Not all the journalism has been collected, not all the letters survive, and not all those that do have been published. To rely on the books and on *The Collected Essays, Journalism and Letters* is almost certainly to overlook some of the uncollected or unpublished things he wrote about language, because he returned to the topic so often. But the books and the collection are enough to show the range of language topics he touched on and how he viewed them, and material from outside the books would probably not greatly alter our notions of the topics or the views.[2]

Preface

I have not tried to take account of everything that has been written about Orwell, and in any event I was not able to consult anything that appeared after the end of 1982. I have limited my references to studies that bear directly on the topics in hand, and especially those that are easily accessible. Where an article has been reprinted, I refer to the reprinted version. My references to language studies are chiefly to those that are recent and non-technical. The subject is too large to pursue in the monographs and scholarly journals that proliferate, and it is so central to modern thinking in many fields that research quickly trickles down to easily-accessible sources such as college textbooks, *Scientific American*, and even weekly news magazines and daily newspapers. They are useful starting-points for their subjects, and most contain further references. By referring to them whenever possible, I mean to show that an informed outlook on language is available to any open-minded reader; a polyglot background or esoteric education is not prerequisite.

I have referred often to the *Random House College Dictionary* to exemplify sound, non-specialist treatment of present-day vocabulary; to the *Guardian* to exemplify current educated journalistic prose; and, in Chapter Seven, to the 1979 House of Lords debate on 'The English Language: Deterioration in Usage' to exemplify recent language watchers' worries and reactions. I have also referred frequently to the *Tracts* of the Society for Pure English that appeared from 1919 to 1948, almost exactly coterminous with Orwell's adult life. They are, though not now at all up to date, examples of the easily-accessible, non-technical sources available to him. They deal with many of the same subjects that he dealt with, so they illustrate how central these concerns were to his time and place. He may well have known about them, and it seems that he even drew on one or two of them freely and without acknowledgment.

That is my cue to acknowledge gratefully those who have given me support and advice during my study, though none is responsible for the facts I have assembled or what I have made of them: The Rockefeller Foundation, for a Humanities Fellowship during the year 1982; Rutgers University, for support and habitation concurrent with the Rockefeller Fellowship; Dr Robert G. Cameron, Executive Director, Research and Development, The College Board; Professor David Crystal, Department of Linguistic Science, University of Reading; James W. Lindsay, former Senior English Master, Swanage Grammar School, Dorset; Professor William Lutz, Editor, *Quarterly Review of Doublespeak*; David McNeill, former New York correspondent, BBC Radio; Peter Phillips, Deputy Headmaster, Dynevor Comprehensive School, Swansea (formerly Head of English, Don Valley High School, Doncaster); Professor Randolph Quirk, Vice-Chancellor, University of London; Michael Smart, Assistant Secretary, Department of Employment; and my family, three generations of women *sine quibus non*.

W.F.B.
New Brunswick, New Jersey
January, 1983

CHAPTER I

Theory of Language

𒀸𒀸𒀸𒀸𒀸𒀸

LANGUAGE stood in the foreground of George Orwell's mindscape. Though he called for social change, he felt keen nostalgia for the age he saw vanishing, and he felt change in language most keenly of all. Oppressed by the guilt he felt for his complicity in the British class system and the British Empire, he charted the barriers that dialect and language difference erected. In his literary criticism he made language a touchstone for good writing and for bad. He thought that literacy and the electronic media with their political and commercial blandishments threatened the subjugation, not the liberation, of the human mind.

Orwell's views of language permeate his writing from the earliest work onwards, but *Nineteen Eighty-Four* (1949) and the essay 'Politics and the English Language' (1946) characterize his outlook for most readers. Many who have never read him know the terminology of *Nineteen Eighty-Four*: 'doublethink' appears in college dictionaries for those who have not read Orwell's definition in the novel; 'Newspeak' became a dysphemism for utterances, notably in politics and advertising, much as 'fascism' had become a dysphemism for political systems (as Orwell observed). Though it is not Orwell's word, 'doublespeak' is transparently derived from 'doublethink' and 'Newspeak' (with assistance from 'doubletalk'); and a *Dictionary*, and a *Quarterly Review*, of *Doublespeak* have appeared.[1] The title of Orwell's last book has become a label for tyrannical invasion of privacy, just as 'Orwellian' (usually as an adjective modifying 'nightmare') has become shorthand for ruthless oppression. But the celebrity of his fictional future language should not conceal the range and complexity of the views on real and present language that he expressed elsewhere.

When he died, aged forty-six, from tuberculosis in 1950, Orwell had achieved international recognition: *Animal Farm* (1945) had been a critical and commercial success, resulting in the 1946 publication of his *Critical Essays*; and *Nineteen Eighty-Four* had been a Book-of-the-Month choice, reviewed in hundreds of journals from the *New Statesman* to *Life*. Orwell's literary reputation, and perhaps his early death, gave his linguistic views a currency they might not have had in other circumstances. 'Politics and the English Language' became a favourite text in American freshman English courses, and was anthologized in many freshman readers and 'taught' in hundreds of classrooms.

But the 'Politics' essay and *Nineteen Eighty-Four* did not simply gather lustre from Orwell's literary fame. Their influence came also from the activist political context in which he had set his linguistic views. Orwell's politics, which he described as 'democratic Social-ist', were never party-line. His political views were widely compat-ible because they were broadly anti-totalitarian. He hated all dogma, political included, preferring to see things as they were and to weigh them accordingly: Rosenfeld summarizes the usual view that 'Orwell was fair, honest, unassuming and reliable in everything he wrote'.[2] But things as they were, and as he saw them, changed, as things and views do; so Orwell was not only independent but somewhat incon-sistent. This is not a book about Orwell's politics as such, but his theory that language is a political force gives his politics a place here just the same. His political stance made him congenial to all but the most blimpish right and the most bolshevik left. Orwell, like the Dickens he wrote about, became 'one of those writers who are well worth stealing'. D.A.N. Jones poses, among his 'Arguments against Orwell', the fact that 'such writers as Robert Conquest and Kingsley Amis, who think themselves to be anti-Communists of Orwell's kind, . . . keenly support the American war . . . in Vietnam,' while at the same time 'two American leftists, Noam Chomsky and Nor-man Mailer, felt able to cite Orwell in support of their own position as opponents of their government's war policy.' Jones concludes, 'It seems that people of almost any political persuasion can find some of their beliefs expressed in Orwell's work, very eloquently.'[3] No one except a few zealots would want to defend what Orwell attacked, and as the particulars of the scene he observed – Sir Stafford Cripps, Konni Zilliacus, and the rest – fade into historical distance, the generalities become even more congenial.

His linguistic views were part of that booty, adopted and repeated by many who could agree on little else. So Orwell is a favourite linguistic authority for politically conservative writers like Lincoln Barnett, who cited *Nineteen Eighty-Four* and quoted the 'Politics' essay with approval. At the same time he has the support of a political liberal like Arthur Schlesinger Jr, for whom 'the control of language is a necessary step toward the control of minds, as Orwell made so brilliantly clear in *1984*.'[4] The vitality of Orwell's linguistic influence, then, has come not only from his wide literary influence, but from his broad political valence and the strong though vague connection between politics and language that he proclaimed.

Orwell's language opinions were influential also because he expressed them much as he expressed his widely compatible political views, in broad generalizations, even exaggerations. Though he complained of others' 'sweeping statements' (e.g., Chesterton's, CE 3.97), critics often note the habit in him: Stuart Hampshire writes of Orwell's 'aggressive exaggeration' and 'ferocious over-statements'. Ringbom characterizes Orwell's essay style as 'assertive, categorical, generalizing'.[5] Orwell's unqualified 'Now, it is clear that the decline of a language must ultimately have political and economic causes' (CE 4.127) is such a statement, one so general that despite his emphatic 'clear' and 'must' it can encompass most viewpoints because it avoids the specifics that might exclude many.

This feature of Orwell's political writing gave his prose a forcefulness and inclusiveness that made him influential. But it also led to superficiality. Orwell's friend, the writer George Woodcock, held that 'these virtues of economy, clarity, fluency, descriptive vividness, are all *superficial* virtues. They do not make up for a lack of deeper understanding,' and he said that while 'occasional articles', including the essay on political language, 'are small masterpieces in a limited field', 'bounded fragments of observation', beyond them Orwell never got under the surface of the problems he treated. For some critics the same faults were true even of the political language essay: Christopher Sykes thought that it contained 'some over-stated views', and Hugh Rank said that its 'massive over-generalizations' appear 'without any supporting data or examples'.[6] Orwell's title and many of his remarks purported to deal with the language as a whole – spoken and written, receptive and expressive. But his real concern was only with political writing and the standard variety of English that is its usual medium; and even there he never proved the case for the causal relationship that was his premise.

'Politics and the English Language', however, and *Nineteen Eighty-Four*, by no means contain all that Orwell said about language. In 1930 he wrote of Edith Sitwell that her 'English is queer and, one must add, precious, but there is a charm in her love of sonorous words for their own sake.' Here, almost twenty years before he wrote *Nineteen Eighty-Four*, Orwell already took language to be a touchstone; if a writer's style was 'queer' and 'precious,' if it had 'a charm' in its 'sonorous words', the reviewer had to say so – and the meaning of his terms would be self-evident. In the twenty years between that review and the end of his life, Orwell never left the subject of language, so our sources for understanding his language views lie in everything he wrote.

Some of these sources, like the remark on Sitwell, are phrases scattered among his writings on other subjects. For much of his writing career Orwell kept to his early habit of revising everything, often three or four times; but during the years when he tried to make a living as a journalist ('columnist' would be closer to the facts) he found, as he ruefully admitted, that he was publishing unrevised pieces (e.g., CE 2.350; cf. 4.149).[7] The scattered remarks about language from this time, even when they balloon into paragraphs, are sometimes heedlessly expressed. In many of them Orwell said things he probably would not have cared to defend after further reflection. Taken together, however, these remarks add up to a fair statement of his outlook on language. Often they are the only source for his views on a particular topic: almost all we know about his views of American English, for example, is in the sum of such scraps.

The longer essays are a different matter. In them he took a position and developed it. 'Politics and the English Language' is the best known, but far from the only one he wrote on language. 'New Words' (1940?) is typical of these pieces, not only for its fine Orwellian inclusiveness – 'Everyone who thinks at all has noticed that our language is practically useless for describing anything that goes on inside the brain' (CE 2.3) – but for its combination of old-fashioned notions about the 'true meaning' of words with its new-fangled interest in the connection between language and mind and the advantages of modern technology for exploring it. Orwell's pamphlet 'The English People', written in 1944 but not published until 1947, includes a long section on the English language, again with some splendid generalizations – 'The temporary decadence of the English language is due, like so much else, to our anachronistic class system' (CE 3.27) – but also with some passages that look forward to 'Politics and the English Language' (1946). The tardy publication of 'The English People' made these passages look back on the 'Politics' essay, and may be one reason why Orwell re-used the 1944 material in 1946.

Orwell's language concerns continued to surface in his 'As I

Please' columns from 1944 onwards, and in more substantial essays like 'Propaganda and Demotic Speech' (1944). But his books, too, reflected these concerns. *Down and Out in Paris and London* (1933) embodies much of the material from early essays like 'The Spike', 'Clink', and 'Common Lodging Houses' (1931–2) and enlarges on Orwell's experience of lower-class varieties of English, especially the transient slang of tramps and beggars. *Burmese Days* (1934) looks further back to his tour as an officer in the Indian Imperial Police (1922–7), but through the perspective of fiction. The Burma of Orwell's novel is a multilingual country where class and language boundaries coincide – where, for example, a Burmese butler is rebuked for learning his English too well, and English women find it best to learn nothing more than 'kitchen Urdu'. Not only the dialogue but the narrative of *Burmese Days* is studded with words from oriental languages, some of them already wholly within the English vocabulary, some on the margins, some far outside. Rosenfeld found 'the pidgin and official English were all excellently reported'.[8]

A Clergyman's Daughter (1935) is a novel that returns to some of the scenes of *Down and Out*, and to some of its themes: in the central episode, a play-like dialogue among tramps and beggars passing the night in Trafalgar Square, the speech of the lower-class Londoners distinguishes them from the title character, the Irish whore, and the fallen clergyman among them. *A Clergyman's Daughter*, also like *Down and Out*, embodies Orwell's early autobiographical essays, especially 'Hop-Picking' (1931), and his growing interest in non-standard varieties of English. And, like *Down and Out* too, this book explores the interest more fully than did its essay origins. *Keep the Aspidistra Flying* (1936), on the other hand, perhaps because it surveys a narrower range of English society, or maybe because Orwell's early interest in language variety had run its course in the three previous books, is more sporadic in linguistic commentary. But when Orwell undertook the assignment that resulted in *The Road to Wigan Pier* (1937), he returned to his old interest. The journals show his awareness of the new (to him) language patterns he found in Yorkshire and Lancashire, and the book expands on it, not only with examples unrecorded in the journals but with theories based on the examples. Here Orwell's linguistic summing-up provides the culmination of his book.

The next three books spanned seven years: *Homage to Catalonia* (1938), Orwell's account of his months in Spain during the Civil

War; *Coming Up for Air* (1939), a novel of the transition of a man from boyhood to middle age and of England from before the First World War to the eve of the Second; and *Animal Farm* (1945), the book that brought Orwell international literary recognition. His reaction to geographical language variety marks the first, to class and chronological variety the second (the third, with its talking animals, scarcely counts as a piece of linguistic observation). But his language commentary during this period was mostly in the essays and journalism, and if we had to depend on these three books as sources for Orwell's ideas about language, we would have a thin time of it. Though Atkins maintained that 'In later life Orwell spent more care and hard thinking on the English language and its possible developments than on any other single subject,'[9] only the later *Nineteen Eighty-Four*, and Newspeak, give his books of 1938–45 some retrospective linguistic interest.

What was the background to Orwell's linguistic observation and commentary? Hodgart reckoned him 'an amateur philologist of genius', but Angus Wilson thought that 'The description of a working-class family in the essay "North and South", like the speech of the workers in *1984*, belongs to the music hall of the nineties' – not even to the musical *My Fair Lady*, it seems.[10] Orwell himself tallied 'In my life I have learned seven foreign languages, including two dead ones, and out of those seven I retain only one, and that not brilliantly' (CE 3.86); not the boast of a Professor Higgins or of the Henry Sweet on whom Shaw based the character, author of *The Practical Study of Languages* (1900). Hodgart's description of Orwell shows that he shares Orwell's linguistic ideas, but it does not prove that those ideas were especially sound.

The seven foreign languages that Orwell learned were the Latin and Greek that he studied in school; the French that he studied and later used when he lived in Paris; the colloquial Hindustani, Burmese and Urdu he learned during his tour of duty in the orient; and Spanish. He worked hard at the classical languages, or was made to work hard, having started Latin at the age of eight and Greek at ten (CE 4.336); but he later acknowledged his ignorance of Latin (CE 2.7), and held 'You forget your Latin and Greek within a few months of leaving school – I studied Greek for eight or ten years, and now, at thirty-three, I cannot even repeat the Greek alpahbet' (RW 137).[11]

Apparently Orwell's French stood him in better stead. His mother's family was French, and his aunt lived in Paris where he stayed with her on the brink of his 'down and out' experience in 1928 (her lover was a Frenchman who taught Esperanto). He studied French at Eton, for a time under Aldous Huxley. Orwell had already excelled at French, as well as Greek and Latin, in the examination he took on entering the Indian Imperial Police in 1922. He later said, however, that he had gone to Paris in part 'to learn French' (CE 1.113). In any event he taught English in Paris (PL 16), as he made a fictional expatriate do in *Burmese Days* (BD 91); he owned a copy of Villon in the original (PL 120); and he offered his services as a translator from French when back in England, laying some claim to knowledge both of the older language and of contemporary slang (CE 1.72, 78). At the same time he offered to do translations from Spanish, and of course he heard and used Spanish during his six months in Spain in late 1936 and early 1937. Yet French appears to be the language that he retained 'not brilliantly'. He admits to 'bad Urdu' and 'bad Spanish' (PL 168; HC 3, 11), and gives no account at all of his using Hindustani and Burmese, though these languages came easily to him when he had to study them in the Police Training School at Mandalay in 1922.[12] These seven languages, even if he had retained lasting mastery of them all, would not have made him a descriptive linguist, only a polyglot; but it does not appear he was even that.

For his studies in his own language, the evidence is even slighter: the hero of *Coming Up for Air* recalls schooldays with the English master's 'voice grating away about predicates and subjunctives and relative clauses' (CA 84), but that is not a very singular memory for someone born just before 1900, like the hero, or just after, like Orwell. As we shall see in the next two chapters, Orwell was alert to linguistic diversity in space and time (dialects and language change), but his background in such specialist matters was not very thorough – not, for example, anything like what he would have learned reading English at a British university in the early 1920s, much less what he would learn doing so now. Even the celebrated 'Appendix' on Newspeak in *Nineteen Eighty-Four*, though it uses some technical terms of linguistic description, uses none that the intended non-specialist reader would fail to grasp; and, after all, Newspeak is an imaginary language.

Orwell knew no more about language, then, than the average Briton of his time and class might have known, and perhaps a trifle less. He did not have a university education, but he had experience of several languages and he read widely. He did not boast about his linguistic knowledge, yet he appears to have been quite confident in his linguistic opinions; and that, too, was about average for a person of his age and background.

The *Tracts* of the Society for Pure English (1919–48) show how common Orwell's language concerns were for his time, place, and class. The first *Tract*, mostly a reprint of the 1913 Prospectus, set out the Society's general position:

> . . . the English language, which is now rapidly spreading over the world, is subject to no . . . guidance, and to very little intelligent criticism . . . .
>
> The promoters of this association . . . are of course well aware of the danger of affectation, which constitutes the chief objection to any conscious reform of language . . . .
>
> [The association] would aim at preserving all the richness of differentiation in our vocabulary, its nice grammatical usages, its traditional idioms, and the music of its inherited pronunciation: it would oppose whatever is slipshod and careless, and all blurring of hard-won distinctions, but it would no less oppose the tyranny of school-masters and grammarians, both in their pedantic conservatism, and in their ignorant enforcing of newfangled 'rules', based not on principle, but merely on what has come to be considered 'correct' usage . . . .
>
> The Society, therefore, will place itself in opposition to certain tendencies of modern taste; which taste it hopes gradually to modify and improve.
> (pp. 5–7)

Not only the general outlook but also the particulars of the manifesto coincide with Orwell's chief concerns: words borrowed from foreign languages, and especially their pronunciation in English; the creation of new words from English resources to meet new intellectual needs; the contribution of the working classes to English vocabulary; the preservation of 'the forms and uses of local speech'; the 'slurred and indistinct way of speaking which is now regarded as correct English'. *Tract* 21 (1925) reviewed 'The Society's Work' in English as the language spread 'all over the world', and restated the question 'Is Reform Feasible?' The members of the Society, and especially the contributors to the *Tracts*, were mostly the kinds of people Orwell avoided: academics, literati, Americans. Even so, as the notes to the following pages will show, the *Tracts* often paralleled his thinking on language, the subject where his views were least independent of his upbringing. In some cases the parallel is so close that the easily-available *Tracts* may have provided the source of his remarks. More often, however, the *Tracts* contain information that

Orwell, to his cost, lacked when he wrote. In any event, the *Tracts* exemplify the lay discussion of English during the years of Orwell's writing.

On a few topics, however, Orwell was not average. These are not the topics for which he has gained his linguistic reputation, and his views on them would not gain him a reputation today. But he was unusual for a practising man of letters then, as he would be now, in holding views on them at all. They are the relation of speech to writing; the relation of expression to understanding (or reception); the relation of utterance to thought; and the relation of linguistic form to linguistic meaning. He discussed other matters at greater length, and his views on these topics sometimes remain only as the unexpressed assumptions of those discussions. But his scanty background in even those linguistic matters that his academic contemporaries studied makes it likely that his views on such more recondite subjects were entirely independent. He was not, after all, an 'amateur philologist of genius', but he had the instincts for psycholinguistics.

In *Burmese Days*, hero Flory's Burman servant, Ko S'la, wakes his English master:

'Will the holy one play *tinnis* this evening?' Ko S'la asked.
'No, it's too hot,' said Flory in English . . . .
Ko S'la understood English very well, though he could not speak it.
(BD 51)

The difference between the servant's receptive competence and his expressive performance is a familiar one: even in our own language we are aware of words we recognize but do not use, words in our passive but not our active vocabulary. And in a second language our grasp of what we hear or read extends beyond vocabulary to tenses, numbers, genders, and whole structures that we would not know how to form. Orwell's observation, which may stem from his own experience, is therefore one we can share even if we don't travel to Burma. Orwell may be exaggerating the observation here, for Ko S'la's remarks are meant to be in Burmese: to understand another language 'very well' if you cannot speak it at all is an unusually large gap between what you can grasp and what you can say, especially if the foreign-language speaker uses colloquial forms and natural speed (see Chapter Four). But if Orwell exaggerated the gap, we are at risk of underestimating it. We can recognize it in a passage like this but then overlook it entirely when, for example, discussing language skills in schoolchildren, evaluating the language they know by the language they use or equating their comprehension with their expression.

It would be a similar oversight to confuse speech and writing simply because both are 'language'. In a 1938 letter to the working-class writer Jack Common, Orwell said:

> The thing is that all of us talk & write two different languages, & when a man from, say, Scotland or even Yorkshire writes in standard English he's writing something quite as different from his own tongue as Spanish is from Italian. I think the first real prole novel that comes along will be spoken over the radio.
> (CE 1.314; cf. 212, 497)

He had no use for 'futile' slogans and speeches that fail 'to notice that spoken and written English are two different things', insisting that the 'variation exists in all languages, but it is probably greater in English than in most' (CE 3.136–7). By the end of 1940 Orwell had a somewhat different view of the outlook for proletarian literature: 'It's a fact that written English is much more colloquial now than it was twenty years ago, and that's all to the good. But we've borrowed much more from America than from the speech of the English working class' (CE 2.40). Orwell had extended his observation to an evaluation: if speaking and writing, the two 'channels' of language, are not the same, then one of them must be better than the other. He rejected, characteristically, the conventional view that written language is the standard to which spoken language must conform; but he accepted the conventional idea that a choice was necessary.

Yet how valid is that idea? We can say 'I was waiting for a bus' but we would only write 'Not wishing to be left alone, I rode in the bus.' Our 'waiting' and 'wishing' are equally good English, but these days 'Not' + '-ing' usually begin written sentences only. The difference is between two forms that language can take, not between a better form and a worse. The difference can blur a bit when the speech is read from a written page, at its worst when a television announcer stares at the camera and says, 'Be with us tonight as x and his band are joined by y and z in a gala extravaganza of fun-filled [etc.].' Whether or not that is good writing, it is simply not speech. We can say 'Be nice' or 'Get with it' but 'Be with us' belongs only to writing, as does most of the rest of that example. Even more specialized examples include the noun phrase that stands alone before its sentence, either the subject ('Miller Lite – it's all the beer you ever wanted') or object ('Your

Buick dealer – see him today'). Both forms emphasize the noun phrase, usually a brand name, in a structure limited to writing that is read aloud.

Orwell appears to have grasped part of the distinction. He joined the two 'directions' of expression and reception with the two 'channels' of speech and writing to give, at least by implication, four areas of language:

	SPOKEN	WRITTEN
EXPRESSIVE	speaking	writing
RECEPTIVE	listening	reading

But if speech and writing are both language but different, then what is language? Something, it appears, common to speech and writing but not wholly embodied in either; otherwise speech and writing would not be different. The physical sounds of speech can be represented, like any other sounds, on an oscilloscope – that way they have a physical reality on a par with the letters of writing, even though the two physical realities look extremely dissimilar. Whatever is 'language' about them, however, is not in either of those physical realities but in something else: the mind. Expression and reception can be so different that Ko S'la understood English 'very well' but did not speak it. The chart maps the surface of language behaviours but not the underlying mental ability that makes all four of them possible.

The hero of *Nineteen Eighty-Four*, in a stressful moment,

> seemed even to have been deprived of the power of speech. His tongue worked soundlessly, forming the opening syllables first of one word, then of the other, over and over again. Until he had said it, he did not know which word he was going to say.
> (NE 143)

In the Appendix, Orwell gave as the aim of Newspeak 'to make articulate speech issue from the larynx without involving the higher brain centres at all' (NE 254; cf. 48), a remark that goes back to 'Politics and the English Language': 'The appropriate noises are coming out of his larynx, but his brain is not involved as it would be if he were choosing his words for himself . . . . And this reduced state of consciousness, if not indispensable, is at any rate favourable to political conformity' (CE 4.136). Orwell hedged a bit on the theory that underlies these passages; he says in the Appendix that Newspeak was intended to make politically divergent thought 'literally unthinkable, at least so far as thought is dependent on words' (NE 246). Orwell believed that Newspeak could erase the concept 'science' by deleting the word from its dictionary (NE 159, 254); but the Burmese girl says ' "At least touch me with your lips, then.["] (There is no Burmese word for to kiss)' (BD 52–3) and gets what she asks for. The episode, however, is an exception to Orwell's general belief that though thought depends so much on words that words can control thought, words are so independent of thought that they can occur without it.

We all have moments in which we speak heedlessly, and we call these moments 'thoughtless'. By that we mean that we were socially inconsiderate or not speaking deliberately. Orwell, however, seems to have meant that, at least theoretically, language could take place without brain activity, but brain activity could be nothing more than language made it. And he seems to have meant more by 'brain activity' than conscious choice of words: he speaks of 'the higher brain centres' in their entirety.[13]

Orwell was not alone in taking this 'one-way street' view of the relationship of speech to language. The American linguist Benjamin Lee Whorf, for example, had an influential theory that we cannot form concepts for which our native language makes no provision. More recent studies, however, suggest that a shared human language ability conditions common underlying language structures in speakers of all languages. The differences among those languages are relatively superficial, then, and unlikely to influence basic mental abilities such as concept formation.

Experiment and writing in this field is both technical and speculative, but it has become so central to language study (almost entirely in the years since Orwell's death) that it cannot be left out of our account. The simple and self-evident two by two table illustrates one of the findings: language is an abstraction that underlies speech and writing, expression and reception; none of the four 'is' language, but language makes them all possible. The abstraction or ability we call language that all four have in common, must reside in the mind. On that assumption we can imagine language without speech or writing, but not speech or writing without language. Of course language informs thought and thought supports language, but it simply does not seem that speech could continue with the larynx cut off from the higher brain centres, or that thoughts depend on specific words to any large extent.[14]

When Orwell turned his attention to the meaning of words, it was usually to changes in their meaning: 'ought one to acquiesce when certain words have their meanings arbitrarily narrowed?' (CE 3.325, 1945). But in 'New Words' (1940?) he tackled the problem of meaning head on, and he did so in two characteristic connections: technical change and language change, and the relation between vocabulary and thought.[15] Orwell's general premise, already quoted earlier in this chapter, was that 'our language is practically useless for describing anything that goes on inside the brain', but that 'it would be quite feasible to invent a vocabulary, perhaps amounting to several thousands of words, which would deal with parts of our experience now practically unamenable to language' (CE 2.3). The waking mind, he held, contains 'a kind of chessboard upon which thoughts move logically and verbally' (CE 2.4). But other kinds of inner life are not so systematic, among them the most important: 'this un-verbal part of your mind . . . is the source of nearly all *motives*,' and liking and judging 'spring from feelings which are generally admitted to be subtler than words.' Only imaginative writing approaches these feelings in language, he went on, and then only by a kind of flank attack, the primary or dictionary meaning of words having little to do with their 'real' meaning in, for example, a poem. One consequence of this strategy, Orwell held, is that the 'art of writing is in fact largely the perversion of words', though the perversion is most thorough when it is least obvious: such a writer as Gerard Manley Hopkins, though he appears to 'twist words out of their meanings', is 'really' trying to use them 'straightforwardly'.

This problem of writers reflects a larger problem, Orwell said: 'if words represented meanings as fully and accurately as height multiplied by base represents the area of a parallelogram, at least the *necessity* for lying would never exist.' As it is, however, 'from the point of view of exactitude and expressiveness our language has remained in the Stone Age.' Orwell's solution was 'to invent new words as deliberately as we would invent new parts for a motor-car engine', so that 'expressing one's meaning' would be simply 'a matter of taking the right words and putting them in place, like working out an equation in algebra'.[16] But Orwell's solution stems from his assumption that meanings exist outside of words and that categories of 'pure' meaning are more distinct than categories of word meaning. The shortcomings of language for expressing inner life are only an accident of its history, Orwell stated; its growth has been slow and haphazard, he agreed, but he did not accept that its present state is beyond human control. Such a view, he continued, stemmed from the 'feeling that any direct rational approach to one's difficulties, any attempt to solve the problems of life as one would solve an equation, can lead nowhere' – perhaps even from a childish superstition that grows to an adult fear of 'too rational thinking' and thus to a belief that 'To reform language is practically an interference with the work of God.'

Part of this argument is not about language at all: it simply dismisses all opponents of any reform as childish, superstitious, and passive enemies of reason and progress. But part of it does make a statement about language: that the reason can construct words adequate for discussing 'motives' much as the reason would design an engine part or solve an equation, so that the language of the feelings would be like the language of 'thinking' (the 'part of our minds for any straightforward intellectual problem') in resembling a 'kind of chessboard'. Such an innovation, finally, would faithfully link language to motive and so remove the need for lying – lies about feelings would be as obvious as illogical argument.

Orwell was not alone in believing that English needed new words for the management of urgent human concerns. In 1948 Raymond B. Fosdick wrote 'We Need New Words and New Faith':

> They are words that will describe new concepts of adaptation, new patterns of tolerance and accommodation. They are words that will represent the implementation of understanding and objectivity, words that will stand for a technique by which human adjustments are accelerated and faith in rational processes becomes effective. Perhaps more than anything else we need words that will give fresh meaning to the concept of patience
> . . . .

Within a few months, Orwell published *Nineteen Eighty-Four*, in which the conduct of human concerns, even the content of human minds, similarly depends on the items in the dictionary.

To avoid the logical circularity of defining new words by means of existing language, Orwell would turn again to technology – in this case the technology of the film:

> All the powerful motives which will not go into words and which are a cause of constant lying and misunderstanding, could be tracked down, given visible form, and named. I am sure that the film, with its almost limitless powers of representation, would accomplish this in the hands of the right investigators, though putting thoughts into visible shape would not always be easy – in fact, at first it might be as difficult as any other art. (CE 2.11)

The explicit points in a discussion often count for less than the underlying assumptions. Here Orwell's proposal tells us little about the film or about English vocabulary, but it says a great deal about his views of language and how language conveys meaning, objective and subjective alike. The same is true of his final arguments, where he added 'A note on the actual form new words ought to take':

> It seems to me probable that a word, even a not yet existing word, has as it were a natural form – or rather, various natural forms in various languages . . . . I suppose there must always be *some* correlation between the sound of a word and its meaning . . . . Now one instinctively makes the gesture that is appropriate to one's meaning, and all parts of the body follow suit including the tongue . . . . Therefore in forming new words one would have to pay attention to appropriateness of sound as well as exactitude of meaning. It would not do, as at present, to clip a new word of any real novelty by making it out of old ones, but it also would not do to make it out of a mere arbitrary collection of letters. One would have to determine the natural form of the word.
> (CE 2.11–12)

The internal flaws in this passage are obvious – if the natural form of a word always arises from the instinctive gestures of the tongue, why does the form differ in different languages? Why does the German say *Zimmer* and the English say 'room'? What about words that have similar forms but different meanings, like *camera* which is a room in Italian (akin to English 'chamber', from French) but a photographic instrument in English? What about words that change their form and meaning? A *camera oscura* or 'dark room' was a box with a lens, mirror and viewing screen that early nineteenth-century artists used for landscape sketching; later sensitized plates took the place of their sketching paper and 'camera' (without *oscura*) became an international word and 'darkroom' became something different. It remains today in television cameras that do not have the chamber-like shape of the original cameras, even in the portable television 'minicam'. The same questions apply to 'grotesque', which is 'the particular style in the painted decoration of architecture . . . . The name *grotesque* was given to it because it was unearthed in the vaulted excavations, which were called *grotte*' (SPE 15 [Bridges, 1923], p. 20). The present-day word has changed its meaning; the new meaning gives rise to the colloquial adjective 'grotty', that is 'ugly, bad', a near-antonym of the painted decoration.

Some of the other flaws are scientific. It seems reasonable, for example, that the position of the tongue and the language sound have a 1 : 1 relationship – for each position a distinctive sound and vice-versa. It still seems reasonable even if we interpret 'tongue' to include all the speech organs, not only the tongue itself but the lips, the velum (the flap at the top rear of the mouth that moves up and down to close or open the passage from mouth to nose), the larynx, the lungs, and all the muscles and nerves that operate them. But even reasonable notions are often illusory, as Orwell himself well knew. Phonetics – the study of speech sounds – shows that several different articulations (arrangements of the speech organs) can produce a given sound. Nor is the sound the speech organs produce in itself linguistically distinctive.

To illustrate the point we can take Orwell's own *Nineteen Eighty-Four* – the title – and the number 1984. Numbers make a convenient illustration because, more than most other words, they occupy in the rational mind 'a kind of chessboard upon which thoughts move logically and verbally'. Numbers are abstractions in themselves but they have clear-cut correlates in the physical world. Arithmetic can consistently and exhaustively state their relationships, avoiding the circularity of explanation through natural human language (an arithmetic lesson is in human language, but the arithmetic itself is not). And numbers so well accord with the chessboard figure that chessplayers can use them to convey their moves in postal matches and tournament records. (The same goes for business graphs and bingo cards.) Numbers are the epitome of everything Orwell claimed for the waking mind. If what he said about the language of the waking mind is not true of numbers, then it is all the less true of other objective vocabulary and still less of subjective vocabulary.

We must begin, then, with the notion '1984' and see how some of the languages Orwell knew represent it. As an idea outside of language, a meaning without specific linguistic form, the concept will appear within pointed brackets {1984}. As the different languages represent the concept, it can appear in conventional spelling with carets < >:

FRENCH <*mille neuf cent quatre-vingt quatre*> 'thousand nine hundred four-twenty four'

HINDI <*unnis sau caurasi*> 'one (from) twenty hundred four-eighty'

GERMAN <*neunzehnhundertvierundachtzig*> 'nineteen hundred four and eighty'

SPANISH <*mil novecientos ochenta y cuatro*> 'thousand nine

hundred eighty and four'
ENGLISH <*nineteen eighty-four*> 'nineteen eighty-four'[17]

The modern languages Orwell knew encode a reality like {1984} from the world outside language in very different forms: an English speaker would have no way of predicting the French and German forms, for example. The individual words are somewhat more similar: the German *neun*, Hindi *nau*, French *neuf*, Spanish *nueve*, all resemble each other and English 'nine' as none, for example, resembles Hungarian *kilenc* {9}. The words differ more, however, than the list suggests. To stay with English and with {84} alone, we have the usual British pronunciation to rhyme with 'claw' and the common (though not universal) American pronunciation to rhyme with the first syllable in 'forever'. Some varieties of Modern English, that is, shed the 'r' sound at the end of 'four' and some others do not. Among those that do, the resulting word may rhyme with 'claw' or with 'know'; we may conveniently enclose the different forms in square brackets when it is the actual pronunciation we mean, [f ɔ̇r], [fɔ:], [fou]. But the changes in pronunciation do not depend only on the variety of English; they can also depend on neighbouring sounds. Among the varieties that shed the sound, it reappears in 'four of them' in much of Britain and American New England, but not in most of the American south-east. In some varieties that lack [r] after a vowel, that is, the [r] reappears before another vowel, but in some others it does not. In any variety, the appearance, disappearance, or reappearance of [r] after a vowel follows regular rules.

But we still have some other differences to account for in even something as short and straightforward as {84}. In many forms of British English the <t> in 'eighty' will sound much like the first sound in 'tea'; in most forms of American English it will sound like the [d] in 'doodle'. But the same forms of American English will keep the 'tea' sound in 'eighteen' and 'sixty', and omit it completely in 'ninety' ([naini], to rhyme with 'tiny'). Since 'eighty' and 'eighteen' both include an underlying {8} and hence <eight>, rules must be at work here too to produce these results.

The rules will have to account for the following familiar American pronunciations:

<twenty> [tweni]   <sixty> [siksti]
<thirty> [θə rdi]   <seventy> [seveni]
<forty> [f ɔrdi]   <eighty> [eidi]
<fifty> [fifti]   <ninety> [naini]

A statement of the rules might be:

1. If the <t> follows <n>, the <t> is lost.
2. If the <t> follows a vowel or <r>, the <t> sounds like [d]. (It follows a vowel in <eighty>: the 'gh' is silent.)
3. If the <t> is in none of the above contexts, it retains the [t] sound in pronunciation.

The rules have a fixed order: the most specific first (dealing only with the context <n>); the more general next (all vowels and some consonants); and finally the most general (everything else, a phonetic 'residual powers' act). So applied, they cover not only this group of related words but all the words in this variety of American English.

The numbers <thirteen>, <fourteen>, and so on up to our original starting-point, <nineteen> as in <nineteen eighty-four>, all retain the [t] sound, but in a different context. In both <eighty> and <eighteen> we have two syllables, stressed on the first: [EIdi], [EIti:n]. But in <eighteen> the second syllable is more prominent than the second syllable in <eighty>. We need to modify our three-point rule above: it applies only when the <t> is after a strong stress and before a light one. If the previous syllable is light or the following syllable anything but light, the change of <t> to [d] won't happen; consider 'beauty' : 'beautician', 'priority' : 'prioritize', among other familiar examples. In ordering our pronunciation rules for <t>, this one about syllable stress has to come before the three about preceding vowels and consonants.

To speakers of other varieties of English, perhaps even to some self-conscious speakers of the English varieties in which these pronunciation rules apply, the rules no more than codify corruption. 'How can a "t" sound like a "d" or like nothing at all? Pronounce it the way it's spelled! You are corrupting our language!' That objection, however, would be hard to sustain. The rules for <t> are on a par with the rules for the retention or deletion of <r> after a vowel, a matter that does not excite much judgmental comment one way or the other, at least in America. The American speakers for whom these rules apply, moreover, are a large majority and include most of the most respected business, governmental, entertainment and even intellectual people in the nation. If they're all 'corrupted', who holds the measure for what's pure?

Most important, however, is the evidence of the rules themselves. They do not look like decay or carelessness at work. They show that the patterns of much American speech are highly regular and rigorous – a few concise rules, correctly ordered, cover a multitude of instances. Real corruption is never as tidy as that. Other rules of the same kind, applied over the course of much time, will likewise explain why 'nine', *nueve*, *neuf*, *nau*, and *neun* are so much alike but still quite different. Do we really wish to say that to the extent that they differ they are corrupt? Is Spanish really corrupt English? That line of reasoning is not very constructive.

The matter of the rules returns us to the place of pronunciation in language. Orwell made pronunciation something nearly equivalent to language when he spoke of the 'natural form' of words stemming from gestures of the speech organs and the separation of the larynx from the brain centres. But we have, in this discussion, found that the utterance is at the surface of a process several layers deep:

UTTERANCE   [nainti:n eidi fɔr]

↑

pronunciation rules

↑

LANGUAGE   <nineteen eighty-four>

↑

language encoding rules

↑

MEANING   {1984}

The matter is not even as simple as that![18] But at least the table shows that the rules are regular ones, that they can hardly reside in the larynx or other speech organs, and so they must – along with the other underlying faculties for language we have already traced to the top of the spinal cord – reside in the mind. Even our pronunciation, though it is the most physical thing about language, shows that our chief language organ is the brain. So the spoken form is not the language form. The language form that encodes the outside reality, and from which the spoken forms in all their variety arise according to regular rules, is an underlying one that we can recover only by study of the surface forms. The rules that derive the various spoken forms from the underlying form have nothing to do with meaning – [siksti] differs in its <t> from [fɔrdi] because <s> differs from <r>, not because {6} differs from {4}.

We traced the spoken word back to its non-linguistic level, which we called 'meaning'. To do so has brought us back to the early paragraphs of Orwell's 'New Words', where he discussed his view of meaning. It is not a small subject, but a review of it in the terms he provides may clarify it somewhat.

Meaning is our name for the content of language, the reflection of the world outside language that language conveys. But of course language does not convey it directly as though language were simply a xerox of nature; the differing versions of {1984} amply show as much. Language, on the contrary, encodes the world it reports. If you don't know the code you simply won't get the meaning, for the code is a set of symbols, and the symbols are arbitrary. Orwell quoted poems by Shakespeare, Housman, and Arnold to show that 'plumb', 'plunge' and 'plummet' are among the words that 'regularly convey certain ideas by their sound . . . . Clearly, apart from direct meanings, the sound plum- or plun- has something to do with bottomless oceans' (CE 2.11). The three are related, it is true, but only by their common derivation from 'plumb' in the meaning 'lead' (Pb) as in 'plumber'; 'plummet', for example, is a 'little lead' ('plumb' with the suffix '-et'). The connection of the three words is with their common original, an arbitrary connection so far as their modern meaning is concerned, and nothing to do with their sound or with bottomless oceans. The fruit 'plum', and the colour, share the sound of 'plumb' but not the connection with lead; they too are unconnected with ocean depths.

So meaning does not give the word a natural form or indeed any particular form at all, and the form does not create a meaning that was not there before the form. Yet at one time or another Orwell held both these contradictory views. He wrote:

> When you think of a concrete object, you think wordlessly, and then . . . you probably hunt about till you find the exact words that seem to fit it. When you think of something abstract you are more inclined to use words from the start . . . . Probably it is better to put off using words as long as possible and get one's meaning as clear as one can through pictures or sensations. Afterwards one can choose – not simply *accept* – the phrases that will best cover the meaning.
> (CE 4.138–9)

Such a view, as Wicker notes, makes language 'merely the garment of thought – something selected from a range of possible choices, like an overcoat in an outfitter's shop'.[19] The upshot, Wicker goes on to show, is that Orwell is a 'naive realist, who insisted that a pre-linguistic experience of undifferentiated sensations gives an immediate knowledge of how things are, and so provides the basis for all certainties'. Orwell believed, that is, in a 'deep philosophical dissociation . . . between language and thought'. But, we have already seen, language has its rise in the mind and is essentially a psychological phenomenon.

So what a sentence 'means' is not really present in the speaker's mind as something separate from the words. When writing instructors point out that 'Writing is a form that thinking takes,' they do not mean that the two activities are distinct but that, on the contrary, we can best work out our thoughts in utterances; writing simply happens to be a form of utterance that is easy to review and alter. Equally the 'true meaning of a word', whatever it may be, is not a quality guaranteed by its fidelity to something outside of language. Such fidelity is most nearly possible with numbers, of course, but the example of {1984} shows how distant the connection is even there; and a number that has no reference to anything outside of language, such as a four-cornered triangle, shows how well language is able to function as an autonomous natural system.[20]

The autonomy of language from the world it reports, and the symbiosis of language and thought, make up the theoretical objection to Orwell's other language tenet. In *Nineteen Eighty-Four* he had the Newspeak lexicographers delete terms from the dictionary so that each word would have only one meaning, and that meaning would be compatible with the party line. Their goal is to make impossible any thought in conflict with the line. This too is a separation of thought and word, but where before Orwell had the thought choose – even create – the words, here he had the thought impossible without the word. The first position makes the word the creature of the thought, the second vice-versa. But the opposite of an illogical idea is not necessarily a logical one.

The vocabulary of a language is not simply what a dictionary contains; the diminution of a dictionary does not restrict speakers to a smaller vocabulary. The growth of English vocabulary was particularly great in the fifteenth century, although as yet English-speakers had no dictionaries in which to record or trace the new words; and when the first English dictionary appeared in the early seventeenth century, its very small size in no way halted or reversed the continuing growth of the vocabulary.[21] Most language-users today employ the dictionary for a restricted range of purposes (chiefly spelling and pronunciation) if at all, and rarely so as to increase their vocabulary – never to reduce it. Daily we hear and use words not in our dictionaries.

Those are practical matters. Even more important is the theoretical limitation of thought by language. Would the disappearance of a word from the vocabulary, whether by its exclusion from the dictionary or otherwise, really leave the corresponding thought unthinkable? No, because language and thought do not have a 1 : 1 relationship. If 'the Greeks had a word for it' and we have not, we can still express what the Greeks did even though we may need more than one word to do so. Wicker's article uses the term 'Cartesian dualism' to describe one aspect of Orwell's linguistic thought. But his article is quite intelligible to readers who aren't familiar with that term, because Wicker goes on to say what it means. The same is true of words like 'honour', 'justice', 'morality', 'internationalism', 'democracy', 'science', and 'religion', the words that Orwell in his Appendix to *Nineteen Eighty-Four* said 'had simply ceased to exist'. People can long for justice without knowing the word for it. For while language is not independent of mind, and thought is impossible to separate from language, a concept does not depend on a *specific* word for its existence. Thought is not, after all, simply the stringing together of slogans.

Two points save Orwell from the full brunt of these criticisms. One is that, clearly, his remarks about 'honour' and the rest in the world of Ingsoc and Newspeak were remarks about the ideas, not the words; *Nineteen Eighty-Four* is concerned with a society, not with a vocabulary. The theory underlying the 'thought-deleting' qualities of Newspeak conflicts with most of the other views Orwell held, even with his most general view about the separability of thought and language. It seems likely that he mentioned the theory here just to satirize a certain kind of idealism.

The second point, one not often remarked on, is that the famous Appendix is written in the past tense:

> It was expected that Newspeak would have finally superseded Oldspeak (or Standard English, as we should call it) by about the year 2050 . . . . The version in use in 1984 . . . contained many superfluous words and archaic formations which were due to be suppressed later . . . . Newspeak was founded on the English language as we now know it, though many Newspeak sentences . . . would be barely intelligible to an English-speaker of our own day.
> (NE 246–7)

The verbs are in the past tense, the words of Standard English 'were due to be suppressed later', but the speaker and his assumed audience ('we') are both speakers of Standard English. Though the novel is 'futuristic', its events are viewed from an even more distant future when Ingsoc and Newspeak have given way to a society and a language more like our own. Newspeak did not, it seems, ever succeed in extirpating Oldspeak and its vocabulary of political morality.

The difference between what Orwell thought self-evident and what well-informed English students now assume about language and mind is not the result of a technical innovation; no way of directly observing the brain's language activities has come into use since 1950. It is a result of changes in the questions we ask and in the answers we accept as 'self-evident' (and 'well-informed'). The changes are not universal. Orwellian beliefs in these matters are doubtless still much more general than those that language students hold. That is probably because a great deal of language activity is unconscious – the way the language centres in the brain monitor another unconscious process, breathing, is just one small example.[22] Nothing as complicated as speech could possibly work unless most of its processes were under unconscious control, so most people regard conscious language activities as simple and conclude that language is a simple matter. A parent will refer, off-handedly, to having taught a child to talk. But reflect, in the perspective of the newer theories of language and mind, what that would entail!

The extremely complicated interaction and feedback that co-ordinate the muscles for breathing during speech (quite a different sort of breathing from the non-speech kind) form only a part of the unteachable 'hidden' language ability that makes the 'obvious' speech activity possible. To take an analogy: vampire bats have a substance in their saliva that prevents the clotting of their victims' blood and permits the bat to get a nice long drink. If we concentrate on the more visible aspects of the bats' approach to nutrition, we overlook invisible but essential species adaptations like the anti-clotting saliva. Someone long ago might have wondered why the poor victim's blood did not simply stop flowing, just as someone might have wondered why people can understand utterances that they can't produce. What has changed is not so much the sources for our answer as the questions we ask.

Most of Orwell's remarks were not addressed to the 'few' or the expensively-educated; yet he regarded their underlying assumptions as self-evident. Orwell's views were, in his time, not eccentric ones. Many linguists and psychologists in the 1930s held views that went by the apt name 'mechanistic', and scorned views that argued for – their phrase – a 'ghost in the machine'; what we now more graciously call 'mentalistic' views. The mechanists were preoccupied with the utterance in its physical (usually audible) form, and with the organs that directly produced it. The chain of sounds from the larynx, of letters from the pen, was to them much more 'real' than any wispy 'meaning' behind them. The theory set out earlier in this chapter, by contrast, holds language to be primarily a mental act and its realities to be psychological, not acoustical. The difference is one of the academic outlook, and Orwell did not take an academic view of this subject any more than of others.[23]

The different outlook has opened a new perspective on language. For Orwell and for the mechanists, language was very nearly the equivalent of what was said or written, so they paid close attention to usages, larynxes, and sounds. That sort of view makes distinctions: one usage, or sound, is not like another. It takes for granted, or overlooks, the underlying language ability that is common to all the usages, larynxes, and sounds. From the new perspective, usages and so forth are relatively superficial and language ability is relatively profound; the most interesting thing about usages is the way they relate to the underlying ability. And that view, in contrast with the older outlook, resolves distinctions.

The new perspective would not have surprised all of Orwell's contemporaries, however. The posthumous work of the Swiss Ferdinand de Saussure, *Course in General Linguistics*, had already appeared in 1916 (in French; the first edition in English was in 1959). Saussure distinguished between *langue*, a set of conventions in a language community, and *parole*, the embodiment of the set in a given utterance. *Parole* would have no meaning without *langue*, but it never reflects *langue* wholly and completely. To this distinction later linguists added an emphasis on the psychological, as distinct from the social, dimension of *langue*. But Saussure had already given a priority to underlying features of language which, after some decades of attention to surface features, modern linguistics has now generally accepted.[24]

So though Orwell might have formed his view of language in accord with a book published when he was thirteen, his view actually reflected more established thinking of his times. What is more, it spanned his life as few of his other views did. The first expressions of it come from 1930 when he had already renounced the life that Eton and the Indian Imperial Police epitomized, but nowhere in his linguistic comments do we hear of a renunciation like that one or a new commitment such as the commitment to Socialism he announced after his sojourn in Spain. On the contrary, he retained throughout his life a distaste for American English for no other explicit reason than its difference from British English, and in 1942 linked his distaste with his educational beginnings:

> Up till about 1930 nearly all 'cultivated' people loathed the USA, which was regarded as the vulgariser of England and Europe. The disappearance of this attitude was probably connected with the fall of Latin and Greek from their dominant position as school subjects. The younger intellectuals [now] have no objection to the American language . . . .
> (CE 2.177)

This in a 'London Letter' to *Partisan Review*, an American publication! The apparent lapse in courtesy is not an example of Orwell's fearlessly controversial journalism, however; it is simply an example of assumptions about which, in his mind, no controversy was possible. Such assumptions remained unchanged longest for Orwell when they dealt with language.

Here the assumption is that Latin and Greek studies, those dominant in the prep school where, by his classical prowess, he gained a scholarship to Eton, benefitted British English until their fall, preserving it from the influence of American English. As a piece of cultural history it is a hasty judgment on a par with 'Up till about 1930 nearly all "cultivated" people loathed the USA': did studies in ancient foreign languages, conducted by perhaps a few thousand people, ever insulate tens of millions in their country, oblivious to those studies, from the influence of a closely-related language variety which they heard and read almost daily? And if only the few thousand felt the influence, what was its significance if the scholarship boy among them, twenty years after he left Eton, could not remember the Greek alphabet? Most of all, even if the studies did influence the few, why did they and why should they?

The answer lies in another underlying assumption of Orwell's, that language is not a subject in which objective knowledge outweighs personal opinion. Few of his sweeping generalizations matched his remarks on language, because rarely in a question of language did he feel the need to pause, to analyze, to qualify. Like the radical teaching assistants of the 1960s, who off-duty carried signs reading 'Question Authority' while in class they condemned split infinitives, Orwell changed his political and social views but left his language views untouched from Eton and before.

As early as 1940, Philip Mairet remarked:

> Orwell is very English in his ability to form judgements of complex human material that are often arrestingly right, though the conscious philosophy behind the judgements seems to be sketchy or non-existent. He is really a sociological writer, but the only traces of sociological theory that his work exhibits are remains of a Marxism which he has almost outgrown and which it is doubtful if he ever more than half accepted.

Orwell relied on 'those limited generalizations of insight which, while not social theory, often tell us more about a given moment of experience than a theory can,'[25] for his criticism of language even more than his criticism of society. He did not test the linguistic hearsay of his time and social class against the rigour of any theory or even any systematic observation. In language, at least, he seems to have thought, things are what they seem, and that is what we were always told they were.

CHAPTER II

Language Change

𒀭𒀭𒀭𒀭𒀭𒀭

IF GENERALIZATION was a characteristic Orwellian mode, nostalgia was a characteristic mood. Edwardian by birth, he made the hero of his most nostalgic book, George Bowling in *Coming Up for Air*, his elder by an even decade and put him in Orwell's own childhood Berkshire.[1] When the heroine of *A Clergyman's Daughter* loses her Anglican faith she has nothing to replace it with, no new values or insights gained on her expeditions outside the rectory. The English administrators of *Burmese Days* are villains, not because they are colonial functionaries but because they are bad colonial functionaries. Winston Smith, in *Nineteen Eighty-Four*, sets himself apart from the Ingsoc Outer Party by buying first an ornate copying book 'of a kind that had not been manufactured for at least forty years past' (NE 9), then an antique paper weight. In his aesthetic criticism Orwell could praise Dickens and condone Kipling, but not Wells and certainly not Dali. For though he came to demand change, his rejection of the present stemmed from a longing for the past more than a confidence in the future.

Henry Popkin quotes Orwell's question 'when I say I like Dickens, do I simply mean that I like thinking about my childhood?' and goes on:

He loved everything Edwardian, everything he had first encountered before 1918 . . . . All of these seemed right, natural, and defensible to Orwell because they were supremely right and natural when he first knew them. It is no great exaggeration to say that Orwell frequently let nostalgia overpower his judgment . . . .

Orwell's Edwardian leanings help to explain the unresolved dilemma of his later years – the conflict between his socialism and the pessimism that found its fullest expression in *1984*.[2]

Orwell himself wrote at the end of his life:

The Language of 1984

> There is a now a widespread idea that nostalgic feelings about the past are
> inherently vicious . . . . In many ways it is a grave handicap to remember
> that lost paradise 'before the war' . . . . In other ways it is an advantage
> . . . . [O]ne is likelier to make a good book by sticking to one's early-
> acquired vision than by a futile effort to 'keep up'.
> (CE 4.445–6, 1948)

Orwell came to England and to Berkshire from India in 1904,
when he was about one. He acquired English, his first language, in
his middle-class Anglo-Indian household in the English home coun-
ties 'before the war'. Both the time and the place combined with his
constitutional nostalgia to confirm his views of language, and especially of language change. So, though – like English literary men for
centuries before him – he called for a committee to create new words,
he did so because he thought language change 'haphazard' and
unlikely to serve present needs without outside direction.[3] In his
other writing, especially 'The English Language' and 'Politics and the
English Language', where he described not so much language change
as its effects, his vocabulary depicts language as an organism in
process ('corrupion', 'decay', 'decadence' and 'decadent', 'decline')
or under attack ('abuse', 'debasement', 'perversion'). Orwell may
have thought these terms simply descriptive, but in fact they are
figures of speech – language cannot decay or suffer abuse like a living
body.

These terms – and Orwell was far from the first English writer to
use them and others like them – arise from an underlying assumption
that a language is an entity; they hypostatize or reify it, treating the
concept as if it were a distinct substance or reality.[4] We already saw in
the first chapter, however, that such a view is not sound. True,
language has substantial or at least physical attributes: it occurs in
sound waves and in marks on a page, and the speech organs include
brain, tongue and larynx. But sound waves are not language and the
speech organs do not contain language as, say, vampire bat saliva
contains anticoagulants. Language is a matter of mind, and mind is
individual.

So to say 'that speaker is abusing the language' is no more than to
say 'I don't like what the speaker is saying', just as to say 'that
election is democratic' is praise and 'that exam was Orwellian' is
dispraise. None really describes the event; it simply describes a
reaction to it. It is literally 'subjective', not 'objective', because it
characterizes the grammatical subject, the describer, and not the
grammatical object, the thing described. The analogy of organic

processes implicit in 'the language is decaying' or 'English has declined since Shakespeare' reaches immediate absurdities: no other processes of conception, birth, maturation, aging and death are also part of language natural history. But if the natural history of language cannot be compared to organic processes like these, it cannot be compared to any. The Orwellian figures of speech again are evaluations, not descriptions, and nostalgic evaluation at that.

So Orwell's viewpoint unrealistically reified language and sentimentally deplored its change. That viewpoint, naturally, came more and more into conflict with Orwell's social and political convictions that change was necessary and – when he was not pessimistic about it – possible. He affirmed, for example, that

> it is worth noticing that prose literature almost disappeared during the only age of faith that Europe has ever enjoyed. Throughout the whole of the Middle Ages there was almost no imaginative prose literature and very little in the way of historical writing: and the intellectual leaders of society expressed their most serious thoughts in a dead language which barely altered during a thousand years.
>
> (CE 4.66)

It is likewise worth noticing that Orwell was speaking of Latin, and his view of Latin was inconsistent; latinity preserved the English of Britain from overseas contamination, but here it symbolizes the dead weight of the past. Orwell was not only inconsistent but wrong; he would fail an undergraduate 'Western Civ' course for his remarks about medieval imaginative prose and historical writing. More to the point, his 'dead language', medieval Latin, 'barely altered during a thousand years' from classical Latin only in comparison with, say, the fifteenth-century French of Villon. In fact, medieval Latin changed from one century to another, developed national and even regional varieties, received and imparted vocabulary in exchange with the vernaculars (including both English and French). As a written, especially as a literary language, it was far from dead. It was a dead language only in that, unlike the spoken Latin of Cicero's age or the French of Villon's or the English of Orwell's, it was the first or native language of no one.

In a sense Orwell's errors of cultural history are beside the point he made here, that a prevailing orthodoxy inhibits fearless thinking and 'to write in plain, vigorous language one has to think fearlessly'. Orwell merely used medieval literary and linguistic history to show that writers in an 'age of faith' do not make large use of mental reservations. He might have chosen a luckier example, however, because he intended this example to demonstrate, not simply to illustrate, so the facts are relevant. And factual mistakes such as these produced failed analogies when Orwell used language change to symbolize social change (as he did again in *Nineteen Eighty-Four*):

> The tendency of mechanical progress is to make your environment safe and soft; and yet you are striving to keep yourself brave and hard. You are at the same moment furiously pressing forward and desperately holding back. It is as though a London stockbroker should go to his office in a suit of chain mail and insist on talking medieval Latin.
> (RW 194)

Again medieval Latin is the unstable middle: without the ageless security of classical Latin or the present reality of Modern English, it was for Orwell a language both mutable and arcane. But medieval Latin was a scholarly language, and medieval scholars had no more distinct opposites than medieval knights; debates between *miles* and *clericus* were a staple among the abundant imaginative prose that contradicts Orwell's earlier generalization. So Orwell's London stockbroker is doubly inconsistent, his medievalism with his office and his Latin with his armour.

Orwell's generalizations about the early history of language in Europe were only slightly more accurate and consistent when he turned to English. He held that

> English is a mixture of several languages, but mainly Saxon and Norman French, and to this day, in the country districts, there is a class distinction between the two. Many agricultural labourers speak almost pure Saxon.
> (CE 2.133; cf. CE 3.24)

Yet the Suffolk passages in *A Clergyman's Daughter* show how little Orwell cared to be saddled with rural types who speak 'pure Saxon': ' "They bells up in the church tower. They're a-splintering through that there belfy floor in a way as it makes you fair shudder to look at 'em" ' (CD 38; cf. 59, 61). Even this brief passage, not field notes but the invention of Orwell himself, contains three words from Old Norse ('they', 'them', 'are'), one from Dutch ('splinter'), one from Low German ('shudder'), one from French ('tower'), and one with an international history all its own: 'belfry' comes from an ancient Germanic word meaning 'high' (the second element in 'iceberg', 'ice-mountain') and another meaning 'protection' (the second element in 'Siegfried', 'battle-protection'); together they gave the compound *berg-frij*, 'high [place of] safety', 'portable siege tower'. Old French borrowed the compound in the form *berfrei*, and Middle English in turn borrowed it as 'berfrey'. But the portable siege tower became obsolete in warfare, so the name devolved on a fixed bell tower. The ancient elements too became obsolete, but the bells – by a process known as 'folk etymology' – seemed to provide a clue to the first element at least, and the word took new form as 'belfry'. That history fits the word for no single category, certainly not for 'pure Saxon'.

Orwell cited Chaucer occasionally, usually as a comic or burlesque writer (CE 2.128, CE 3.285–6, 302); Chaucer supplied the motto for *Down and Out in Paris and London*, 'O scathful harm, condition of poverte!',[5] and a macedoine of Middle English on the theme of springtime opens Chapter Eleven of *Keep the Aspidistra Flying*. But Orwell ended that passage 'And so on and so on and so on. See almost any poet between the Bronze Age and 1850' (KA 222), about as dismissively as he could; and in fact little early English before Shakespeare was important to him. So, when he looked out of his window in the spring of 1947, he found 'Of all passages celebrating spring, I think I like best those two stanzas from the beginning of one of the Robin Hood ballads,' and quoted verses that included 'The woodwele sang and would not cease.' He went on,

> But what exactly was the woodwele? The Oxford Dictionary seems to suggest that it was the woodpecker, which is not a notable songster, and I should be interested to know whether it can be identified with some more probable bird.
> (CE 4.312–13)

Orwell's definition came from some less probable 'Oxford Dictionary' than the OED, which gives as its first definition the Golden Oriole, a notable songster indeed, and cites this very passage.[6] Like Orwell's mythical modern country labourers with their 'almost pure Saxon,' who tell us something about his knowledge of the early language but not much about rural speech, his candid puzzlement over 'woodwele', along with his preference for the Robin Hood ballads (c. 1600) among 'all passages celebrating spring', confirms that Orwell was not at home in early English, in its literature, or in modern reference books that elucidate them.

Such comments may appear carping or ungracious, but they are germane. Orwell's poor grasp of language history, like his temperamental nostalgia, helped form his attitude toward language change. And his attitude, not surprisingly, was almost uniformly disapproving. He was against the creation of new words whether by borrowing from foreign languages or by extension of English resources. He resisted changes in meaning. Though a declared enemy of nationalism, he retained an 'English for the English' viewpoint; though a critic of the social status quo, he decried change in language.

Orwell's attitudes towards language change crop up sporadically in his writing, mostly his essays: he did not write at length on any one of them as he did about 'New Words' or 'Politics and the English Language'. And so he was not always consistent about them; he favoured the deliberate creation of a new terminology for subjective states, and he scorned the 'archaic words' and 'stilted bookish language' of official wartime writing – words like 'peril', 'valour', 'might' (noun), 'foe', 'succour', 'vengeance', 'dastardly', 'rampart', 'bulwark', 'bastion' (CE 3.135; cf. 209–10) and 'lackey' (NE 77). Even so, he objected less to the words themselves than to political speeches where they miss the demotic note, and where 'the main weakness . . . is [the] failure to notice that spoken and written English are two different things.' Orwell found no inherent fault in such words, only a lack of soapbox decorum.

His comments on innovations in English vocabulary, by contrast, suggest that he found them objectionable in themselves, just as innovations. Many words, for example, begin their life in English as one part of speech and then branch out into others. Linguists call such change 'functional shift' or more simply 'conversion', and Orwell – though he probably did not know those terms – certainly knew the phenomenon. He commented that

> the vocabulary is made much larger . . . by the practice of turning one part of speech into another. For example, almost any noun can be used as a verb: this in effect gives an extra range of verbs, so that you have *knife* as well as *stab*, *school* as well as *teach*, *fire* as well as *burn*, and so on. (CE 3.24)

So far this sounds like commendation. But a few pages later Orwell observed that 'American has some of the vices of English in an exaggerated form. The interchangeability of different parts of speech has been carried further . . .' (CE 3.28), a clue to his otherwise unexplained condemnation of 'bad usage – for example, the disgusting verb "to contact" ' (CE 3.326; the *Guardian* (29 July 1982, p. 24) quoted a Government Minister to the effect that his department 'had conducted a worldwide search and contacted 16 companies'). Orwell did not say how he knew that American English uses conversion more freely than does British English, and he treated 'vices', 'bad usage', 'disgusting' as self-explanatory terms. Yet those terms raise the very questions a discussion like his should deal with.

A word like 'time', for example, can be a noun or a verb with closely-related meanings; such conversions are so common that the brief sentence 'Time flies like an arrow' contains several and hence has more than one possible meaning:

> Time is an entity that flies past as though it were an arrow.
> Determine the speed of flies the way you would that of an arrow.
> A breed of flies called 'time flies' (cf. 'May flies', 'fruit flies', etc.) enjoy an arrow.

Other sets of words created by conversion do not carry the meaning of one part of speech into the other: 'express' is a mode of conveyance as a noun, 'the overnight express'; it is something quite different as a verb, 'express yourself candidly' or 'express the juice from that orange'. The noun 'expression' (and the adjective 'expressive') share only the meaning of the verb. Even words from the same arena of meaning shift unpredictably in conversion, for 'doctor' (verb) is not to 'doctor' (noun) what some meanings of 'nurse' (verb) are to 'nurse' (noun); the same is true of noun-verb pairs like 'father' and 'mother'. In many cases the word changes meaning and accent alike: 'rebel' (noun and verb) changes the accent from the first syllable to the second, while 'attribute' (noun and verb) changes both accent and meaning, as does 'contract' (noun and verb). But 'comment' ('since . . . the author must occasionally comment, one's own comments unavoidably become those of the narrator', CE 4.512) has the same stress pattern as 'contact', and in any event stress was not an explicit part of Orwell's protest (he seems to have noticed stress only once and then in a different context: NE 253). So why is 'contact' a 'disgusting' verb?

Like any other writer in English, Orwell found conversions already abundant in the language when he first came to use it. From our perspective some of his usages, though not in themselves 'bad', are more rare than others: 'the Home Guard is in practice officered on a class basis' (CE 2.151). But of course Orwell used conversion daily, as do we. A noun like 'orbit' can become a transitive verb with the spacecraft as the subject ('The spacecraft orbited the earth') or the object ('The Soviets have orbited another spacecraft'). But Orwell's distaste for conversion survived the evidence of its productivity in English, and became one of the features of 'Newspeak' (and the reason for his not calling it 'Newspeech'):[7]

> The grammar of Newspeak had two outstanding peculiarities. The first of these was an almost complete interchangeability between different parts of speech. Any word in the language (in principle this applied even to very abstract words such as *if* or *when*) could be used either as verb, noun, adjective, or adverb. Between the verb and the noun form, when they were of the same root, there was never any variation, this rule of itself involving the destruction of many archaic forms. The word *thought*, for example, did not exist in Newspeak. Its place was taken by *think*, which did duty for both noun and verb. No etymological principle was involved here; in some cases it was the original noun that was chosen for retention, in other cases the verb. Even where a noun and verb of kindred meaning were not etymologically connected, one or other of them was frequently suppressed. There was, for example, no such word as *cut*, its meaning being sufficiently covered by the noun-verb *knife*.
> (NE 247–8)

One clue to Orwell's distaste for conversion is his remark here 'Between the verb and the noun form, when they were of the same root, there was never any variation.' The example he gave is 'thought/think', which is indeed a noun-verb pair from the same root with variation between the two forms. Many other such pairs exist: 'food/feed', 'drift/drive', 'bath/bathe' are only a few. (These examples list the noun before the verb, although historically the noun comes from the verb in some of them, as it does in 'thought/think'.) Many other reputable pairs in English, however, have no variation: from the first page under letter 'B' in the RCD come 'baa', 'babble', 'baby' ('Baby me, baby'), and on the second page is the protean 'back' that has no formal variation in the four parts of speech it can be (noun, transitive and intransitive verb, adjective, adverb). Since some intransitive/transitive pairs in English do show variation ('fall/fell', 'sit/set', etc.), we can say that 'back' really fills five possible forms with one.

Yet Orwell objected to such commonplaces, and especially to the artificial regularity that resulted in the 'destruction of many archaic forms'. That is easy to believe; English once had a verb based on 'cool' that, had it survived, would have given Modern English 'keel', as it still has 'food/feed', 'blood/bleed', 'doom/deem', and the rest.

Analogy with more common forms like 'baby' and 'back', however, eventually destroyed 'keel' and many others like it; no medieval Newspeak lexicographers had a hand. But Orwell did not really know or care so much about early English that he would have made analogy his bête noire. He took such changes in the medieval language for granted; changes in his contemporary language, on the other hand, he found more disturbing. In effect he wanted change to stop, as it does – and does only – in a dead language like classical Latin. And that is the heart of the matter, for Latin noun/verb and other related pairs always show variation between the forms. It is this variation that Orwell took as a self-evident good in language, though it makes the formal system of English a self-evident 'bad'.[8]

Another productive source of new vocabulary in English is derivation, the process that makes a new word – often in a different part of speech – by affixing: 'verbs and adjectives . . . turned into their opposites by means of the prefix *un–*' (CE 3.24), for example, or 'the formation of verbs by adding *ise* to a noun' (CE 3.27). And derivation is again a feature of Newspeak, that artificial variety of English in which Orwell enshrined all the usages he hated most, whether trivial or essential, of means or of end:

> Adjectives were formed by adding the suffix *-ful* to the noun-verb, and adverbs by adding *-wise* . . .
>
> In addition, any word . . . could be negatived by adding the affix *un-*, or could be strengthened by the affix *plus-*, or, for still greater emphasis, *doubleplus-* . . . It was also possible, as in present-day English, to modify the meaning of almost any word by prepositional affixes such as *ante-*, *post-*, *up-*, *down-*, etc. By such methods it was found possible to bring about an enormous diminution of vocabulary.
>
> (NE 248)

Here, as in his discussion of conversion, Orwell used some of the same examples that he had used in 'The English Language', so his views were consistent – and his pet peeves the same – in the years (1944–8) that separated the compositions. Orwell's language views are often simply his reactions to individual words, elevated to the level of high principle. As a result the principle is frequently in conflict with the general drift of the language. The prefix 'un-' does not, for example, always and everywhere 'negative' the following word:

He was usually happy.
He was unusually happy.

At a certain age.
At an uncertain age.

Other derivations show even more marked drift of meaning: 'profess', 'professor' and 'professional' show little overlap of meaning among the formally related verb, noun and adjective/noun; even formally-related noun pairs like 'solidity' and 'solidarity', 'conservationist' and 'conservative', are not synonyms (cf. CE 4.272).

A principle in conflict with the drift of the language could, by the same token, also be in conflict with Orwell's own habitual practice. Jacintha Buddicom recalls that the young Orwell was particularly adept at coining 'undictionary' words.[9] And derivation of a verb from a noun by adding –ise, for example, quite reputable in words such as 'realize' and 'mesmerize', was a process the more mature Orwell seems to have found both useful and pleasant. He had no qualms about the well-established 'anglicised' (e.g., CE 2.99) and the more recent 'fascised' (e.g., CE 1.378, 386; CE 2.119, 228) and 'Marxised' (CE 1.512); and he apparently played with this form of derivation in a 1943 letter to Rayner Heppenstall:

> I wonder would you feel equal to featurising a story? We do that now abt once in 3 weeks. I featurised the first 2 myself . . . I could send you a specimen script & no doubt you could improve on my technique of featurisation.
> (CE 2.305)

If he had any objection to present-day 'privatise' (opposite of 'nationalize', with derived nouns 'privatising' and 'privatisation') it would probably have been political, just as any objection to 'editionise' (publish [a newspaper] in variant regional editions) would have been journalistic; linguistically his practice, if not his theory, was consistent with both words.

Orwell was equally at home with more far-ranging sorts of derivation; he provided '*Daily Worker*-ful' (BD 199), 'Nancitude', 'Scotchification' and 'aspidistral' (KA 14, 37, 154), 'su-superior' and 'art for art's saking' (RW 213, 211). He would have felt familiar such metaphorical derivations as the *Guardian*'s 're-jig', for from the noun 'blimp' (a stuffy conservative, personified in the fictional 'Colonel Blimp') he had the abstract nouns 'blimpishness' (e.g., CE 2.230, 277) and 'blimpocracy' (e.g., CE 2.116, 209, 212), and the verb 'blimp' by conversion, with derivational prefix and suffix: 'it is a question of unblimping' (CE 2.352).

Orwell lumped 'the formation of verbs by adding *ise* to a noun' together with 'certain American usages' (CE 3.27), perhaps because he wanted to blacken its repute. He did something like that when he defamed phrasal verbs:

> whereas English alters the meaning of a verb by tacking a preposition on to it, the American tendency is to burden every verb with a preposition that adds nothing to its meaning (*win out*, *lose out*, *face up to*, etc).
> (CE 3.28)

'Every' is an Orwellian exaggeration: phrasal verbs are usually formed only with verbs of one syllable, as Orwell's examples show. (To be even more exact, we should say 'particle' for his 'preposition'. If the word following the verb really is a preposition, then the two do not form a phrasal verb. 'Please stand in the corner' and 'Get up to five pounds free' are not phrasal verbs, but 'Please stand in for me while I'm gone' and 'What are you getting up to?' consequently are.)[10]

The 'every verb' generalization reappears in 'the American habit of tying an unnecessary preposition on to every verb' (CE 3.326). But one writer's necessity may be another's burden: for Orwell, the radio audience would 'listen-in' (e.g., CE 2.119), a fully conjugatable verb (e.g., 'Listened-in to Cripps's speech' CE 2.418) that can produce a noun by derivation ('half an hour's listening-in to the B.B.C.,' KA 48), though that would now seem one word too many for most Americans and Britons alike. Many writers would also settle for 'tying an unnecessary preposition to every verb' without 'on', come to that.

Orwell was satirizing colonial administrators when he wrote that 'The civilians in Burma had a comforting theory that "sticking by one's job" (wonderful language, English! 'Sticking *by*' – how different from 'sticking *to*') was the truest patriotism' (BD 67). Most of the satire is in the viewpoint rather than the phrasal verbs, however, for despite his animadversions Orwell generally used phrasal verbs without self-consciousness. An exception may be Julia's remark in *Nineteen Eighty-Four*, ' "we've got to fix up about the next time we meet" ' (NE 113) – a hint perhaps of the lovers' failure to evade the effects of Newspeak even in their secret moments together. The hint is a very subtle one all the same, if Orwell intended it at all; elsewhere he could be just as redundant without apparent overtones ('After his hoof had healed up,' AF 110, is equal to 'After his hoof had healed'; just as 'which I can't dodge out of', CE 4.382, is equal to 'which I can't dodge'), and – especially in colloquial phrases – often to good stylistic effect: 'not quite strung up to the effort' (CD 106); 'to land ourselves in for centuries of semi-slavery' (HC 178). He even managed to combine conversion ('button', verb from noun), derivation (prefix 'un-') and phrasal verb in one word, and used it to describe – again without apparent satirical intention – someone else's style: 'This is a tendency to play tricks with syntax and produce unbuttoned-up or outright meaningless sentences' (CE 4.157).

Present-day phrasal verbs remain equally protean. A student who has had the maximum number of loans has 'loaned out', not the same as older 'lend out' or more recent 'max out' meaning 'reach and pass one's maximum performance'; cf. 'veg [vedʒ] out', 'become torpid as though in a vegetative state', and 'hulk out', 'go into a frenzy like the title character in the television series *The Incredible Hulk*'. A shampoo that 'lathers in extra body and manageability' also exemplifies conversion ('lather' as verb) and phrasal verb. Phrasal verbs remain idiomatic, too: 'in' and 'out' are antonyms, but 'fill in' and 'fill out' (a blank or form) are virtually synonyms; while to be 'all set up' is the opposite of 'all upset'. Older 'fall down' gives 'downfall' but newer 'melt down' and 'fall out' give 'meltdown' and 'fallout'; likewise 'breakthrough' and 'kickback'. The verb/noun is 'shoot out', but 'shoot off' gives 'offshoot'. The verb 'take out' gives two nouns, 'takeout' if it is food but 'outtake' if it is edited film.

Orwell's 1940 phrase 'he had the first draft vetted' (CE 2.355), illustrates the beginnings of a related process, for present-day 'positive vetting' has a technical sense to 'investigate [a candidate's] background aggressively, not depending only on leads the candidate or others provide'. It produces a full range of verb forms, including the *Guardian*'s 'had been positively vetted' and 'only customary positively to vet'. Such fixed phrases, though not phrasal verbs, are kindred extensions of the vocabulary.

Conversion, derivation and phrasal verbs are resources for expanding English that Orwell regarded as disagreeable features in the modern language. In the parlance of Saussure he took them as synchronic features ('the facts of a linguistic system as it exists at one point in time without reference to its history' RCD s.v. 'synchronic'), not as diachronic features ('the changes in a linguistic system over a given period of time' RCD s.v. 'diachronic linguistics'). But all three are features of linguistic change, and – given his attitude towards such change – he would probably have liked them even less had he seen them in the diachronic perspective.

The diachronic perspective did not help him understand borrowing. 'One mystery about the English language is why, with the biggest vocabulary in existence, it has to be constantly borrowing foreign words and phrases' (CE 3.130); 'English is also, and to an unnecessary extent, a borrowing language . . . in most cases an English equivalent exists already, so that borrowing adds to the already large stock of synonyms' (CE 3.24). The case against borrowing foreign words is a very old one. Almost four centuries before Orwell, the Cambridge classicist Sir John Cheke was 'of this opinion that our own tung shold be written cleane and pure, vnmixt and vnmangeled with borrowing of other tunges' (1557).[11] Cheke's 'opinion' and 'pure', among other words in the passage, are borrowings; but by the time he learned the language they were no longer new borrowings so he regarded them as native English words. Orwell's more recent complaint shows that such protests are not very successful, and so does his practice. For him 'mystery', 'language', 'vocabulary', 'existence', 'constantly', 'phrases', 'unnecessary', 'extent', 'equivalent', 'large', 'synonyms', among others, are familiar English terms; yet all were at one time borrowed words. And Orwell could not have written these passages in anything like this form without them, and so they are not really 'unnecessary'. Synonyms, words with the same 'meaning' as symbols of the world outside language, are rarely interchangeable or redundant: they supply the alternatives for adjusting speech or writing for style, tone, audience, occasion, and so forth (see Chapter Three).

Orwell did not see the diachronic perspective in the synchronic scene, so his views of borrowing turn out to be merely views of very recent borrowing. Orwell's question as to why English, 'with the biggest vocabulary in existence, . . . has to be constantly borrowing foreign words', again shows his disposition to accept the linguistic status quo but to protest further change: in fact, the vocabulary of English became 'the biggest' partly through borrowing. So Orwell observed borrowing of 'any foreign word that seems to fill a need, often altering the meaning' and gave as an example 'blitz': 'The word "blitz" now used everywhere to mean any kind of attack on anything . . . "Blitz" is not yet used as a verb, a development I am expecting' (CE 2.381, 1941); 'As a verb this word did not appear in print till late in 1940, but it has already become part of the language' (CE 3.24,

1944). The word is German for 'lightning' as in the compound *Blitzkrieg* 'lightning-war'; the English word is borrowed and short-ened from the compound, so 'blitz' in English first means any sort of 'overwhelming all-out attack' (RCD s.v.), not 'lightning'*per se*. That is the source of its meaning in sports as both noun and verb: 'a linebacker blitz,' 'blitz the quarterback'. But there it has achieved a further change, for the object of the verb can be either the blitzee or the blitzer: when a linebacker blitzes the quarterback, he rushes the opponent's player; but when a team blitzes the linebacker, they cause their own player to rush the opponent. That too is a development familiar in the diachronic story of English. Does a 'sticker' stick or is it stuck? In 'lockjaw' does the jaw lock or is it locked? How about a 'liftback' car? Modern English intransitive phrasal verbs often replace transitive verbs ('hurry up' and 'close up' for 'hurry' and 'close'), and intransitive verbs become transitive ('Fly Eastern'; 'Shop A & P'; 'Bike Europe'; 'Dive Florida', that is 'Do your scuba diving in Florida waters'), providing the basis for further develop-ments like 'Shop into Boots'.

Although several of the words that Orwell employed to discuss borrowing were from Latin and Greek, it was 'the encroachment of Latin and Greek' that he most disliked (CE 3.26; cf. CE 4.131, 132, 136, 138). The place of Latin in his views, we have already seen, was conditioned by his nostalgia, his early education, and his attitude towards social class (probably also by his deeply-felt anti-Catholicism, although he never made the connection directly). These are important concerns, but they are not strictly linguistic concerns. Nevertheless he wrote

> many necessary abstract words, especially words of Latin origin, are
> rejected by the working class because they sound public-schoolish,
> 'tony' and effeminate. Language ought to be the joint creation of poets
> and manual workers, and in modern England it is difficult for these two
> classes to meet. When they can do so again – as, in a different way, they
> could in the feudal past – English may show more clearly than at present its
> kinship with the language of Shakespeare and Defoe.
> (CE 3.29)

The passage raises questions it does not answer. How 'many' words, and 'necessary' for what? Which ones do the working class reject? If the needy can reject them, are they really necessary? Orwell's 'public-schoolish' and 'effeminate' are not answers; they are merely symptoms of his increasing discomfort about Eton and his lifelong hostility towards gays. His statement that 'Language ought to be the joint creation of poets and manual workers' is populism that recalls certain statements of Whitman; neither writer said how poets and manual workers 'create' language, or how they could keep other classes of society from taking a hand.[12] Orwell also did not say when, or how, poets and manual workers met in the feudal past, or how he found out about it; he was, again in good company, yearning for a 'Golden Age' of the English language that is somehow always just far enough in the past to be out of living memory.[13] 'When they can do so again' is idealist pie in the sky pure and simple, as is the future of English Orwell hinted at. And, finally, the kinship of Shakespeare with that or any other form of English (Defoe seems to be only a make-weight here) is an attempt to invoke a sacred name above dispute.[14]

Implicit in Orwell's criticism of Latin borrowings was his rule for the pronunciation of foreign words in English:

> Sometimes it is necessary to take over a foreign word, but in that case we should anglicise its pronunciation, as our ancestors used to do. If we really need the word 'café' (we got on well enough with 'coffee house' for two hundred years), it should either be spelled 'caffay' or pronounced 'cayfe'. (CE 3.131; cf. 16)

The SPE in 1929 thought

> A man, speaking or writing, is at liberty to introduce a French word whenever he chooses, and he may be tempted to do so for lack of an English word which exactly suits his shade of meaning . . . When such French words are used in literature, they are printed in italics with their foreign accents, as Greek words would be, and however well we may be accustomed to them they are French words and not English . . .
>
> If this be not done . . . if popular tea-shops paint their title of CAFE over their doors [without the accent] the word will be pronounced like *chafe* and *safe* . . .
> (32, pp. 373–4; cf. 61 [1943], pp. 12, 18)

The pronunciation of 'garage' that Orwell commended, 'garridge', is now current in Britain but not in the United States, where something closer to the French original is still attempted; in 1921 'garage' still retained its French pronunciation in Britain.[15]

Orwell's rules, which already applied to 'café' among some varieties of English within a few years of Orwell's writing this (1944), applies automatically to older borrowings: well-established words from Latin are not pronounced now as they were in classical times, any more than they are formed the classical way (we say 'museums', not 'musea') or retain their classical meanings or part of speech. Newspeak 'plus' is an adjective prefix with adverbial force ('plusgood'); in Latin *plus* could also be a noun, while in Modern English it can also be a preposition ('Two plus two') or a connective ('Plus, she knows calculus'). But the pronunciation of 'plus' – and 'alias', 'item', 'transpire', and thousands more – depends on the variety of English the speaker uses, not on command of Latin. That is less true of newer borrowings: *cul de sac* remains a noun, the plural of *beau* is still *beaux*, and *fiancée* doesn't yet rhyme with 'fancy'.

Orwell's argument about the relative merits of 'coffee house' and 'café' is a familiar one – why go abroad for what we already have at home? Like many such arguments, however, his depended on a view of nationhood and not on a grasp of language history. It was consequently both weaker and stronger than it might have been. From the OED Orwell would have learned that 'coffee house' had been an English term since the early seventeenth century, not the mid-eighteenth as he seems to have thought. The information would have made his argument stronger. But he would also have found that English writers used 'café' to describe continental and other foreign (not just French) establishments from the early nineteenth century; by 1893, the OED comments, it was 'recently introduced in this country for the name of a class of restaurant'. The question of 'café' in English was already long settled when Orwell confronted it. That information makes his argument weaker. Foreign words keep coming into English for a variety of reasons – need and fad are only two of them – and like other immigrants, most of them become naturalized before they are ever noticed. In the case of 'coffee house' and 'café', RCD now defines the former as a species of the latter: a coffee house is 'a café specializing in serving different kinds of coffee'. Whatever jobs 'café' may have stolen from the older (and longer) 'coffee house' a century and more before Orwell wrote, by the time he made his comments the two terms were well on their way to amicable demarcation of roles. New words, including borrowed words, do not really add to the stock of synonyms for long, as Orwell claimed.

Orwell's practice sanctioned even larger possibilities for expanding the English vocabulary though his theories did not. Orwell's example 'stick by' and 'stick to' has parallels in other pairs like 'stand by' and 'stand for', part of a phrasal verb family including 'stand up', 'stand out', 'stand against', 'stand down', 'stand back', and 'stand in (for)', all of them different in meaning from the sum of their parts as – for example – 'stand on' is not. The phrasal verbs are versatile because some can be either transitive or intransitive, with different meanings: 'Stand by your beliefs' but 'Stand by for further news'. And the nouns based on them provide still further words: 'standing by with a stop-watch' leads to 'a great standby' (CA 83, 44). Adjectives too come from these phrasal verbs when the 'preposition' travels from the end and fuses to the beginning: 'standing up very straight' leads to 'a fine, upstanding . . . chap' (CA 50, 112). Another kin of the phrasal verbs are the verbs, some of them very old in English, like 'withstand' and 'understand'. Even more remote products of phrasal verbs can result from a simple combination like 'fall' + 'off', with a derived noun 'off-fall' that, in the course of time, yields 'offal' by wear and tear. The noun 'offal' is exactly parallel to 'decay' historically (from Latin *de* + *cadere*, 'off-fall', by way of French), but as usual the formations have developed different meanings; 'off' itself is derived from 'of' with change of form and meaning, and 'after' is another derivation from 'of', even more changed.

The Old English 'stand' descended from an unrecorded word, something like **sta-*, current in parts of Europe perhaps five thousand years ago. From the same original came Latin *stare* and from that Latin *statuere*: *stare* had the past participle *status*; *statuere* had *statutus*. From the latter we have borrowed 'statute' and 'statutory'. From the former we have 'status' itself, 'stative' (and 'stature'), 'statue' (and 'statuary', 'statuesque'), 'station' (and 'stationary', 'stationer', 'stationery'), 'statistics' (and 'statistical', 'statistician'). From Latin *status* came French *estate*, which gave us our 'estate' and 'state', both the noun (giving 'stately', 'statehood', 'statesman', and so forth) and the verb (giving 'statement'). Our 'stasis' and 'statis' come from a Greek verb related to both the Latin and the Old English.

All these Modern English words descend from a few words in Greek, Latin, and the early Germanic ancestor of English. Among their cousins are many more words still, even less obviously kin in form and meaning. The 'stet' in 'obstetrics' also comes from the word that gave us 'stand'; the obstetrician 'stands in the way' of the exiting newborn. 'Circumstances' stand around; a 'contrast' stands against, its final 'st' the only vestige of the earlier word. Also related in one fashion or another are 'steed', 'stud', 'stow' (noun and verb), 'stool',

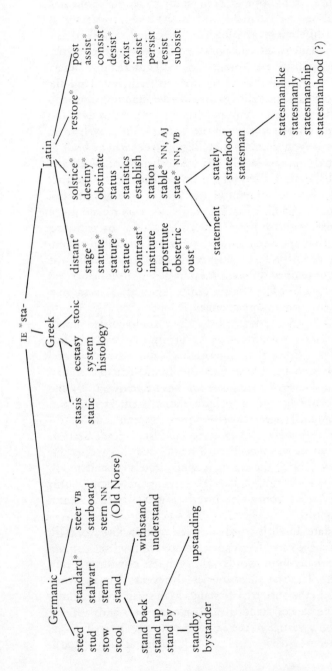

Some of the many Modern English words related by common descent from Indo-European *sta-, 'stand', both native (from Germanic) and borrowed (from French). Words followed by an asterisk entered English from French. A single original word gave rise to all these forms, and more, in different languages, and in different words formed by sound change, derivation, compounding, inflection, and conversion. Not represented on the chart are all the different parts of speech these words can be ('prostitute' can be ('prostitute' can be a verb), or all the different meanings of each word ('stand' can mean 'tolerate').

'stage', 'distant', 'institute', 'oust', 'prostitute', 'superstition', 'stal-wart', 'stem', 'obstinate', 'stable', 'starboard', 'stern', 'restore', 'insist', 'system', and at least as many more Modern English words as already listed here. When Orwell declared 'A writer isn't judged by his "status", he is judged by his work' (CE 2.229), he dipped into a rich source of English vocabulary; when an American Civil Liberties Union functionary said, in 1982, 'We need statutory standards,' he double-dipped.

For English it is. The noun 'state' comes from Latin by way of French, but the suffixes '-ly', '-hood', '-man' are native to English. Our suffix '-man' is the same as our noun 'man', but it does not have the stress of the noun and so though we can hear the difference between 'man' and 'men', the difference between 'statesman' and 'statesmen' is discernible only in the spelling – singular and plural both sound as if they ended [mn]. The suffix '-hood', on the other hand, is not the same as the modern noun 'hood' (which comes from a word related to 'hat'). Instead the suffix comes from an Old English noun that meant 'condition' or – what else – 'state'. In the diachronic perspective, then, 'statehood' is a tautology, a redundant word that says the same thing twice. But the historical perspective is not the only one, and for us 'statehood' says one thing and says it only once ('only once' is also historically redundant: both words come from 'one').

The suffix '-ly' also derives from another word, 'like'; something 'manly' was 'man-like' in the language a thousand years ago. By that token, 'likely' is just as redundant as 'statehood', and so – come to that – is 'fulfill', which is just two words (the adjective 'full' and the derived verb 'fill') clapped together; compare Orwell's 'fullwise' (NE 40). But language soon finds jobs for all the extra population it spawns or adopts, and 'like' has gone one way while the suffix '-ly', even more changed in form by lack of stress than was the suffix '-man', has gone quite another. So we can have not only 'state', 'statehood' and 'stately' and 'statesman', but also 'statesmanlike', 'statesmanly', 'statesmanship', and probably 'statesmanhood'. The combination of these native English suffixes with words borrowed from Greek, Latin and French is a rich source of strength to the English vocabulary, and a continuing one: it involves not only bor-rowing but conversion, derivation, and change of meaning, chief sources of 'the biggest vocabulary in existence'.

Orwell had less to say about some of the other ways that new words have come into English. He noted that 'adjectives can be made more emphatic or given a new twist by tying a noun to them; for example, *lily-white*, *sky-blue*, *coal-black*, *iron-hard*, etc.' (CE 3.24), but his practice was more creative than his examples: 'one of the loudest-lunged patriots in France' (HC 57) and 'nasty, poodle-faking, horseless riffraff' (BD 202) both use participial adjectives for their second element. Orwell readily adopted other compounds – collocations of two words – such as 'world-picture' (CE 4.313), but he gave fullest rein to the possibilities of compounding in the book where he vilified it: *Nineteen Eighty-Four*. The largest part of the words Orwell called 'neologisms' (CE 4.473) in the novel are compounds, usually of two nouns:

doublethink	goodthink	crimethink	oldthink
oldspeak	newspeak	duckspeak	speakwrite
crimestop	thoughtcrime	facecrime	sexcrime
goodsex	bellyfeel	prolefeed	joycamp
ownlife	dayorder	blackwhite	

Only about two dozen such terms appear in the course of the novel and in the Appendix, although Orwell gives several pages to description of the 'B vocabulary' that was 'in all cases compound words' (NE 249). Other terms in Newspeak are not strictly compounds, which are by definition two whole words joined together, but blends, combining one word and part of another, or parts of two words:

Minitrue	Minipax	Minilove	Ingsoc	Pornosec
artsem	thinkpol	Recdep	Ficdep	Teledep

Again, the novel gives the impression that it abounds in these words, but in fact they are relatively few. They are, moreover, not in themselves especially inimical to Orwell's English or ours. From 'bicycle' (two-wheel cycle) we have 'bike'; at a seaside resort you may hire a 'quike' (four-wheel cycle), unless you are a 'workaholic' and remain at the office. You may send a 'Telemessage' by British 'Telecom', perhaps about the extraction of 'biogas' from 'biomass'. You pray with a 'televangelist' to avoid the perils of 'oilgate' (a scandal about oil that reminded some of the American Watergate scandal), of a 'hittile', that is 'a missile so accurate that it could actually hit the target . . . instead of merely exploding alongside it' (*Guardian*, 14 July 1982, p. 3; neither 'Watergate' nor 'missile' has origins that imply the later developments), above all of a 'Euroshima'.

As with blends, so with compounds. The modern formation

'Doublespeak', as we already noted, was not among Orwell's inventions, but one his readers have invented easily enough – not because they have learned his technique for neologism but because his technique is one very common in English.[16] It has given us traditional words like 'blackbird' and 'bootstrap' and new words like 'gridlock', 'lifestyle', and 'Skillcentre'; on the model of 'blackmail' we have 'greymail', the threat to embarrass the prosecution if they continue legal proceedings. Orwell was hostile to compounds when they were reductive or, to his thinking, ugly. Neither effect is desirable, but neither is caused by compounding or blending. In themselves (as in 'themselves') both are perfectly regular and well-established kinds of English word-formation; they are reductive or ugly only when they are inept.

Ambiguity is inherent in compounds; few are self-explanatory. Why, for example, is 'gridlock' a 'locking of the grid' while 'keyboard' is a 'board on which there are keys' and 'bootstrap' a 'strap attached to a boot'? In each the second noun is the category that the first noun 'modifies', but the modification is never the same twice. If an 'icebox' is a box that contains ice, what is a 'pothole' – a stash? Like phrasal verbs and many other language structures (even phrases: an 'electric fire' is conflagration of electric origin in the US, but an electric space-heater in the UK) compounds are 'idiomatic' in that their meaning isn't simply the sum of the meanings of their parts. Compounds composed of verb + noun are rarer but include old ones like 'scarecrow' and newer ones like 'stopgap'. A 'wardrobe' is now chiefly an item of furniture in Britain but, by metonymy, the garments it encloses in America. For someone with Orwell's belief in the 'mental chessboard' theory of language, such uncertainty cannot have been pleasing. Yet despite the uncertainty, the productivity of compounds is enormous: to obtain discount tickets, get a 'Railcard'. To catch a crook, see the 'photofit' (composite photograph, successor to the composite drawing 'Identikit'). To get a job, go to the 'Jobcentre', which you find by asking for the 'labour exchange' just as in New York City you find the 'Avenue of the Americas' by asking for 'Sixth Avenue'; even the pronunciation of compounds is unpredictable.

Orwell lumped together with blends like 'Minilove' others composed of the first letter or letters of several words: 'Pornsec', 'Ficdep' (pornography section, fiction department) among them ('artsem' for artificial insemination is on a somewhat different pattern). He commented,

As for the kaleidoscope of political parties and trade unions, with their tiresome names – P.S.U.C., P.O.U.M., F.A.I., C.N.T., U.G.T., J.C.I., J.S.U., A.I.T. – they merely exasperated me.
(HC 47)

Even in the early decades of the twentieth century, telescoped words and phrases had been one of the characteristic features of political language; and it had been noticed that the tendency to use abbreviations of this kind was most marked in totalitarian countries and totalitarian organizations. Examples were such words as *Nazi, Gestapo, Comintern* . . .
(NE 252)

Words formed this way are called 'acronyms' if we pronounce them as one word, 'initialisms' if we pronounce them one letter at a time: 'radar' is an acronym (for Radio Detecting and Ranging), CIO is an initialism (for Congress of Industrial Organizations); 'But to reject US-inspired arrangements in GATT, the IMF, the OECD, or elsewhere begs the question' (*Guardian*). These examples, unlike Orwell's, suggest that acronyms and initialisms aren't notably characteristic of totalitarianism. Again, Orwell seems to have objected partly on aesthetic grounds, partly because words like 'Nazi' have bad associations, and – although the reason is only implicit – partly because he felt that language embodies reality and so a truncated word can embody only a deformed reality.

In fact acronyms and initialisms, though they do not form a large proportion of Modern English vocabulary (not a large proportion but a large number; a sizeable dictionary of them has had to be repeatedly revised),[17] fit the language perfectly well. A clear sign is their adoption as words, often without the user's knowing the original form or even that the word is not the original form. For most users 'radar' is simply radar; its origin is beside the point. 'PCV' is an initialism for 'pollution control valve', but it frequently occurs in both popular and technical use as 'PCV valve', without the user's realizing that 'v' already signifies 'valve'. The 'Strategic Arms Limitation Talks', likewise, are usually called the 'SALT talks'; many who use the term do not know what the acronym stands for or that the phrase is redundant. So also 'Sam missiles', 'IRA accounts'; they reproduce in acronyms the redundancies found in words like 'fulfill', 'likely', and 'statehood', and in phrases like *Medieval Age* (name of a book).

The English vocabulary also grows by the adoption of proper names, as Orwell observed in his satires on advertising (pp. 144–5).

Generic and proprietary drug names are especially fecund, though not many of these are likely to follow 'aspirin' into the general vocabulary. A more homely list is composed of bathroom and wash-day products, whether English words like 'Dot', adaptations from English like 'Jif', borrowings from abroad like 'Persil' (French, 'parsley') or outright coinages like 'Radox'.

Two courses of language change are more difficult to chart, especially for the amateur language critic: pronunciation and meaning. Of the former Orwell had understandably little to say. (The Orwell who predicted the advent of decimal currency in Britain knew that '10d' was pronounced 'ten pence' but might all the same have been surprised to find that '10p' is pronounced 'ten [pi:].' Present-day 'cwt' is still pronounced 'hundredweight'.) He made, to be sure, lengthy attempts to represent non-standard English in his essays and novels, using a kind of phonetic spelling. But these were in the synchronic, not the diachronic perspective; he was little concerned with non-standard pronunciation as an aspect of language change, a sign of the linguistic system in a constant state of becoming. Only, perhaps, in one 'As I Please' column and hence in a relatively unde-veloped form did he remark that

> there is the general slovenliness of modern English speech with its deca-dent vowel sounds (throughout the London area you have to use sign language to distinguish between 'threepence' and 'three-halfpence') and its tendency to make verbs and nouns interchangeable.
> (CE 3.109)

Even here the critic's presuppositions distort his view, giving 'slovenliness' and 'decadent', linking sound changes with grammar – not as systems but as symptoms. In fact most sound changes that result in homophones, 'sound-alike' words, do not bring anything like serious confusion.[18] Many present-day speakers of British Engl-ish pronounce <l> after a vowel with lips rounded, so that 'stall' sounds like 'store'; but if context does not differentiate the words, an initial vowel in the next word may, so that 'stall (out)' does not sound like 'store (up)'. Sometimes it is the grammatical context that distinguishes homophones. 'Away' (from 'on way') sounds like 'a way' (from 'one way'), but 'Let's go away' and 'Let's find a way' are instantly distinct because 'away' usually follows intransitive verbs, 'a way' transitive ones.

Orwell regarded words as labels on fixed meanings, so he usually explained changes in meaning when he noticed them: 'slicked back in what people used to call a "smarm" ' (CA 113), for example, though we may wonder what he meant by a 'knocking-shop' (CA 180). The fullest treatment again comes in an 'As I Please' column. It is difficult to condense something already so compact, but the salient points are these:

> If one cares about the preservation of the English language, a point one often has to decide is whether it is worth putting up a struggle when a word changes its meaning.
>
> Some words are beyond redemption. One could not, I imagine, restore 'impertinent' to its original meaning, or 'journal', or 'decimate'. But how about the use of 'infer' for 'imply' . . . which has been gaining ground for some years? Ought one to protest against it? And ought one to acquiesce when certain words have their meanings arbitrarily narrowed? . . . Constant use of such phrases as 'intimacy took place twice' has practically killed the original meaning of 'intimacy', and quite a dozen other words have been perverted in the same way.
>
> Obviously this kind of thing ought to be prevented if possible, but it is uncertain whether one can achieve anything by struggling against the current usage. The coming and going of words is a mysterious process whose rules we do not understand . . . for example the word 'car', which had never had any currency in England except in high-flown classical poetry, but was resurrected about 1900 to describe the newly invented automobile.
>
> Possibly, therefore, the degradation which is certainly happening to our language is a process which one cannot arrest by conscious action. But I would like to see the attempt made.
> (CE 3.325–6)

Again the strong opening – the preservation of the English language is at stake. Words are 'perverted', the language is 'degraded'. Orwell felt uncertain 'whether one can achieve anything by struggling against the current usage', as Fowler felt 'It is perhaps another piece of presumption to suppose that one can do anything to help a language into right and divert it from wrong tracks' (SPE 26 [1927], p. 194). Yet Orwell's examples do not even support his charge against 'current usage'. He considered 'infer' to mean 'conclude or judge from premises or evidence', 'imply' to mean 'indicate or suggest without express statement, as something to be inferred' (RCD s.v. 'infer', 'imply'). In a discourse the speaker would imply and the listener would infer. But those meanings are simplifications of what the words have meant in English since their introduction in the early sixteenth century – both, apparently, by the scholar-saint Sir Thomas More (the poet laureate Skelton had used 'infer' in a quite different sense, now obsolete, a few years earlier). It was also More who first used 'infer' in the sense here given for 'imply'! In this he was followed by Spenser's schoolmaster Mulcaster later in the sixteenth century, by Milton in the seventeenth, and by James Mill and Sir Walter Scott in the nineteenth, among others. Orwell was misled by his reification of language and by his label theory of meaning, most of all by his not having looked into a historical dictionary for information about change of meaning (which would also have softened his 'never any' generalization about 'car').

The history of a word always involves change; it sometimes also involves erroneous intervention, not least by those whose classical education has not taught them to leave well enough alone. The ptarmigan, beloved of Orwell's wealthy Scottish schoolmates, gets its name from Gaelic *tarmarchan*; the initial 'p' seems to have been the idea of someone who had 'pterodactyl', 'Ptolemy', or just 'ptomaine', in mind. A 'cutlet' is a 'small rib' from French *côtelette*; like german *Schnitzel*, however, for the same piece of meat, English 'cutlet' seems to assume *côtelette* means a 'small cut', the assumption that makes 'turkey cutlet' intelligible.

But error is not the only cause of change, even far-reaching change of meaning. Latin had a noun *cardo* ('hinge') that gave an adjective *cardinalis*: something 'cardinal' was important because everything hinged on it. That is the meaning of 'cardinal vowels' and 'cardinal numbers'. But 'cardinal priests' were 'attached to their particular church in a stable relation, as a door to a building by its hinges' (*Oxford Dictionary of English Etymology*). When the priests took to wearing red vestments, 'cardinal' was applied to other red things, including red birds. The major league baseball Cardinals are named after the birds, not the colour or the prelates or the status or the hinges. Like 'cardinal', 'nominal' is an adjective from a noun, *nomen* ('name' or 'noun' itself). So 'nominal' can mean 'in name only': board measurements are usually 'nominal' because the finished board will be smaller after planing. A 'nominal' charge is 'small' or 'moderate', not a full charge for the goods or service. A nominal suffix, on the other hand, goes on a noun. And in National Aeronautics and Space Administration parlance, 'all functions are nominal' means they are normal, not that they are only moderate or will be smaller after planing.

Orwell knew that meaning change was not restricted to such changes of referent. He wrote of 'Britisher',

> This word was used for years as a term of opprobrium in the anglophobe American press. Later on, Northcliffe and others, looking round for some substitute for 'Englishman' which should have an imperialistic and jingoistic flavour, found 'Britisher' ready to hand, and took it over. Since then the word has had an aura of gutter patriotism, and the kind of person who tells you that 'what these natives need is a firm hand' also tells you that he is 'proud to be a Britisher' – which is about equivalent to a Chinese Nationalist describing himself as a 'Chink'.
> (CE 3.327; 'As I Please', 2 February 1945)[19]

This kind of change elevates (or 'ameliorates') the meaning of the word. It happened also with 'Yankee', which has gone through several periods of use as 'a term of opprobrium' but now – depending only a little on who uses it, and of whom – is generally neutral or laudatory.

As Orwell also knew, however, the opposite tendency is more common, casting a previously neutral or laudatory word in an opprobrious role. He wrote a lengthy 'As I Please' piece (CE 3.111–14) on the 'unanswered question . . . "What is Fascism?" ' Unlike most of his 'As I Please' columns, this one devoted its entire twelve hundred words or so to one subject, during the course of which Orwell listed eight groups to which he had seen ' "Fascist", applied in all seriousness . . .' The groups ranged from war resisters to supporters of the war, from Trotskyists to Catholics, from Conservatives to Communists. Orwell lamented that 'in internal politics . . . this word has lost the last vestige of meaning' and 'It will be seen that, as used, the word "Fascism" is almost entirely meaningless.'

His lament was not really over loss of meaning, however, but over a shift of meaning from objective definition to subjective reaction. Orwell knew as much:

> even the people who recklessly fling the word 'Fascist' in every direction attach at any rate an emotional significance to it. By 'Fascism' they mean, roughly speaking, something cruel, unscrupulous, arrogant, obscurantist, anti-liberal and anti-working-class . . . That is about as near to a definition as this much-abused word has come . . .
>   All one can do for the moment is to use the word with a certain amount of circumspection and not, as is usually done, degrade it to the level of a swearword.[20]

The changes of meaning Orwell remarked on here are degradation as he aptly noted (sometimes called 'pejoration'), and generalization. Both changes, in the gloomy world we inhabit, are common: 'lewd' used only to mean 'not educated' but now has nothing to do with education; 'ostracize' used to mean 'banish in consequence of a vote using pieces of shell [compare 'oyster'] as ballots' but is now far more general. To 'ostracize for lewdness' nowadays is not at all what it was. The verb 'harvest' meant 'to gather (a crop or the like)' (RCD), but can also mean 'to remove for transplanting (a liver or the like)' and 'to hunt so as to reduce in number (deer or the like)'. 'Lust' has gone the other way; it once meant simply 'pleasure', and has taken on its modern meaning by the process called specialization, like Orwell's 'intimacy'. Such changes may impede rational political discussion but they facilitate political invective (compare the discussions of 'Trotskyist', HC 176 ff.; CE 1.274; CE 3.327; *Guardian*, 2 August 1982, p. 10, and 3 August 1982, p. 1). That may not be an improvement but it is a fact, and to go on using 'Fascist' (or 'Britisher', 'Yankee', 'intimacy', 'lust', 'lewd', 'ostracize') as though nothing had happened will neither help rational political discussion nor restore the word to its former aura of meaning.

'Former' here simply means 'previous'; it does not mean 'original' and certainly not 'true'. For many words the original meaning is long lost, and for few is any earlier meaning more 'true' than the present meaning. Orwell's 'aspidistra' provides an example. Though formed on classical elements, it is not a classical word: the OED Supplement (1933) cites its first appearance as 1822. It is derived from Greek *aspid-*, 'shield', and *(tup)istra*, from Greek *tupis* 'mallet' and *-tra*, an instrumental suffix (*tupis* is related to *tupos*, 'blow [as of a hammer]' and gives modern 'type', 'that which is struck'). An 'aspidistra' is then a shield-shaped member of a plant family whose forms recall a mallet. Whether a plant can really resemble a shield or mallet, or both at once, is not the question. 'Aspidistra' simply means 'aspidistra', and a reflective gardener might well think of different comparisons. Most who know nothing of the word's etymology recognize the plant without trouble. And Orwell's 'aspidistral' (which the OED 1972 Supplement credits to him) refers only to the plant, not to the shield or the mallet.

The present meaning remains a meaning. When a London entrepreneur opens a hair dressing salon 'partly to dispel "the myth of black hairdressing as a back-street business" – a view which he considers was fairly accurate at the time' (*Guardian*, 4 August 1982, p. 9), 'myth' simply means 'belief' without the usual suggestion of uncritical acceptance. When, years earlier, the *Daily Worker* demanded the British Admiralty to 'sweep the mad dogs from the seas', however, Orwell commented 'Clearly, people capable of using such phrases have ceased to remember that words have meaning' (CE 3.110; also later on p. 110, 331–2, and CE 4.272). His comments of this kind often referred to mixed or dead metaphors, but they stemmed from Orwell's more general belief that words have distinct and correct meanings like labels, and that any alteration of them is simply mislabelling. Yet meaning has always changed in living languages as a glance at any page of his dictionary would have reminded Orwell. The skilful writer does not respond by holding out against language change, but by recognizing and implementing it. To those who follow horse racing, a 'track record' is the speed record for a given track, and 'That horse holds the track record' means that animal set that record. More recently 'track record' has come to mean something less technical and specific, very nearly the same as 'record': 'this country's track record', for example, or 'a viable track record', 'a proven track record', even 'a bad track record'. 'Course record' (from golf) has not yet changed like 'track record', but to insist that a 'track record' can only be excellent, or that it pertains only to the track and not to the horse, is to invite the criticism that you 'have ceased to remember that words change meaning'.

Change of referent can bring change of pronunciation and lead to a new word in the language. Orwell wrote of his heroine's 'cosmos' (CD 308), to rhyme with 'gross'. But we can write of the New York 'Cosmos' (of the North American Soccer League), to rhyme with 'grows': one 'Cosmo', two 'Cosmos'. And words can change meaning, form, or both by sound attraction with other words. Orwell wrote 'At a pitch I could be a tolerable road-sweeper' (RW 32); later he wrote 'when the pinch comes' (RW 211). If the former is not just a typographical error, it is an error of the kind that has changed the language substantially. When a chairperson wrote in a draft that a programme, after a good start, had 'foundered' for lack of administrative support, a linguist member of the committee corrected him: 'It should be "floundered" '. The dictionary holds with the chairperson, but the dictionary itself may soon be in error if the popular opinion of the member – common among those who do not know the sea – spreads much more. The same is happening with 'flout/flaunt', 'mitigate/militate', 'veracious/voracious', 'eminent/imminent'. And the same happened long ago when, to name but one instance out of many, the stylish whiskers on the American Civil War general A.E. Burnside became so popular as 'burnsides' that they were known where he was not, and his name posed a mystery that ignorance solved by reversing it; as the whiskers appeared on the side of the face, 'sideburns' made sense so far as that half of the word was concerned. As for the other half, the language already had a word 'sideboard' (piece of dining room furniture) that fitted nicely – the whiskers looked more like boards than burns, apparently. Both changes were a form of 'folk etymology', the 'modification of a linguistic form according to a falsely assumed etymology' (RCD s.v.). In one perspective such changes are mistakes, but only those actually underway attract the censure of observers. Those already established – which include respected vocables like 'gooseberry' – are sanctioned by an unwritten linguistic grandfather clause ('ignorance is bliss' variety). Those newly in use – which include 'palimony', compensation to a former domestic partner who was not a spouse and hence not entitled to 'alimony' – seem to fill a need in the language, and that is all the sanction they require.

Of all language change, change of meaning is the most rapid and continuous. Inflections are relatively stable: an old plural like 'shoon' is slow to become 'shoes', and the '-en' suffix is even slower to leave the language – it remains in 'oxen', 'children', and a few other words. Words themselves come and go, but every word has several pronunciations and many have several meanings. It is theoretically possible to list the words, though it is a job that even the huge OED did not pretend to have completed; and to list the pronunciations would not be out of the question, since the language has relatively few distinctive sounds and the way they differ from one variety of English to another is fairly predictable. But to list the meanings of all the words is hardly even theoretically possible, not only because they are many but because they are continually changing. To resist changes in meaning is to fight for something we would not recognize as language and could not use as we use English.

A word that takes on a new meaning may take on a new form with it. The new form usually follows the pattern of most words in that form class ('part of speech'). Though 'medium' as an English noun has the plural 'mediums' ('She paints in several mediums', or 'He consulted several mediums'), the Latin plural 'media' now means 'that which mediates between a news source and its audience', hence the 'print media' or 'electronic media', often as an English singular; the Latin plural ending in -a is now unfamiliar in English, so that 'media' often appears as a singular with the plural 'medias'. In the sense 'not good', 'bad' has an ancient superlative 'worst'; in its more recent sense 'stylish and suave', it has the more 'regular' superlative 'baddest'. The two senses of 'bad' are ambiguous in the positive degree but differentiated in the superlative degree, just as 'media' may be the plural of 'medium' or the singular of 'medias'. Structure changes more slowly than vocabulary; structure arranges words into phrases, clauses and sentences, and while the words can change readily, the arrangements can't. And we are more aware of words than of structures. The arrangement of words in 'nineteen eighty-four', as we've already seen, is characteristic of Modern English; other modern languages use different arrangements. Yet we are not so analytically aware of 'nineteen eighty-four' as we are of 'contact' (verb), 'concertize', or 'Newspeak'.

Modern English structures for the negative are complicated, but we become aware of their complications only when we run into an unfamiliar version. The version may be from a different variety – many British varieties fuse 'will' with the pronoun where American varieites would fuse it with the negative:

> BR: You'll not see me here again.
> AM: You won't see me here again.

But the British version differs from the American only where the subject is a pronoun and the verb is 'will' or 'shall'. If the subject is a noun, or the verb is not 'will/shall', the British version will be the same as the American, e.g., 'Dad can't do it.' Other differences may be obvious if the version is old enough; English a thousand years ago made the negative a prefix to 'will' instead of a suffix, giving *nillath ge* ('not willeth ye').

In most varieties of Modern English the rule for negation, interrogation, and emphasis adds a form of 'do' with the negative suffix:

> I want to see you.
> I don't want to see you.
>
> Come here.
> Don't come here.
>
> He runs marthons.
> Does he run marathons?
>
> I wish you would stop.
> I do wish you would stop.

A different rule applies when the verb is a form of 'be' or one of the 'modal auxiliaries' ('will', 'shall', 'may', 'can', 'must', 'do', and – in some varieties – 'have', 'dare', 'need'):

> I am angry.
> I am not (I'm not) angry.
>
> I can read Hindi.
> I cannot (I can't) read Hindi.
>
> I dare say.
> I dare not (daren't) say.

Orwell's English had the same rule for these verbs, and for 'use' as well:

> 'Used you not . . . to do horrible things . . .?' (CD 296)
> 'Surely that usen't to be there?' (CA 210)

It also added 'have' both as an auxiliary and as a main verb:

> 'I had not to wash the plates . . .' (PL 67)
> 'When the private soldier had not a cigarette, the general had not one either.' (HC 87)

The second example, with 'have' as a main verb, would seem familiar now only if fused: 'When the private soldier hadn't a cigarette . . .' But for many speakers it would seem even more familiar with 'do' and a negative suffix: 'When the private soldier didn't have (BR: 'hadn't got') a cigarette . . .' That is even more true of the first example, where the auxiliary 'have' now seems archaic and 'I didn't have to wash the plates' would be far more familiar.

The rule that exempts 'be' and the modal auxiliaries from the insertion of 'do' in negatives is not an irregularity or an exception; in fact it takes precedence over the insertion rule so that 'do' appears only if the main verb is *not* on the 'be' and modal auxiliary list. And because 'be' and the modals occur in a great many sentences, ordinary discourse suspends the general insertion rule quite frequently. All the same, the insertion of 'do' in negatives is general to every verb in English save a very few, and even in the short time since Orwell wrote the list of exemptions has grown shorter. Words like 'have', which belong on both lists, now behave more often like main verbs even if they function as auxiliaries; the same is true of 'dare' and 'need'. For Orwell the developments of the last generation would have seemed 'errors'. They were departures from the negation system of his English, and such structures are a deeply-rooted, slowly-changing aspect of a language. Yet the changes are now part of our negation system, and the drift of the changes in the direction of greater uniformity is probably inevitable: if you don't remember all the other verbs on the list with 'be', it is the pattern of the general rule that you will use.

Analogy, which levelled 'have' into the general non-auxiliaries, and, in Newspeak, 'thought' into 'think', easily levels superficial sound-alikes (homophones) into look-alikes (homographs): 'cite' and 'site' become identical to 'sight' not only in pronunciation but in print. The reader may have an unfavourable opinion of this development, and surface features commonly receive most of the attention, favourable or not. The changes in 'have', because they are more profound, have been slower and hence receive less attention. Their effects on the structure of the language, all the same, are more important.

Other changes still taking place affect the plural and possessive of nouns. British English uses a plural verb with many mass nouns ('The crew are hoping'; 'Ford were not'). British written English often omits the apostrophe on the possessive of proper nouns ('Barclays Bank', but 'Williams and Glyn's Bank') and sporadically on common nouns ('This weeks special'). So we find '. . . the head of CBI's ecnomic team and the chairman of the giant Reckitt & Colman combine . . . At Reckitts . . .'²¹ Though the literal error 'ecnomic' disarms confident analysis, 'Reckitts' appears to be neither true plural nor true possessive but a replacement for both, visible again in 'Clarks help parents' (that is, Clark Shoe Company; compare 'Teachers College Press' in New York). The replacement, if it is completed, will aid the many writers for whom the apostrophe is intractable. In 1982 a leaflet describing the 'EasyFiler' database management program used 'it's' as a possessive adjective and 'use's' as a third-person singular verb; and an advertisement in *TV Guide* promised 'The Most Special Walton's Movie of All . . . "A Day for Thanks on Waltons Mountain" '.

Those problems do not occur in Orwell's prose (e.g., 'Boys' Weeklies'), and neither do the possessive noun forms in '-s'. They are innovations, but the forms of written English he used were generally conservative even for his day, reflecting his middle-class education before the First World War and especially his language views. His view of language was a reaction, not a description or an analysis. His nostalgia shaped it, not his curiosity or knowledge about the early language, even such as the OED offered. He accepted, consequently, the English he learned as if it were unchanged from its origins, but despite a few comments to the contrary, he regularly protested further change as if it threatened the fabric of the language. Our knowledge of the early language, on the other hand, shows that Orwell's English was the product of centuries of change, and our knowledge of modern British and American English shows that it has continued to change even since Orwell wrote.

CHAPTER III

Language Variety

𒀭𒀭𒀭𒀭𒀭

FROM LANGUAGE CHANGE comes language variety. Sometimes the variation is slight, unnoticeable; sometimes it is marked; sometimes it is extreme, so the differences mask any similarities. The example of 'eight' from Chapter One will serve.

Orwell knew English language varieties like [eit] and [ait] that rhymed with 'bait' and 'bite' (compare his remarks on 'face' and 'fice', p. 93). He knew foreign language varieties like German *acht*, Spanish *ocho*, French *huit*, Hindi *ath*, and Latin *octo*. And he probably knew that they are not all varieties on the same level; that, for example, just as [eit] and [ait] are pronunciation varieties of <eight>, so *ocho* and *huit* are lineal varieties of the ancestor *octo*. Two are living pronunciations of <eight> and two are living descendants of *octo*. But while the Spanish and French pair descend from a common ancestor recorded in Latin *octo*, the German and English pair descend from an unrecorded ancestor: unlike Latin, the 'parent' language they have in common, now called Germanic, was never written down. The Latin family, and other examples, have enabled linguists to develop techniques for reconstructing the lost ancestors of many modern words. Their results do not really yield words; they yield only theories. A theory is a scenario to explain some known facts. In the case of German and English, a word like **ahto* would explain both *acht* and 'eight'. The reconstructed form seems remote from the modern forms, but it fits well with other words that entered German and English from Germanic, like *nacht* and 'night'.[1]

Hindi *ath* too seems remote from modern *acht*, 'eight', *ocho* and *huit*. Records show, all the same, that it descends not from Latin *octo* but from Sanskrit *ashtau*; Sanskrit was the ancient language of India, a written language roughly contemporary with Latin and a bit older than Germanic, related to both. Records, reconstruction, modern languages and their varieties together enable us to construct a historical 'tree' for {eight} in these languages:

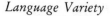

Language Variety

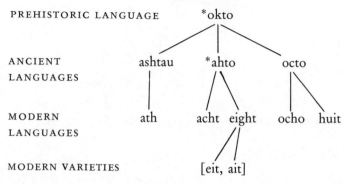

PREHISTORIC LANGUAGE *okto

ANCIENT LANGUAGES   ashtau   *ahto   octo

MODERN LANGUAGES   ath   acht eight   ocho huit

MODERN VARIETIES   [eit, ait]

The tree-chart shows that language changes, and that the change is always in the direction of greater variety. For Latin *octo* also gave Italian *otto* and Germanic *ahto* also gave Old Norse *átta*, to name only a few among many; and the modern pronunciations of <eight> are more than the two listed in this chart. The three ancient forms are also varieties of a common ancestor. Like Germanic *ahto* it was a word in an unwritten language, and we have only a theoretical knowledge of its form: most theories converge on something like *okto*, name the language Indo-European, and give its heyday as sometime about 1500 BC.

The chart shows something else about variety: first, that every language is a variety descended from some other less varied language; second, that change is patterned, not random; third, that the pattern is not explainable in terms of 'facility' or 'sloppiness' (we do not know why Sanskrit found *ashtau* a more appropriate version of *okto* than *ahto*, but it almost certainly had nothing to do with the anatomy, temperament or environment of the speakers); finally, that observation and reconstruction enable us to 'stack' the varieties that come from change in several layers. The chart above shows these layers historically, diachronically. The chart on the next page shows them descriptively, synchronically.

The synchronic levels are not all the same sort. The bottom and the top are easier to define – the individual can't be subdivided (which is what 'individual' means), and the language can't be extended; otherwise it includes some varieties not intelligible to a speaker of another variety, and in such a case we would usually say they are not the same language. In between, however, it is a matter of definition: we can make our regional varieties the right size for a large nation or for a

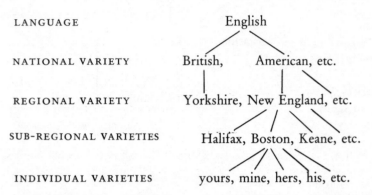

small neighbourhood. However we define it, these varieties of a language are usually called 'dialects'. That term is useful so long as we do not start thinking that one of these dialects is any more the 'language' than any other; for, as the chart shows, 'language' is simply the properties that make the dialects mutually intelligible. It is the sum of the parts, and no part is the sum more than any other. In fact, unlike the language, the dialects do not really have autonomous existence; a dialect is only what we define it to be, and it need not even be regional (it could be class, occupational, age, or some other kind).[2]

But if a language is the sum of its dialects, what is a dialect? It is the sum of the features common to the individual language systems of its speakers. What each of us speaks is not a language, or even a dialect, but an idiolect. We may all be English speakers in the sense that our language systems are mutually intelligible, but since 'English' is only a title for what makes them so, we cannot be said to speak it. In fact 'English' is a *langue* and what we speak is *parole*. The same is true of dialects, though in them the *langue* has more rules (a dialect is more restricted than a language).

We see the chart, however, from our viewpoint as idiolect-speakers. The language we use is central to us, and varieties that depart from our usage seem alien; the greater the departure the more alien. When the variety is beyond the horizon it is foreign even though it may be kindred, so – for example – if we are to understand German we must learn it deliberately. We don't have to learn the English of our elders, our neighbours, or our transatlantic cousins. Their language may have unfamiliar features, but it isn't foreign.

Yet the very unfamiliarity can breed contempt. The German

speaks another language; that is as it should be. But why do our elders, our neighbours and our visitors make such a mess of the language we share? Why don't they speak proper English? We could glance at the chart to remind ourselves that they do not speak proper English because no one speaks 'English'; that English as a generalization is unspeakable, and the least rule-governed level of language variety. We could but, most often, we do not.

In *Keep the Aspidistra Flying*, the down-at-heel poet-hero, passing the day in a public library, picks up a women's paper:

> It was an American paper of the more domestic kind, mainly adverts with a few stories lurking apologetically among them. And *what* adverts! . . . A panorama of ignorance, greed, vulgarity, snobbishness, whoredom and disease . . .
> Christ, what muck!
> But of course it was an American paper. The Americans always go one better on any kind of beastliness, whether it is ice-cream soda, racketeering or theosophy.
> (KA 234–5)

The reaction was in accord with Orwell's view (p. 46) that 'American has some of the vices of English in an exaggerated form', and (p. 39) that anti-American feeling disappeared in connection 'with the fall of Latin and Greek . . . as school subjects'. He explained the second remark, 'The younger intellectuals have no objection to the American language and tend to have a masochistic attitude towards the USA, which they believe to be richer and more powerful than Britain' (CE 2.177). For the certainties of Latin and Greek, that is, the new intelligentsia had substituted the anxieties of masochism. Orwell later wrote to *Partisan Review* 'about Anglo-American relations':

> During the period 1935–9 the Left intelligentsia were taken in to a surprising extent by the 'anti-Fascist' antics in which so many American newspapers indulged. There was also a tendency to crouch culturally towards America and urge the superiority of the American language and even the American accent. This attitude is changing, however, as it begins to be grasped that the USA is potentially imperialist and politically a long way behind Britain.
> (CE 2.278–9)

Orwell clearly thought the transatlantic English-speaking nation not only rich and powerful but corrupt and even criminal. Of a bandit in Mark Twain's autobiographical *Roughing It*, he said:

It is perfectly clear that Mark Twain admires this disgusting scoundrel. Slade was successful; therefore he was admirable. This outlook, no less common today, is summed up in the significant American expression 'to *make good*'.
(CE 2.327)[3]

The comment is Orwellian; sweeping 'perfectly clear' and 'no less common today', self-explanatory 'disgusting', the tawdry syllogism, and – most to our present purpose – the discovery of national moral habits in national speechways.

The American impact on British English was not something Orwell could easily measure. He believed that 'there are great numbers of English people who are partly Americanised in language and, one ought to add, in moral outlook' (CE 3.219). Yet in a 1936 letter to Henry Miller he wrote, 'I noticed also when I worked in the bookshop that it is harder and harder to sell American books in England. The two languages are drifting further and further apart' (CE 1.229). But the meaning of the impact was something else: 'On the whole we are justified in regarding the American language with suspicion. We ought to be ready to borrow its best words, but we ought not to let it modify the actual structure of our language' (CE 3.29).

Orwell acknowledged some virtue in 'the American language' (as he called it, not 'dialect' or 'variety'; see also CE 3.217). In *Homage to Catalonia* he recalled the moment the sniper's bullet hit his neck, and 'The American sentry I had been talking to had started forward. "Gosh! Are you hit?" ' (HC 185). It is literary dialogue like this that he must have meant when, writing of a passage in Miller's *Tropic of Cancer*, he said 'The American language is less flexible and refined than the English, but it has more life in it, perhaps' (CE 1.156). Even here his praise was doubly faint. In the course of his essay on 'The English Language', by contrast, Orwell repeatedly turned to America for examples of the worst tendencies in Modern English. He began with simple description,

> There is no such thing in English as declension of nouns, and there is no gender. Nor are there many irregular plurals or comparatives. Moreover, the tendency is always towards greater simplicity, both in grammar and syntax.
> (CE 3.25)

Different schools of linguistic description would take different views of this passage; many would want to adjust the blanket statement of the opening sentence, the meaning of 'irregular', 'simplicity', the distinction between 'grammar' and 'syntax'. But in any event Orwell's remarks were descriptions. He followed them immediately, however, with evaluations that he offered as though they too were merely descriptive:

> Long sentences with dependent clauses grow more and more unpopular, irregular but time-saving formations such as the 'American subjunctive' (*it is necessary that you go* instead of *it is necessary that you should go*) gain ground . . .

The first remark is simply impressionistic: among writers or speakers? Of which countries or classes? What is the numerical equivalent of 'more and more unpopular'? The second statement is, if meant as historical observation, backwards: the formation that Orwell said was 'gaining ground' is actually older than the one he believed was losing ground. The whole demands paraphrase: 'I like long hypotactic sentences and verb phrases; to the extent I feel their use declining, I mean to blame the decline on the Americans.'

Orwell implied that he was unreceptive to American pronunciation. When he addressed the subject directly he went even further:

> As to accent, it is doubtful whether the American accent has the superiority which it is now fashionable to claim for it. The 'educated' English accent, a product of the last thirty years, is undoubtedly very bad and is likely to be abandoned, but the average English person probably speaks as clearly as the average American. Most English people blur their vowel sounds, but most Americans swallow their consonants. Many Americans pronounce, for instance, *water* as though it had no T in it, or even as though it had no consonant in it at all, except the W.
> (CE 3.29)

Again the reader seems to recognize what Orwell meant – the British pronunciation of 'laboratory' and 'secretary' is notoriously one syllable shorter than the American because the penultimate vowel is 'blurred' in Britain, and some Americans do make an invertebrate monosyllable out of 'water'. But those examples do not exhaust the differences in pronunciation, and others seem to contradict them: most British pronunciations of 'missile', 'futile' and similar words have vowels less 'blurred' than the commonest American pronunciations; most American pronunciations of [r] after a vowel, as in 'water', do not 'swallow' the consonant as most British pronunciations do. The generalizations are too broad, founded on too few examples.[4]

The historical comments were, as usual with Orwell, not even up to the standard of the synchronic: language changes continuously, so all varieties of pronunciation are 'the product of the last thirty years' or of any other spell you choose, and all are 'likely to be abandoned'. Those are truisms, but not distinctively true of the educated English accent when Orwell wrote in 1944. His contention that the 'educated' English accent was 'undoubtedly very bad' omits to say 'undoubted' by whom or 'bad' for what, but those oversights too were usual in his language judgments.

The spread of American in London and other urban centres Orwell attributed to modern mass media: 'In the big towns they are being more and more Americanised in speech through the medium of the cinema' (CE 2.178; cf. 3.58). Even the impact of colloquial English on writing reflected the spread, for Orwell thought 'we've borrowed much more from America than from the speech of the English working class' (CE 2.40), perhaps because he thought the literati borrowed both directly from America and indirectly through the Americanized British workers.

With American English, as with most language topics, Orwell concentrated on vocabulary. He allowed that

> many American words and expressions are well worth adopting. Some are necessary neologisms, others (for instance, *fall* for *autumn*) are old words which we ought never to have dropped. But it ought to be realised that on the whole American is a bad influence and has already had a debasing effect.
> (CE 3.28)

The effect, Orwell went on, involves conversion and phrasal verbs, but also derivations like '*beautician*, *moronic*, and *sexualise*'. American 'often replaces strong primary words by feeble euphemisms' – 'the word *death* and various words that go with it (*corpse, coffin, shroud*)' are 'almost unmentionable'. Of course conversion, phrasal verbs, derivation, and euphemism are resources in British English as well, so Orwell's objection here is not to the structure of American English but to American ways of implementing that structure.

Of the resources themselves, he said

> above all, to adopt the American language whole-heartedly would probably mean a huge loss of vocabulary. For though American produces vivid

and witty turns of speech, it is terribly poor in names for natural objects and localities. Even the streets in American cities are usually known by numbers instead of names. If we really intended to model our language upon American we should have, for instance, to lump the lady-bird, the daddy-long-legs, the saw-fly, the water-boatman, the cockchafer, the cricket, the death-watch beetle and scores of other insects all together under the inexpressive name of *bug*. We should lose the poetic names of our wild flowers, and also, probably, our habit of giving individual names to every street, pub, field, lane, and hillock. In so far as American is adopted, that is the tendency.
(CE 3.28–9)

Orwell was, to be sure, using 'city' in the British sense, 'a municipal unit of considerable size'. Yet even in an undoubted city like Trenton, the capital of New Jersey, numbered streets are almost unknown. Orwell's examples from the nomenclature of entomology were no improvement. In the 1930s survey for the *Linguistic Atlas of the Eastern States*, one test item was the local name for the insect variously called the 'dragon-fly', 'devil's darning-needle', 'mosquito hawk', 'spindle', 'snake doctor', 'snake feeder', 'snake heeder', 'snake guarder', 'snake servant', 'snake waiter', but never 'bug'.

Orwell's remarks about American vocabulary were ill-informed, then, in ways that published works like the DAE or Mencken's *American Language* (1919, 1921, 1923, 1936 and supplements), or even the SPE *Tracts*, could have remedied.[5] His lack of information did not inhibit Orwell, however, any more than it inhibited his remarks about American grammar and pronunciation. He really did not want to know. His views of American English were no more rigorous than his other linguistic views, and they were deformed by his considerable bias against American social and political institutions.

It is not in isolated words like American 'bug' or British 'knock-on' (not in RCD, *American Heritage* or *Webster's Seventh New Collegiate Dictionary* but obvious enough to British readers for unexplained use in the *Guardian*, 'He was referring to the knock-on effects') that the important differences between British and American English lie. Instead they lie chiefly in patterns of pronunciation and grammar, like the distinctive features of any two related varieties of a language. Where they do lie in vocabulary, it is in vocabulary expressive of important national institutions. Patterns of pronunciation, both individual sounds like the <l> in 'stall' and the overall 'melody' of the sentence, are a concrete but rather specialized subject. So are patterns of grammar, some of them already touched on in this book. To return only to the intricacies of 'do', both US and UK English have the question 'He does, does he?' but for UK 'He could do' US has 'He could'. At a less formal level, UK has 'We do snacks in the evening' where US has 'He's doing smack on the weekend'. The first set of differences is one of grammatical pattern, the second of word meaning.

'Programme' (US 'program') is not a new word in English: it meant 'public notice' in the seventeenth century, from Greek *pro* 'before' [viz., the public] + *gramma* 'writing'. In the nineteenth century it was 'a descriptive notice or plan of intended proceedings', and in the twentieth the proceedings themselves: a radio programme, a concert programme, a social programme. A computer program is also a 'plan of intended proceedings' (though more exactly it is a set of instructions). It has become an extra word in many phrases: 'an established program of research' is simply 'established research'. But elsewhere it is shorthand for longer phrases like 'government operations providing funds and training to assist the indigent' in political demands for 'more programs'. That is notably a US development closely akin to the development of 'scheme' in the UK: the Federated Superannuation Scheme for Universities, for example. (The noun 'scheme' in the US has most of the bad overtones of the verb.) But the US use of 'program' is beginning to appear in Britain, both in journalistic prose where it is a synonym for 'scheme' ('In all, 553,000 young people entered the programme in the year to April 1, 1982, when fewer than 3,500 of the year's school leavers were still awaiting . . . a place in the scheme') and in official titles where it has a shade of different meaning ('The plan was announced as the Manpower Services' Commission gave its approval to a new Community Programme Scheme'). The UK sense of 'programme' as distinct from 'scheme', it appears, will express a difference between American and British social institutions.

The causal connection between society and its language was one Orwell habitually assumed and put to evaluative use. Yet neither the direction nor the arena of the causality are explicit in Orwell and those who share his views. Does a corrupt society produce a corrupt language or vice-versa? By Orwell's standards or those of most other moderns, the society of Elizabeth I was 'corrupt'; but it was precisely for his language that Orwell defended Shakespeare against detractors (e.g., CE 4.300–1). Is a primitive language always and only characteristic of primitive cultures? Modern society has not become simpler in the last half-century, but Orwell said that grammatical simplification had been 'gaining ground'. What, if anything, is 'primitive' in the language of a Burmese peasant is not, as Orwell must have learned to his cost, the structure. 'Corruption' and 'simplicity' turn out to be impressionistic reactions, not linguistic descriptions. Talk about language variety turns into mere name-calling if it is only misinformation, false assumptions and outright bias.

Orwell has received credit for founding the study of 'popular culture' in such works as 'Boys' Weeklies' and 'The Art of Donald McGill'.[6] But Orwell's interest in boys' newspapers and seaside postcards was less for their demotic origin – he explicitly branded the boys' papers an instrument of class oppression – than for their unconventional aesthetic criteria. The criteria in themselves were not a guarantee of artistic success; an artist could succeed or fail by them as by any other canons (he blasted the vogue for sex and violence in 'No Orchids for Miss Blandish'). But they were not the classical and neoclassical canons, and so when Orwell took them seriously he helped put them on the intellectual map.

The same outlook gave him special interest in British slang. 'The BBC dialect' or 'educated English' was a variety that he associated with class privilege. He lacked the technical means to record other varieties, but slang always interests amateur language-watchers because it is mostly a matter of vocabulary – it involves next to no grammar or phonology, so it is easy for the untrained to describe. And it is 'colourful': it is the vocabulary of a group apart, more volatile than the slowly-changing standard vocabulary. Orwell had unusual opportunities to observe slang, and his outlook enabled him to profit from them. He did not ignore or deride non-standard varieties of English, and he was particularly alert to slang.

He stood up, as he would, for British slang against American.

> English people of all classes now find it natural to express incredulity by the American slang phrase *sez you*. Many would even tell you in good faith that *sez you* has no English equivalent. Actually it has a whole string of them – for instance, *not half, I don't think, come off it, less of it, and then you wake up*, or simply *garn*.
> (CE 3.29; cf. CE 3.322)

But he unselfconsciously used American 'bumped off' (HC 119, 120),[7] and he seemed, despite his theoretical bias in favour of colloquial style and his literary reputation for direct prose, rarely to use a

British slang phrase without calling attention to it: 'It was an idea that "took on", as the saying goes' (CE 3.171), for example. When a character in *A Clergyman's Daughter* is directing a schoolboy play, he says:

> 'Put a bit of life into it, can't you? . . . Don't drone! Say it as if it meant something! You look like a corpse that's been buried and dug up again. What's the good of gurgling it down in your inside like that? Stand up and shout at him. Take off that second murderer expression!'
> (CD 68)

Orwell heralded the passage 'He strode up and down, haranguing the children in a vehement slangy style,' as if readers might miss the slanginess without that cue.

Orwell's literary slang was sometimes little more than an after-thought. He used 'cit' on only one occasion, apparently, and then twice in the same sentence ('He would be a law-abiding little cit like any other law-abiding little cit – a soldier in the strap-hanging army,' KA 238). He did not italicize it or comment on it, but he did not use it elsewhere. He used 'shoot the moon' often in the first part of *Down and Out in Paris and London* (e.g., 21, 39) but rarely elsewhere. Even though the OED records 'cit' in this sense ('Short for *citizen*; usually applied . . . more or less contemptuously') from 1644, and 'shoot the moon' from 1836, Orwell did not really draw either word into his working literary vocabulary.

It was not from the vantage-point of omniscient narrator that Orwell made his most acute observations of slang, however, but from his experiences as the Old Etonian turned tramp. His early journals are rich with the argot he heard on the road, in the common lodging houses, and in cells (e.g., CE 1.92–3). He went, moreover, beyond mere cultural enrichment. As early as 1931 he included in his hop-picking journal a list of 'New Words (i.e. words new to me) discovered this time' (CE 1.70–1), and when he quoted the jailhouse graffito 'Detective Smith knows how to gee; / Tell him he's a cunt from me' (CE 1.88; cf. CD 172), he added the antiseptic note '("Gee" in this context means to act as an *agent provocateur*).'

When he came to write *Down and Out in Paris and London* (1933), the two pages of the tramp journal entry on slang expanded into five (174–8), and the mere list grew into an annotated catalogue. 'I want,' Orwell said, 'to put in some notes . . . on London slang and swearing. These (omitting the ones that everyone knows) are some of the cant words now used in London' (PL 174). The journal list of seventeen words now returns as thirty-six, including most of those in the first account, and other words not on either list are scattered throughout the book though perhaps not all (e.g., 'skilly', p. 139) are now 'ones that everyone knows'. That is no great or original achievement, all the same; glossaries of underworld slang had been among the more popular publishing ventures of the 1590s, and interest in cant had grown so since that Farmer and Henley's *Slang and its Analogues* (1890–1904) comprised seven volumes. The Society for Pure English published a pamphlet by Eric Partridge on 'Slang' (1940); Partridge's *Dictionary of Slang and Unconventional English* had already (1937) appeared. Smith had urged the literary interest in slang.[8] The difference between Orwell's 1931 journal and his 1933 chapter, then, was his growing grasp of the subject, not his contribution to its study.

He observed that 'About half of these words are in the larger dictionaries' (PL 175), and with the help of the dictionaries he went on to guess the origins of some:

'Glimmer' [which Orwell defined as 'one who watches vacant motor-cars'] (with the verb 'to glim') may have something to do with the old word 'glim', meaning a light, or another old word 'glim', meaning a glimpse; but it is an instance of the formation of new words, for in its present sense it can hardly be older than motor-cars.

OED gives 'glime' as 'to look askance or shyly', which would suit the furtive lookout a glimmer keeps. Partridge cites Orwell's discussion as a source, 'mostly London . . . since ca. 1910' as a place and date, and the verb 'glim' in meanings like 'see' or 'observe one sharply' as the origin.[9] So 'glimmer' is not an 'instance of the formation of new words' but a relatively small extension of meaning required by the crime, not by the invention of cars. Present-day 'supergrass' is an important police informant in the UK, but in the US it is 'potent marijuana'. Both words arose through language change, not developments in law enforcement or hallucinogenic horticulture.

Orwell went on to a discussion of swearing, another life-long interest; Ruth Pitter recalled that

He used to put in a fair number of rude words in those days [ca. 1928] and we had to correct the spelling. I would have thought an Old Etonian knew every word there was and a few more. He certainly couldn't spell the London rude words.[10]

In 1933, however, he was much hampered in his published text by the need to spell his examples with dashes: 'For example, ———. The Londoners do not now use, or very seldom use, this word in its original meaning; it is on their lips from morning till night, but it is a mere expletive and means nothing' (PL 177). Orwell made this rather blunted observation in the course of showing how 'A word becomes an oath because it means a certain thing, and, because it has become an oath, it ceases to mean that thing.' The point is valid but not restricted to swearing: the observation is as true of euphemism as it is of dysphemism, so that 'toilet' is no longer the little cloth (diminutive of French *toile*) the fastidious put on their shoulders or table when brushing their hair (British motorway rest areas now include a 'Unisex Disabled Toilet').

From his point about swearing Orwell went on to make a more general point about insults: 'Evidently a word is an insult simply because it is meant as an insult, without reference to its dictionary meaning' is about as close as he ever got to accepting that usage might depart from dictionary labels and yet prevail. He concluded his chapter:

> These are a few notes that I have set down more or less at random. It is a pity that someone capable of dealing with the subject does not keep a year-book of London slang and swearing, registering the changes accurately. It might throw useful light upon the formation, development and obsolescence of words.
> (PL 178)

The pity is that it has still not been done, and that Orwell did not do it. The job would have been difficult for him: it demands training in phonetics, a grasp of language history and an enlightened view of language change. But Orwell had the interest, and he had the experience in the casual wards and the streets. More to the point, he had – as he showed in this chapter and almost never elsewhere – the insight that slang is not a language phenomenon by itself. It is an aspect of the 'formation, development and obsolescence of words'. Changes in it reflect more general changes in meaning, in patterns of borrowing, in the influence of culture on language. The use of it reflects larger systems of social conduct. Orwell's interest in slang aroused in him the most intelligent (because most independent) expression of his linguistic concerns.

It also provided some of the most creative expressions of his human concerns, such as Nobby's long speech to Dorothy:

'Only we're just a bit in the mulligatawny, see? Because we ain't got a brown between us, and we got to do it on the toby . . . and got to tap for our tommy and skipper at nights as well . . . But you go into partnership with us, and you'll get your kip for a month and something over – and *we'll* get a lift to Bromley and a bit of scran as well.'

About a quarter of this speech was intelligible to Dorothy. She asked rather at random:

'What is *scran*?'

'Scran?' Tommy – food. I can see *you* ain't been long on the beach, kid.'
(CD 103)

Only nine of the eighty-one words in this quotation are slang ('mulligatawny', 'brown', 'toby', 'tap', 'tommy', 'skipper', 'kip', 'scran', 'beach'), not 'three quarters' of it; eight are nouns, one is a verb. 'Function words' like articles, conjunctions, pronouns, prepositions, and other grammatical words such as parts of 'to be', are all perfectly standard, as is their arrangement in the sentence. Those properties of language, essential to intelligibility, are, unlike slang, very slow to change. But only 'toby', 'kip', and 'skipper' were among the three dozen words Orwell had listed in *Down and Out in Paris and London*, so if they do not actually render three-fourths of the speech unintellgible, they do represent an increment in his expressive slang vocabulary of only two years earlier.

Orwell's notes on dialect other than slang were less systematic: sometimes brief, more rarely developed; sometimes journalistic, sometimes fictional. But they are recurrent, from 'The Spike' (1931) to *Nineteen Eighty-Four* (1949). Often they refer to non-standard varieties but do not record them: *Coming Up for Air*'s hero-narrator reacts to 'very broad accents' of pre-war Berkshire farm lads and the changes time brought:

In the Thames Valley the country accents were going out. Except for the farm lads, nearly everyone who was born later than 1890 talked Cockney . . .

She . . . [a]nswered in an accent you could cut with a spade. Lancashire. There's lots of them in the south of England now.
(CA 65, 115, 214; cf. CD 216)

In the diary he kept on his trip north, Orwell also noted variety in similar terms: 'Accent in Sheffield not so broad as in Lancashire' (CE 1.192; cf. 175, 198, 201, 212). When he wrote *The Road to Wigan Pier*, then, he amplified these notes as he amplified much he had noted in the diary (e.g., 'their own broad lingo', RW 176).[11] Terms like 'broad accent' and 'not so broad' are, however, subjective; the breadth of the accent is in the ear of the observer, so 'not so broad' just means 'not so different from mine'. Had Orwell left his remarks at that, they would have done nothing for the value we set on the observations or the observer.

The difference between the diary and *The Road to Wigan Pier*, however, is that the book covers the material of the diary in its first section and then devotes a second section to political autobiography, beginning with a stunning explanation of his title: 'The road from Mandalay to Wigan is a long one . . .' The submerged parallel here ('The Road to ʹ×ʺ') not only explains the last syllable of the title Orwell chose, but demonstrates a subtle ear.[12] As a child, he recalls, he found the cacophony of 'bad accents' ringing in his ears: ' "common" people seemed almost sub-human. They had coarse faces, hideous accents and gross manners'; 'I was still revolted by their accents' (RW 126, 140). Biographers have made much of Orwell's delicate sense of smell. His sense of hearing also set him apart: 'God knows there are worse smells and sounds' (CA 63).

On the road with tramps, he learned that his delicate ear was not commonplace:

> many people have no ear for accent and judge you entirely by your clothes . . . Some people [at back doors] were obviously surprised by my 'educated' accent, others failed to notice it; I was dirty and ragged and that was all they saw.
> (RW 154–5)

His fellow tramps were often no more discriminating:

> A tramp is used to hearing all kinds of accents among his mates, some so strange to him that he can hardly understand them, and a man from, say, Cardiff or Durham or Dublin does not necessarily know which of the south English accents is an 'educated' one. In any case men with 'educated' accents, though rare among tramps, are not unknown.
> (RW 155)

Orwell employed his 'good ear' critically during his northern journey, where he observed regionalisms of negation (' "one bed does nowt" '), double negation (' "they can't do nowt" ', both RW 55), and forms of the definite article (' "They wouldn't never have collected t'pieces" ', CE 1.177–8), deducing

There seem to be 2 ways of dealing with the 'the' here. Before consonants
it is often omitted altogether ('Put joog on table' etc); before vowels it is
often incorporated with the word, e.g. 'My sister's in thospital' – th as in
thin.
(CE 1.175)

The observation was reasonably accurate but not sufficiently self-
aware. Southern 'educated' English likewise has two ways of 'dealing
with' the definite article, analogous to the more obvious two ways it
deals with the indefinite article; like the Yorkshire forms Orwell
reported, both are governed by the following vowel or consonant
sound. Before consonants 'the' has the vowel sound of 'but'; before
vowels, the vowel sound of 'beat'. These forms are not reflected in
spelling as the forms of the indefinite article ('a', 'an') are, and they
are so habitual to educated speakers of southern English that most
who use them do not notice them.

Orwell carried his 1936 observations with him to the end of his life;
he wrote in a 1947 'As I Please' column about 'Nu Speling, in
connection with which somebody is introducing a Bill in Parlia-
ment',

To begin with, unless the scheme were rigidly enforced, the resulting
chaos . . . would be fearful . . . [T]he huge labour of respelling the entire
literature of the past would have to be undertaken. And again, you can
only fully rationalise spelling if you give a fixed value to each letter. But
this means standardising pronunciation, which could not be done in this
country without an unholy row. What do you do, for instance, about
words like 'butter' or 'glass', which are pronounced in different ways in
London and Newcastle? Other words, such as 'were', are pronounced in
two different ways according to individual inclination, or according to
context.
(CE 4.304–5)[13]

Orwell also made jottings on northern regional vocabulary: 'starv-
ing' (i.e., freezing, RW 70); 'flashes' (i.e., stagnant pools, CE 1.177);
'cannel' (a kind of flammable rock, CE 1.182); and 'I notice that the
word "spink" (for a great tit, I think, but at any rate some small bird)
is in use here as well as in Suffolk' (CE 1.212). All of these he would
have found in Wright's *English Dialect Dictionary* (1898–1905),
much as he found the facts of mine work in the *Colliery Year Book
and Coal Trades Directory* for 1935 (RW 40, n.). But in neither work
would he have found such a passage as this, so he had to write it
himself:

As you travel northward your eye, accustomed to the South or East, does not notice much difference until you are beyond Birmingham . . . It is only when you get a little further north, to the pottery towns and beyond, that you begin to encounter the real ugliness of industrialism . . .
(RW 105)

Orwell's ear aided his eye and recorded the difference. It was not simply a difference of sounds or words, but a difference of life, one wholly unlike that of the south or east. He later wrote that

Exaggerated class distinctions have been diminishing over a period of about thirty years . . . but . . . [t]he great majority of the people can still be 'placed' in an instant . . . [T]he most striking difference of all is in language and accent. The English working class, as Mr Wyndham Lewis has put it, are 'branded on the tongue'.
(CE 3.4–5)

It is this sense of 'difference', not of quaintness and surely not of ugliness, that makes the northern speech important to Orwell. And it was through this sense that he came to the notion that another pattern of national varieties would have to arise before the class system, and the ugly differences it made, could end.

In his 1940 diary Orwell worried that government leaflets, though 'getting much better in tone and language', still had 'nothing in really demotic speech, nothing that will move the poorer working class or even be quite certainly intelligible' (CE 2.355–6; cf. 397–8), a problem he returned to in his 1944 essay 'Propaganda and Demotic Speech' (CE 3.135–41). The essay is less practical, more aesthetic and more theoretical than the diary: it raises many of the issues of Orwell's 1946 essay 'Politics and the English Language', and it spends more space on the differences between speech and writing. But it has in common with the diary its belief that

some day we may have a genuinely democratic government, a government which will want to tell people what is happening, and what must be done next . . . It will need the mechanisms for doing so, of which the first are the right words, the right tone of voice.
(CE 3.140)

It was an optimistic belief; the Newspeak of *Nineteen Eighty-Four* is its pessimistic counterpart.

As a result, Orwell was more interested in class varieties, and features that cut across regional varieties, than in regional varieties themselves. In this his social sense separated him from most amateur and many professional dialecticians, who had found regional 'dialects' the only or at least the only interesting kind. Northern interested Orwell because the north was a depressed region. When he turned his interest to other regional varieties, such as the occasional 'base Dublin accent' (CD 114; cf., e.g., 170ff., PL 139), Scots (e.g., BD 191, KA 52) or the Suffolk around Knype Hill in *A Clergyman's Daughter*, it was transiet and superficial compared with the attention he paid to class varieties in passages like the Trafalgar Square scene from the same book (see Chapter Five).

To convey everything that went to make up the differences, the linguistic features of the two Englands – vocabulary, grammar, pronunciation, sociolinguistic outlook – Orwell took the initial aspirate [h] as the shibboleth, the class password in one direction and the symbol of separation in the other. It is not only the most reliable marker of non-standard dialect in his transcriptions; it becomes the linguistic equivalent of class chains in his argument. Orwell's pages are spattered with the ' that replaces initial [h], in the speech of countryfolk ('rustics bawling " 'Ail Mary!" ', CD 74), northerners (' "when it's 'ot" ', RW 55), Londoners (' "'ave a try" ', KA 11): it is a national working-class feature, not a regional feature. The upwardly-mobile George Bowling of *Coming Up for Air* recalls that, when a boy, his family was 'inclined to drop our aitches if we were at all excited' (CA 68; cf. 111), but when he returns to the Berkshire village of his boyhood and sees his first love keeping shop, he remarks

> How bad her accent had got! Or maybe I was just imagining that, because my own standards had changed? . . . I swear she never used to drop her aitches. It's queer how these women go to pieces once they're married. (CA 245; cf. CE 1.439)

In the diary he kept in the north, Orwell – no pedant – even allowed himself one of his rare footnotes: he met a man he thought was 'Hennessey' but later learned 'His name is Firth. I got it as Hennessey because he was introduced to me as Hellis Firth. (*E*llis Firth – people here very capricious about their H's)' (CE 1.205, n.).

So he wrote in his 1940 'Boys' Weeklies' that 'no one in a star part is ever permitted to drop an aitch' (CE 1.480), in an unpublished 1948 poem 'As solid as Gibraltar Rock / My aitches still do stand,'[14] and in *The Road to Wigan Pier* about 'Everyone who has grown up pronouncing his aitches and in a house with a bathroom and one servant'; the pronunciation of initial [h] is part of 'the chasmic, impassable quality of class-distinctions in the West' (RW 129). Then, in the final pages of his book, Orwell enlarged on [h], its symbolism and its revolutionary potential. He held that 'manners and traditions learned by each class in childhood are not only very different but . . . generally persist from birth to death,' so that you get 'anomalous individuals' such as 'millionaires who cannot pronounce their aitches' (RW 224; cf. 225). The economic realities, he went on, make middle-class people with incomes below £200 a year members of the working class, despite their cultural affinities. Socialism is as much for them as it is for the working class: 'They must not be allowed to think that the battle is between those who pronounce their aitches and those who don't; for if they think that, they will join in on the side of the aitches' (RW 227). Political alignments, he said, must reflect economic realities and not cultural symbols.

> I cannot proletarianise my accent or certain of my tastes and beliefs, and I would not if I could. Why should I? I don't ask anybody else to speak my dialect; why should anybody else ask me to speak his? It would be far better to take these miserable class-stigmata for granted and emphasise them as little as possible.
> (RW 229)

With an 'effective Socialist party' there will come a struggle, 'conceivably a physical one', and

> then perhaps this misery of class-prejudice will fade away, and we of the sinking middle class . . . may sink without further struggles into the working class where we belong, and probably when we get there it will not be so dreadful as we feared, for, after all, we have nothing to lose but our aitches.
> (RW 231–2)

And that is how Orwell ends his book; his last word is 'aitches'.

Orwell saw language variety as the product of social division, not of language change:

> The temporary decadence of the English language is due, like so much else, to our anachronistic class system. 'Educated' English has grown anaemic because for long past it has not been reinvigorated from below.
> (CE 32.7)[15]

Orwell's 'due to' might stir the dust in some freshman composition classes, but his picture of a bloodless aristocracy and a vigorous working class would raise cheers in the Lawrence seminar. The class struggle surfaces as a dialect struggle, and since 'English regional snobberies are nationalism in miniature' (RW 114), the aristocrats are a local variety of the nationalists who

> consider it a duty to spread their own language to the detriment of rival languages, and among English-speakers this struggle reappears in subtler form as a struggle between dialects. Anglophobe Americans will refuse to use a slang phrase if they know it to be of British origin, and the conflict between Latinisers and Germanisers often has nationalist motives behind it. Scottish nationalists insist on the superiority of Lowland Scots, and Socialists whose nationalism takes the form of class hatred tirade against the BBC accent and even the broad **A**.
> (CE 3.367)

But somewhere between the national language pride that he deplored because it was expansionist, and regional language pride that he lauded because it was anti-BBC, Orwell's sympathies shifted. He repeated that

> In Scotland and northern England snobbishness about the local accents does exist. . . . Many a Yorkshireman definitely prides himself on his broad **U**'s and narrow **A**'s, and will defend them on linguistic grounds. In London there are still people who say 'fice' instead of 'face', but there is probably no one who regards 'fice' as superior.
> (CE 3.21–2)

As a result of this linguistic pride, Orwell believed,

> In a Lancashire cotton-town you could probably go for months on end without once hearing an 'educated' accent. . . . All the Northern accents . . . persist strongly, while the Southern ones are collapsing before the movies and the BBC. Hence your 'educated' accent stamps you rather as a foreigner than as a chunk of the petty gentry. . . .
> (RW 114)

Orwell seems to have regarded cockney as the working-class variety par excellence: it was the linguistic underdog, a shame even to those who spoke it; it was a national class accent rather than a regional accent; and it offered the nation a chance to 'lose its aitches' along with its chains of inherited class disadvantage. He was on poor historical ground when he held that cockney 'seems to have come up in the [eighteen] forties (it is first mentioned in an American book, Herman Melville's *White Jacket*)' (PL 176). The attestations of cockney as a distinctive lower-class London variety of English go back further than that: much depends on what features you mean and what evidence you accept, but the language Chaucer gave to his London publican Harry Bailey c. 1390 appears to have cockney features.[16] Orwell went on, 'Cockney is already changing; there are few people now who say "fice" for "face", "nawce" for "nice" and so forth as consistently as they did twenty years ago.' (In 1944 he said the opposite; see p. 93.) Cockney was indeed changing, like 'educated' English; all varieties change, and cockney had felt the catalytic metropolitan influences of other dialects as provincial varieties never do, without the reinforcing metropolitan influences of prestige as the 'educated' variety did.

Orwell clearly found the regional accents of the working class valid and vital, and he was receptive to their vocabulary. He was less receptive to non-standard (un-'educated') grammar, possibly because many of his language ideas had been founded on dead languages where pronunciation was not an issue but grammar incessantly was. So the intelligence and pride of the crippled pavement artist Bozo baffled him:

> Bozo had a strange way of talking, Cockneyfied and yet very lucid and expressive. It was as though he had read good books but had never troubled to correct his grammar. . . . I repeat what he said more or less in his own words.
>
> (PL 161)

The verbatim transcript of this interesting informant, however, is almost pure standard English. An occasional non-standard verb form occurs, as in ' "It don't follow that because a man's on the road he can't think of anything but tea-and-two-slices," ' but the sentence survives its intricacies intact – the two negatives are 'correct', and Orwell doesn't quote Bozo using redundant negation anywhere in the lengthy quotations – so it is hard to know what Orwell found so incorrect about the man's grammar. Orwell's reaction to Bozo is important because it respected the man and his mind even though it balked at his grammar, and because Bozo's accent was 'Cockneyfied' even though Orwell's transcription hardly showed it. (Elsewhere he represented it with some care: ' "Ot c'n I do f'yer!" – that approximately was what it sounded like' [KA 200; cf. 15]; ' "Coo, 'e's fair bin

bathing in it! – What you bin doing of, eh?" ' [CD 1.87].)
In 'The English People' Orwell proposed a way

> to remove the class labels from the English language. It is not desirable that
> all the local accents should disappear, but there should be a manner of
> speaking that is definitely national and is not merely (like the accent of the
> BBC announcers) a copy of the mannerisms of the upper classes. This
> national accent – a modification of cockney, perhaps, or of one of the
> northern accents – should be taught as a matter of course to all children
> alike. After that they could, and in some parts of the country they
> probably would, revert to the local accent, but they should be able to
> speak standard English if they wished to. No one should be 'branded on
> the tongue'. It should be impossible, as it is in the United States and some
> European countries, to determine anyone's status from his accent.
> (CE 3.34)

Orwell saw in this national accent, artificially founded on working-
class varieties, a new 'standard English', and took a view that is now
called 'bidialectal': the school should teach children mastery of the
standard variety so they can opt for it in addition to their local
accent.[17] For it is accent that Orwell meant; here as elsewhere he took
the grammatical structure of the language to be invariable, and he
recognized only a few variants of vocabulary.

Orwell's view here revealed an 'activist' attitude towards language
variety that his attitude towards language change had foreshadowed.
He repeatedly proposed resistance to change (e.g., 'the degradation
which is certainly happening to our language is a process which one
cannot arrest by conscious action. But I would like to see the attempt
made' CE 3.326; cf. 3.29). The resistance, by implication, was the
task of individual writers and the example they gave. The foundation
of a national accent, on the other hand, would be the task of the
schools and the instruction they give. The national accent would lend a
radically different meaning to the phrase he often used in derogation,
' "educated" English'.

Orwell did not say how to achieve the modification of a working-
class accent, but his frequent contrast of working-class accent with
that of BBC announcers gives a hint: by the time Orwell was writing
this passage (1944), the BBC – where Orwell worked 1941–3 – had
long been using a guide to pronunciation compiled for them by a
committee of outside authorities.[18] He had also suggested a 'field
experiment' to 'formulate the rules of spoken English', accepting that
spoken English – unlike the written variety where the rules were

already formulated – 'is full of slang, it is abbreviated wherever possible, and people of all social classes treat its grammar and syntax in a slovenly way' (CE 3.137). Orwell's suggestion made characteristic use of modern technology: record a dozen speakers talking *ex tempore*, and some conversations among three or four people. Let a stenographer reduce the recordings to writing,

> word for word, with such punctuation as seems appropriate. You would then – for the first time, I believe – have on paper some authentic specimens of spoken English. Probably they would not be readable as a book or a newspaper article. . . .
> (CE 3.139)

The size of Orwell's proposed sample is small, and his directions for transcription and analysis are naive. But his project represents a practical suggestion in a field where he was often speculative or simply a passive spectator.

Not every detail of these 1936 and 1937 proposals has come about, but Orwell's remarks foreshadowed some of the most recent statements about language variety: that people have the right to their own language; that the language of the dominant class is a cultural attribute without special expressive or logical adequacy; and that differences in language, as typified by non-prestige features of pronunciation, are superficialities best accepted and not dwelt upon.[19] But Orwell's stand is not the same as that of present-day American educators. Orwell anticipated the overthrow of the British ruling class, and he meant his egalitarian linguistic views to unite the working class with the 'sinking' middle class against the upper class whose native dialect is 'BBC'. He did not propose that all dialects were created equal; he took a somewhat bolshie stand that the 'educated' variety was moribund and that the 'stigmata' of lower-class varieties, loss of initial [h] in particular, play into the hands of the ruling class when they divide the workers from their natural allies in the lower middle class.

Orwell described a static language picture: every speaker uses a consistent variety of language and uses it all the time. Even the [h]-less millionaire, though his speech is inconsistent with his new social station, has a self-consistent form of language that derives from his old social background. Most characters in Orwell's books are like that: even the Outer Party of *Nineteen Eight-Four* constitutes a kind of linguistically homogenized equivalent of Orwell's middle class.

And so – if we are to believe him – was Orwell himself. His only departure from the accent he learned in his cultivated middle-class household and at Eton was the cockney he used as part of his tramp disguise, and he did not always care (or remember) to sustain it: 'After I had mixed with these people for a few days it was too much fag to go on putting on my cockney accent, and they noticed that I talked "different" ' (CE 1.64).[20]

He noticed, for his part, that the northern miners 'all of them, except in moments of great animation, softened their northern accents for my benefit' (RW 156; cf. CE 1.178). A few of the people he met in the north spoke usually with 'very little accent' or 'like a leading article' but in a working men's club or a communist meeting their accents became 'much broader' (CE 1.198, 201, 212). In *Burmese Days*, one eastern character even shifts from one language to another as he speaks, and one European 'deliberately exaggerated his cockney accent, because of the sardonic tone it gave to his words' (BD 22). But these characters are unusual in Orwell; most of those who varied their speech appear in his non-fiction, and in his fiction characters speak an unvaried form of language: the characters in Trafalgar Square, for example, or Dorothy's uncle ('He was one of those people who say "Don't you know?" and "What! What!" and lose themselves in the middle of their sentences', CD 207; cf. 208, 216, 303; BD 19).

One reason is the difference between 'real life' and fiction. In life the individual creates the discourse, but in fiction the discourse – including dialogue – creates the character. Orwell's consistent characters speak a consistent form of the language: however much the northerners may have adapted their speech to Orwell, when Mrs Wayne identifies herself with Dorothy she does not shift to Dorothy's variety of English (CD 167). Orwell knew literary consistency had its drawbacks:

> The speech of 'educated' people is now so lifeless and characterless that a novelist can do nothing with it. By far the easiest way of making it amusing is to burlesque it, which means pretending that every upper-class person is an ineffectual ass.
> (RW 157)

The second reason lies in the difference between Orwell's outlook and ours. His descriptions of language variety were static: one individual, one class, one region, will use one form of language. But we have learned that language varieties are dynamic.[21] No one talks the same way all the time, and a speech community comprises not a single homogeneous variety of language but rather a repertoire of language varieties that members of the community share. A speech community provides several ways of saying the same thing, and members of the community use this redundancy for their expressive purposes. Of course a community cannot speak; only an individual can do that. But individuals equally cannot invent the community's repertoire; they can only employ it. Orwell was interested in slang and swearing. He knew these forms did not provide unique referential resources, that their special capacity was expressive. Every speech community, every language, includes slang and swearing, but 'in London . . . the men do not usually swear in front of the women. In Paris it is quite different' (PL 178). Different speech communities, that is, distribute functional varieties in different ways.

The 'expressive' use of language by choice of a variety involves more than just vocabulary, pronunciation, syntax and morphology; and as the example from *Burmese Days* shows, it can even involve choice of language. In many communities where the repertoire includes several languages, multilingual speakers may draw on a structured distribution of functions among them. An office conversation in New York, Miami or Los Angeles will be in English but comments and asides may, for some speakers, be in Spanish. In Paraguay the conversation would be in Spanish but the asides in Guaraní, an indigenous language.

Choices in vocabulary can involve considerable delicacy. We can speak to a teacher about our 'children', but if we talk about our 'child' the singular has an emotional colouring its plural lacks, probably because 'children' is the plural of 'son' and 'daughter' not marked for gender, leaving 'child' a different role to play. Or, a parent may say to a child 'Listen, darling' or 'You listen to me, young lady.' The imperative mood of the verb is grammatical with or without the subject personal pronoun, and 'young lady' is an acceptable phrase. But the pronoun, and the phrase, are not usual in ordinary domestic address. The speech community assigns different roles to them, as it also does to choices in pronunciation. Many English-language communities, for one familiar example, provide a choice between '-ing' and '-in' ' ('Whatcha doin'?'; 'Nothin' '), but in some '-ing' is almost unavailable, and in a few '-in' ' is rare.

So the speaker's grasp of *langue* includes the ability not only to form utterances in the language but also to choose socially appropriate variants from the repertoire. The social context (formal, familiar, etc.) usually predicts the choice, and the choice reciprocally identifies the context. When the variant is predictable from the context it is 'unmarked' and probably unnoticed; when it is unpredictable it is 'marked' and pushed to the foreground of the listener's attention. A marked choice is open to misunderstanding just the same, because listeners have to interpret it from their own patterns of choice so as to grasp the speaker's intent or social background. The teacher will not react to 'son', 'daughter', or 'children', the unmarked forms; but the marked form 'child' will trigger an attempt to interpret the choice 'I want to talk to you about my child.' (A further nuance involves medium: 'child' has distinctive emotive force only in speech, and in writing that strives for colloquial tone.)

In stratified societies, the choice may be between the prestigious forms of the in-group and the stigmatized forms of the out-group: a formal context will call for the prestigious variety. Speakers also make such choices as part of their presentation of self or 'impression management', so people try to sound like those they identify with. Usually people try to sound like the prestigious in-group, but a speaker may choose stigmatized variants because they stand for positive values of the out-group: sincerity, toughness, trustworthiness. In addition, out-group speech can be a secret code among its members, but then the speech is no longer part of the community repertoire even though its special forms are referentially redundant. Orwell's remark that 'About a quarter of [Nobby's] speech was intelligible to Dorothy' (CD 103), though the fraction is an exaggeration, shows that he knew the difference between non-standard and slang: to outsiders, non-standard reveals who you are and where you came from: slang hides what you are saying.

It was of course to the social divisions in the English-speaking community that Orwell paid special attention: 'middle-class people cannot afford to let their children grow up with vulgar accents' he said succinctly (RW 125), and at greater length:

> In the south of England, at any rate, it is unquestionable that most working-class people want to resemble the upper classes in manners and habits. . . . Above all, throughout southern England there is almost general uneasiness about the cockney accent. . . . Even a person who claims to despise the bourgeoisie and all its ways will still take care that his children grow up pronouncing their aitches. . . .
>
> As things are at present, nearly every Englishman, whatever his origins,

feels the working-class manner of speech, and even working-class idioms, to be inferior. Cockney, the most widespread dialect, is the most despised of all.
(CE 3.21–2, 27)

Against the vital despised cockney Orwell ranged the moribund educated or 'BBC' variety. He observed its quibbles over mealtime nomenclature:

> 'Luncheon, Dorothy, luncheon!' said the Rector with a touch of irritation. 'I do wish you would drop that abominable lower-class habit of calling the midday meal *dinner*!'

The quibble is Orwell's ironic implementation of class affectations, for though Dorothy and her father command the dialect they do not command the money:

> Meanwhile, she had got to settle about the meat for today's dinner – luncheon. (Dorothy was careful to obey her father and call it *luncheon*, when she remembered it. On the other hand, you could not in honesty call the evening meal anything but 'supper'; so there was no such meal as 'dinner' at the Rectory.)
> (CD 34, 37; cf. 320; CA 147; RW 141)

Such speech, the speech of 'everyone who was brought up with a mincing accent and in a house where there were one or two servants' (RW 167–8), has its advantages. For Dorothy, penniless in London, 'her educated accent, which had made it impossible to get work as a servant, was an invaluable asset to her as a beggar' (CD 201; cf. 163), and 'If you talk with a BBC accent you can get jobs that a proletarian couldn't get' (CE 2.209; cf. CE 4.54). But the advantages result from the social affinities of the accent, not from any inherent qualities it has. On the contrary, Orwell found it inherently unaesthetic and ineffective.

> The 'educated' accent, of which the accent of the BBC announcers is a sort of parody, has no asset except its intelligibility to English-speaking foreigners. In England the minority to whom it is natural don't particularly like it, while in the other three-quarters of the population it arouses an immediate class antagonism.
> (CE 3.139–40; cf. 3.1)

In the hospital in 1949 after two years of hearing almost nothing but working-class or lower-middle-class Scots, he overheard the voices of some upper-class English visitors:

> And what voices! A sort of over-fedness, a fatuous self-confidence, a constant bah-bahing of laughter abt nothing, above all a sort of heaviness & richness combined with a fundamental ill-will – people who, one instinctively feels, without even being able to see them, are the enemies of anything intelligent or sensitive or beautiful. No wonder everyone hates us so.
> (CE 4.515)

That is bigotry, but the penultimate word perhaps saves it.

Orwell brought his assumptions about class to the question of slang, as he did his assumptions about borrowing, and about American English:

> American has gained a footing in England . . . most of all because one can adopt an American word without crossing a class barrier. From the English point of view American words have no class label. . . . To the working classes . . . the use of Americanisms is a way of escaping from cockney without adopting the BBC dialect, which they instinctively dislike and cannot easily master. Hence, especially in the big towns, working-class children now use American slang from the moment that they learn to talk. And there is a noticeable tendency to use American words even when they are not slang and when an English equivalent already exists: for instance, *car* for *tram* . . . *automobile* for *motor car*.
> (CE 3.27–8)

The changes that Orwell outlined here were changes in the variety of English he knew best. They were also changes in the English-speaking community, for they added new choices among redundant terms, and they redrew the geographical and class boundaries for a number of choices. Young working-class Britons adopted the American variants to avoid the associations of cockney, which they did not want, and of upper-class British, which they did not like or really grasp.

> Any word or usage that is supposedly cockney is looked on as vulgar, even when, as is sometimes the case, it is merely an archaism. An example is *ain't*, which is now abandoned in favour of the much weaker form *aren't*. But *ain't* was good enough English eighty years ago, and Queen Victoria would have said *ain't*.
> (CE 3.27)

Again the changes arise from linguistic variety and result in redrawn variety boundaries; Orwell viewed them here in diachronic perspective. But some of Orwell's other historical notes, like his observation that 'No born Londoner . . . now says "bloody", unless he is a man of some education' because 'The word has, in fact, moved up in the social scale and ceased to be a swear word for the purposes of the working classes' (PL 176), would not be confirmed by attentive observers then or now.

Both 'ain't' and 'bloody' adjusted their boundaries, the former downwards and the latter upwards. Both words had and retain referential equivalents in the speech community's repertoire, but both have shifted their functional roles. It was the expressive meaning of their choice or rejection that changed. 'Ain't' lost its reputation, alas; 'bloody' lost its lower-class tang (at least according to Orwell). Someone, sometime, introduced 'bloody' as an expletive unique to his or her idiolect. Its adoption by a wider group was the first adjustment of its boundaries, and its migration from the working class to the middle class was another. We do not know why language changes as it does – why <k> became <h>, for example, or why the Indians finished up with *ath* instead of 'eight'. But we know that language change results from language variety just as it causes language variety: synchronic variety in the speech community leads to diachronic change in the language when variants are redistributed to different social contexts (like 'ain't') or to new sets of speakers (like 'bloody').

Orwell's suggestion of a 'national accent' that students would learn alongside their regional variety followed two tracks in its later history: the investigation of non-standard English and the educational responses to non-standard speakers. The two are connected, naturally, but the connection has sometimes been tenuous. Some study of non-standard English varieties has been a continuation of efforts already under way when Orwell wrote. The *Linguistic Atlas of the United States and Canada* (LAUS) continues to publish the results of earlier surveys and to carry out new ones. Other American surveys, more or less independent of LAUS, have also appeared. In Britain, *The Linguistic Atlas of England* (1978–) has begun publication. But Orwell was not a great reader of reference books, and his interest in non-standard English centred on class dialects, not regionalisms. It is among class dialects that the modern study of language variety has made the greatest progress since Orwell wrote. The progress has come with the realization that no one speaks the same way all the time, that the variety choice available to the individual is defined by the community's language repertoire. That repertoire is largely composed of class varieties, not of regional dialects. Progress has also come with a practical concern for the welfare of the classes that Orwell championed: the chronically poor, the socially disenfranchised, the down and out.

Among the speakers whose characteristic non-standard variety has received the most study, American blacks stand out because their variety is most distinctive, had received least study until Orwell's death in 1950, and has received most in the years since. The increasing attention began among academics with typical leisureliness, but when practical social concern brought unprecedented government help for work with the 'disadvantaged', study began to pick up speed. The year 1972 stands out as a pivotal date, with the publication of both J.L. Dillard's 'lay' treatment of *Black English* and William Labov's scholarly study of *Language in the Inner City*.

Dillard's book takes chiefly the diachronic view: it surveys the history of the subject, but even more it turns to African history to explain the distinctive features of Afro-American English (AAE) that everyone had recognized but almost everyone had attributed to black isolation in America (though a few connected the linguistic features with genetic features). Dillard brought together views scattered in out-of-the-way academic papers that traced many AAE features of vocabulary, grammar and pronunciation to African language origins. Compatible with newly-felt and expressed black pride, these views raised serious questions about educational responsibility. Should teachers treat such a cultural heritage as a 'disadvantage'?

Labov's book, by contrast, is synchronic. It is not the product of the author's reading among academic papers but a report of his team's fieldwork among black adolescents. Its first section is 'The Structure of the Black English Vernacular', far longer and more technical than Dillard's chapter 'On the Structure of Black English'. Labov, like Dillard, concluded by asserting what had long been overlooked: that the logical and linguistic resources of AAE are expressively adequate, its grammar and phonology perfectly regular, different though they are from the resources and regularities of standard American English.

Neither 1972 book is the last word (just as neither was its author's first publication) on its subject, but taken together they represent the total revaluation of a major non-standard variety of English. They showed Afro-American English to be substantial and coherent, not just a product of 'disadvantage'. Some of Orwell's approaches to non-standard came close to theirs, especially to Labov's: like him, Orwell designed 'elicitation experiments' to capture the features distinctive of casual speech that careful writing did not mirror; and like Labov, he believed that moments of excitement produce the most natural version of an individual's language:

> Suddenly he began writing in sheer panic, only imperfectly aware of what he was setting down. His small but childish handwriting straggled up and down the page, shedding first its capital letters and finally even its full stops.
>
> (NE 11; cf. CA 68, 111; RW 156; CE 1.178)

More recent views hold a socially-motivated choice of formal speech to be just as 'natural' as the more casual style, since both draw on the community's language repertoire to accomplish individual linguistic goals.

Academic progress typified by Dillard and Labov's books found practical application in 1979 when both scholars appeared as witnesses in the 'Ann Arbor' case.[22] In 1977 the parents of eleven black school children in the Michigan university town had brought suit under the 1974 Equal Educational Opportunities Act, holding that the Afro-American English the children spoke was a 'barrier to learning standard English as defined by Federal law' and hence that the school system, by failing in its legal responsibility to help the children overcome the barrier, was denying their civil rights – resort to litigation to protect civil rights had grown rapidly following the Second World War. The complicated suit took two years to come to court and a month to be heard. It alleged that AAE, no disadvantaged deviant of standard English, was a language in its own right and so came within the provisions of the (quite recent) law regarding foreign-language speakers in American schools; like them, the Ann Arbor children faced an linguistic barrier in learning to read standard English. Failure to treat AAE as a separate language meant treating it as 'inferior', the plaintiffs held. The defence too rested on this issue: the school system held that AAE was a 'vernacular' or 'dialect', not a language, and hence the case had no legal standing.

Labov testified for the plaintiffs that children who speak AAE should learn standard English as though it were a foreign language – not quite the same thing as saying that standard English *is*, for an AAE speaker, a foreign language. His testimony is easiest to understand in the light of statements like the *New York Times* editorial on the case that appeared on 18 June, a few days earlier. The *Times* writer found it 'sad that the courtroom must become the forum' for such matters. Though the editorial showed no special knowledge of language, it pronounced AAE a 'deviation from standard English', held it 'no more slovenly than . . . Pennsylvania Dutch', and insisted that its young speakers 'become fluent in standard English to compete in the job market'. The *Times* confused 'deviant' with 'different', however; it suggested that AAE and Pennsylvania Dutch were alike 'slovenly'; it misleadingly implied that if the children lost their black 'dialect', their black faces would be no economic handicap 'in the job market'; and it left unexplained why, if varieties as different as Kennedy's New England and Carter's Deep South had not barred their speakers from the White House, a lucid variety like AAE should bar its speakers from the job market. And the *Times* held that AAE is not a language.

So to insist, as Labov did, that AAE is a language is really to insist that, *pace* the *Times*, AAE is a regular, logical, coherent linguistic system. To teach the standard form to AAE speakers 'as though it were a foreign language', then, would be to introduce them to a new system, not to 'correct' their own. That is an attractive plan. Yet most post-pubescent students are unsuccessful at gaining real mastery of a foreign language: command of vocabulary is sometimes secure, but control over grammatical structures is less sure, and pronunciation is rarely authentic. Even younger students have trouble gaining a grasp of a foreign language through classroom instruction (see Chapter Four).

Fortunately the differences between AAE and the textbook standard – whatever pundits agree that is, or whatever it really is locally – are not so great as that. Most of them are in the surface forms, not in the deeper underlying structures. They involve performance, not competence, which is just as well, since competence cannot readily be taught. And it is only surface features that most language critics care about. Orwell remarked that 'It would be far better to take these miserable class-stigmata for granted and emphasise them as little as possible' (RW 229), but he also found baffling Bozo's 'strange way of talking, Cockneyfied and yet very lucid and expressive' (PL 161); Orwell's commitment to standard English made it difficult for him to admit that a non-standard variety could be 'lucid and expressive'. Somehow the stigmatized surface features implied an illogical, limited mind. Labov showed otherwise in his book, notably in the chapter on 'The Logic of Nonstandard English'.

Labov also had a chapter that answered the question 'Is the Black English Vernacular a Separate System?' in the affirmative, as 'a distinct subsystem within the larger grammar of English. . . . But the gears and axles of English grammatical machinery are available to speakers of all dialects, whether or not they use all of them in everyday speech' (pp. 63–4). That is what we meant by 'mutually intelligible' when we defined 'language', and such is obviously the case with young speakers of AAE, who spend long hours each day watching television and decoding its version of standard without any difficulty. A speaker of one variety who can handle the speech of another variety will find the writing even easier to handle because it is more regular and allows more time for decoding.

Despite such research, and even such everyday evidence, a sensible person – and a good writer – like Jean Stafford could say about black English,

> Theirs is a lingua franca that they are free to use among one another, but if they are not making themselves understood outside their group, they can expect nothing but misinterpretation. There has to be an official language, an acceptable language.[23]

The statement itself seems to include several misunderstandings: some, like the meaning of 'lingua franca' and the grammar of 'among each other', are easy to correct. But Stafford does not really 'misunderstand' black English, any more than blacks misunderstand standard. It is blacks' 'impression management', not meaning, that encounters misinterpretation outside their group. The remedy does not lie in an official language but in a changed attitude towards blacks. Stafford's remarks reflect a social stance at worst, at best a correctable ignorance of the difference between language expression and reception.

The difference between expression and reception, speech and writing, however, did not figure in the Ann Arbor decision. The judge ruled not only that speakers of AAE have difficulty in speaking standard English, but also that the children's expressive speech was a 'barrier' to their receptive mastery of writing. He also implicitly accepted, although it was not an issue in the case, that the writing most students encounter is significantly closer to the spoken standard than to spoken non-standard; but Orwell's suggested elicitation experiment and his recognition that in spoken English 'people of all social classes treat its grammar and syntax in a slovenly way' (CE

3.137) had long ago shown that the written standard differs widely from the spoken form of all varieties. Implicit in the court's muddle of the spoken and written, the expressive and receptive, is the judgment that AAE is indeed a different language. For though speakers of non-standard, as Labov pointed out, have other subsystems of English available to them, at least receptively, speakers of foreign languages do not. English is not a subsystem of Burmese, so even a competent Burmese speaker, unlike a speaker of AAE, has to learn English in order to read it.

For speakers of a non-standard subsystem like the Ann Arbor litigants, on the other hand, an overhaul of expressive speech won't solve the problem of receptive reading, and even if it did the effort would be hugely inefficient. At a quite early age such speech patterns are deeply fixed, and any subsequent attempt to alter them in the classroom requires a great deal of time, a great deal of extra-curricular reinforcement, and a great deal of student commitment to the idea that the new variety, whether it joins or replaces the old, will really make a difference in the whole range of human interaction – not just in 'the job market'. No school system can readily meet any of these requirements, so attempts to rearrange their language system will rightly strike students as something between a risible misunderstanding of the language and an arrogant assault on their entire culture.

Not that 'poor English' is entirely in the ear of the auditor. But it is not something that you can simply label with Orwell's (and the *New York Times*'s) word 'slovenly'. More often it is inability to take a full role in the repertoire of the speech community, to have the same choices that other speakers have. The result is ineptness in suiting the language to the occasion or to the medium – in failing to see, for example, as Orwell had long since seen, that the spoken and the written languages are far different. Sophisticated members of the speech community do not, though they may think they do, employ a unique and invariable set of rules in all their discourse; on the contrary, the more cultivated they are the more choices they make among varieties. Less sophisticated members of the community are not deficient in the variety they have but in the varieties they do not have. And among the most important rules about the missing varieties are those that tell when to use them. 'Poor English' is often simply inept choice or misguided impression management; it is both when a university student writes a literary essay in the style of a registrar's announcement, though we do not often regard that as 'language deficit'.

Nor is spoken 'good English' the monopoly or even the staple of the middle class. Orwell thought speakers 'of all classes treat . . . grammar and syntax in a slovenly way', but Labov showed that

> The proportions of grammatical sentences vary with class backgrounds and styles. The highest percentage of well-formed sentences are found in casual speech, and working-class speakers use more well-formed sentences than middle-class speakers. The widespread myth that most speech is ungrammatical is no doubt based upon tapes made at learned conferences, where we obtain the maximum number of irreducibly ungrammatical sentences.[24]

The *Quarterly Review of Doublespeak* (8.1, November 1981) quotes then President-elect Ronald Reagan as saying 'If what I understand, if it is true, that I was told what I understood, yes, I thought that made sense.'

So Orwell's guess about the outcome of his proposed experiment was probably right, but only because he and most of those he listened to were middle-class speakers. He did not anticipate Labov's findings, which contradict many common opinions about language: about its uniformity, about 'correctness', about connections between speaker status and variety prestige. They are not easy findings to convey in a classroom, much less in a courtroom. But Orwell would have had other reservations. He did not say how the schools would undertake the task of teaching his 'national accent'; he probably did not think of the courts as enforcers of his suggestion. Even in *Nineteen Eighty-Four* where a 'national standard' complete with vocabulary, grammar and pronunciation was the goal of the authoritarian government, and where political and even sexual conduct were under the closest scrutiny, he made no provision for linguistic enforcement. Orwell would have felt one way about some features of the Ann Arbor arguments, and another way about some others; and after all he was somewhat inconsistent in his own views. But he apparently never dreamed that the course of language would become the concern of national laws like the Equal Educational Opportunities Act of 1974, or of court cases like the Ann Arbor case of 1979, as it increasingly has in the years since he died; for him language remained a matter of individual discernment and individual initiative. The shift to legislation and litigation, as the Ann Arbor case also showed, even when it concerned a non-standard variety of English, arose from a concern with English as a second language. That is the topic of the next chapter.

CHAPTER IV

Language Mixture

🔲🔲🔲🔲🔲🔲

IN ASIA and on the Continent Orwell found himself a linguistic outsider. The English-speaking world was divided into nations and their national varieties: America, England, Scotland, Ireland. England was further divided into regional and class dialects: northern and southern, cockney and 'educated'. As a native speaker, Orwell knew the varieties of English and the features that set one apart from another; he could describe them and evaluate them, preferring British to American, 'demotic' to 'educated'.

But abroad he could do nothing of the sort. Like many travellers, he commanded only one variety of the foreign language and was almost oblivious to the others. His comments rarely went further than remarks on the languages; newly in Spain, he noted

> I was having the usual struggles with the Spanish language. . . . nobody even among the officers spoke a word of French. Things were not made easier for me by the fact that when my companions spoke to one another they generally spoke in Catalan.
> (HC 11)

When he came to Barcelona in late 1936,

> Servile and even ceremonial forms of speech had temporarily disappeared. Nobody said 'Señor' or 'Don' or even 'Usted'; everyone called everyone else 'Comrade' and 'Thou', and said 'Salud!' instead of 'Buenos días'.
> (HC 5)

A few months later, he found 'The "revolutionary" forms of speech were dropping out of use' (HC 114). But that was the extent of his comment on foreign-language dialects, and it scarcely measures up to a tithe of what he had to say, for example, about Yorkshire pronunciation alone.

Abroad Orwell perceived the multilingual, not the multidialectal, in language mixture. He treated it most thoroughly where it was most exotic and most polyglot, in *Burmese Days*. Burma was truly an 'occupied territory' with an English-speaking ruling class, but some of them had learned colloquial Hindustani (an Indo-European language) and Burmese (not an Indo-European language). Many also used Urdu, closely related to Hindustani. Among those they ruled the linguistic mix produced everything from a crowd shouting 'in three or four languages' (BD 251) to the solitary 'Hindu youth, who lived his life in almost complete silence, because he spoke some Manipur dialect which nobody else understood, not even his Zerbadi wife' (BD 76).

Certainly Orwell's hero and surrogate, Flory, is at home in this polyglot scene, commanding not only the languages but the social registers. He says to a Burmese carter, ' "Come here, if you please, O venerable and learned sir! We have lost our way. Stop a moment, O great builder of pagodas!" ' (BD 58). Most of the other Europeans, however, avoid the native languages as far as their position permits, preferring when possible to let the burden of polyglottism fall on their subordinates. Orwell once wrote that 'My grandmother lived forty years in Burma and at the end could not speak a word of Burmese – typical of the ordinary Englishwoman's attitude' (CE 4.114, a letter of 14 March 1946). Their attitude was typical as well of the memsahibs in *Burmese Days* (e.g., BD 72, 88, 287), but Orwell's letter omits the point that his novel makes: 'nice women found kitchen Urdu quite as much as they needed' (BD 118), and his heroine Elizabeth, even before her arrival in Burma, had 'learned some of the more necessary Hindustani phrases, such as *"ider ao," "jaldi", "sahiblog"*, etc' (BD 96); reciprocally, it is in Hindustani, not her native Burmese, that the Burmese bureaucrat's wife longs to talk 'to English ladies' (BD 143). So Elizabeth, in Burma less than a fortnight, declines when Flory tries 'to induce her . . . to learn Burmese . . . (Her aunt had explained to her that only missionary-women spoke Burmese)' (BD 118). Her linguistic soul-mate is obviously not the Burmophone Flory but the young English officer Verrall whose 'Urdu consisted mainly of swear-words, with the verbs in the third person singular' (BD 202); and it is he who becomes her lover.

Polyglottism not only describes the scene of *Burmese Days*, then, but also the characters. We know something about Flory because in a multilingual Burma that frowned on Burmese and used English, Urdu and Hindustani as lingua francas, at leisure he taught Elizabeth

Burmese to court her, and under pressure 'His Urdu deserted him, and he bellowed in Burmese' (BD 252). Other characters are likewise defined in part by their roles in the multilingual society. The native official U Po Kyin schemes to become a member of the European club; his dialogue, even when we are meant to understand that it is in Burmese, is habitually macaronic: ' "Well, Ko Ba Sein, how does our affair progress? I hope that, as dear Mr. Macgregor would say" – U Po Kyin broke into English – " 'eet ees making perceptible progress'?" (BD 9). U Po Kyin has picked up the macaronic habits of his 'educated' masters: ' "You have no strategy, Ko Ba Sein. One does not *accuse* a white man; one has got to catch him in the act. Public disgrace, *in flagrante delicto*" ' (BD 262), but he has not quite grasped them all: ' "I am – what is that expression Mr. Macgregor uses? *Agent provocateur* – Latin, you would not understand" ' (BD 139).

Other Burmese show real, but unacceptable, proficiency; the Burmese butler at the European club apologizes to one of his masters 'I find it very difficult to keep ice cool now,' and receives the rebuke

'Don't talk like that, damn you – "I find it very difficult!" Have you swallowed a dictionary? "Please, master, can't keeping ice cool" – that's how you ought to talk. We shall have to sack this fellow if he gets to talk English too well.'
(BD 26)

U Po Kyin and Flory form two points of a linguistic traingle in the novel with the Indian physician Veraswami on the third. Veraswami, like U Po Kyin, is a native with ambitions to join the European club; like Flory, he is a foreigner in Burma. But he cannot speak Burmese like U Po Kyin or English like Flory. His Burmese is 'villainous' (BD 145), and his English is the stilted variety associated with studious and somewhat obsequious Indians: speaking, 'His voice was eager and bubbling, with a hissing of the s's'; writing, 'The doctor's epistolary style was queer. His syntax was shaky' (BD 37, 224; cf. 49). The examples Orwell gave bear out his description:

'Useless, useless. You have not the mind of an intriguer, Mr. Flory. *Qui s'excuse s'accuse*, iss it not? It does not pay to cry that there iss a conspiracy against one.'
(BD 149)

'The *so-called* weiksa, who is no other than a circus conjurer and the *minion* of U Po Kyin, have vanished for parts unknown, but six rebels

have been Caught. . . . If you could witness the abominable Conceited-
ness and the *lies* he is now telling . . . you would find it veritably Nause-
ous I assure you.'
(BD 224–5)

This style, sometimes called 'Babu English' ('Inky, the Indian boy
. . . is also the comic babu of the *Punch* tradition,' CE 1.471), is
shared by two other outsiders in the community, Eurasians whose
mixed (and illegitimate) parentage denies them acceptance by white
or Burmese; but their command of the style is even less secure than
Veraswami's:

'Also how on occasion of bishop's visit little half-brother and I dress in
longyis and sent among the Burmese children to preserve incognito. My
father never rose to be bishop, sir. Four converts only in twenty-eight
years, and also too great fondness for Chinese rice-spirit very fiery noised
abroad. . . .'
(BD 120)

Several steps further still from native command of English is
pidgin, not a first or native language but a rudimentary mix of
elements from several languages, useful for limited exchanges as
when sampan-wallahs compete for the heroine's patronage:

'Don't you listen him lies, missie! Nasty low fellow! Nasty low tricks
him playing. Nasty *native* tricks!'
'Ha, ha! He is not native himself! Oh no! Him European man, white
skin all same, missie!'
(BD 96)

Furthest of all from native English is Burmese with a few English
words and names scattered in it, the pronunciation suitably adjusted:
'*tinnis*' (for 'tennis', BD 51); 'Porley' (for 'Flory', BD 12, 273).
What Orwell reported in the range from monolingual English
colonial to monolingual Burmese subject he also, though less deliberately, reported in the range from foreign word in its original
language to foreign word naturalized in English. Some of the narrator's language is sufficiently remote from his English-speaking
readership that it requires translation:

By degrees the general suspicion of him crystallised in a single Burmese
phrase – '*shok de*'. . . . *Shok de* means, approximately, untrustworthy,

and when a 'native' official comes to be known as *shok de*, there is an end
of him.
(BD 283)

Much of the Burmese and other exotic language, however, gets no
explanation, either because it is self-explanatory in context or
because it is already part of English vocabulary. The Burmese functionary U Po Kyin, for example, 'was dressed in a *gaungbaung* of
pale pink silk, an *ingyi* of starched muslin, and a *paso* of Mandalay
silk' (BD 14); Orwell put the Burmese words in italics and none
appears in the OED, but the general reference to clothing explains
them as the more abstract context cannot explain *shok de*.

When Orwell wrote of the 'invisible *chokra* who pulled the punkah rope' (BD 26), he italicized *chokra* but left it unexplained, assum-
ing that its meaning ('a young servant') was known. When he wrote
of 'the verandas . . . curtained with green bamboo chicks', the 'dusty
skulls of sambhur', and 'A punkah, lazily flapping' (all BD 20),
however, he italicized none of the words. To his readership 'chicks',
'sambhur' and 'punkah' were as familiar as 'veranda' and 'bamboo'
are to us although they probably retained overtones of the orient that
'veranda' and 'bamboo' no longer do. (Orwell wrote of the 'veran-
dah' [sic] at his Gloucestershire sanatorium in 1949, CE 4.513.) But
Orwell's idea of his readership was true only for his time and place:
chokra and 'chicks', though in the OED Supplement, are not in the
RCD.

OED records 'shiko' as an English verb from 1858, before its first
use as a noun (1886), although in Burmese it is a noun ('The posture
of prostration with joined hands and bowed head assumed by a
Burmese in the presence of a superior', OED; not in RCD). When
Orwell used it as an English word, he gave it English verbal inflections and no italics or explanation ('Ba Taik . . . shikoed low', BD
102; cf. 160); with the derivational suffix '-ing', he made it a noun
('the constant shikoing', BD 159) which takes an English inflection
('there were shiko-ings', BD 59). To treat a foreign word this way is to
make it a full member of the English vocabulary, along with 'bamboo' and 'veranda'. Such words lie at the opposite end of the scale
from *shok de*, a foreign phrase wholly outside English. Between the
two extremes lie the italicized words found only in large English
dictionaries, like *chokra* and the items of Burmese clothing; and the
unitalicized words like 'sambhur' and 'punkah' found in a college
dictionary but unfamiliar to most American and British readers in
1984.

Orwell's acquaintance with this range of words (by no means all the oriental words in *Burmese Days*) could have helped him understand how borrowing increases English vocabulary, but it did not. He seems, instead, to have taken the status quo – his status quo, which is not ours – for granted, but to have resisted any further borrowing while it was still at the *shok de* stage. On the other hand, Orwell could comment insightfully on borrowings from oriental languages when he saw them in the context of his traditional western education:

> [T]ake the word 'barnshoot' – a corruption of the Hindustani word *bahinchut*. A vile and unforgivable insult in India, this word is a piece of gentle badinage in England. I have even seen it in a school text-book; it was in one of Aristophanes' plays, and the annotator suggested it as a rendering. . . . Presumably the annotator knew what *bahinchut* meant. But, because it was a foreign word, it had lost its magical swear-word quality and could be printed.
>
> (PL 178)

'Barnshoot' is not a 'corruption' but a typical folk etymology, and Orwell contradicted his notion that a foreign slur loses its sting in English: when an Indian addressed him as *tum* in a London flophouse, it was 'a thing to make one shudder, if it had been in India' (PL 168), though he earlier reported with pride that a cockney had called him 'mate' (PL 129). Hindi *tum* is very 'familiar', even more than English 'mate'; it is the pronoun a European might use to a rickshaw-wallah.[1] Orwell's reaction to his countryman's informality, paradoxically, was naively free of class bias, but his reaction to the Indian's remark still revealed the Old Etonian under the tramp's rags. Perhaps that was because he borrowed the 'mate' episode from Jack London's *The People of the Abyss*.[2] Or perhaps it was because Orwell had a native speaker's security with English, its varieties and their overtones, but – well as he knew Hindustani – remained bound by the literal force of its honorifics, a stranger as much to its nonce familiarities as he was to the flop-house.

Orwell's compatriots, in any event, were no polyglots in his eyes. They would not learn the indigenous languages of the Empire, and perhaps they could not:

> [T]he English are very poor linguists. . . . A completely illiterate Indian will pick up English far faster than a British soldier will pick up Hindustani. . . . There are some tens of thousands of Indians who speak English

as nearly as possible perfectly; yet the number of Englishmen speaking any Indian language perfectly would not amount to more than a few scores.

[T]he peculiarities of the English language make it almost impossible for anyone who has left school at fourteen to learn a foreign language after he has grown up. In the French Foreign Legion, for instance, the British and American legionaries seldom rise out of the ranks, because they cannot learn French, whereas a German learns French in a few months. English working people, as a rule, think it effeminate even to pronounce a foreign word correctly. This is bound up with the fact that the upper classes learn foreign languages as a regular part of their education.
(CE 3.25–6, 3–4; cf. CE 2.65)

Orwell's first remarks were not very penetrating – it is, after all, usually the subject peoples who learn their rulers' language, and not the other way around – but they attempted only description. His second, more analytical statement made two points. One was the psycholinguistic observation that the English language as such disables its speakers from natural language-learning after puberty, so that while those who remain in school can learn French as Orwell did, those who live among its speakers cannot acquire it as German 'legionaries' do. Such a remark must be hearsay, since Orwell never served in the French Foreign Legion, and the stony monolingualism of his comrades in Spain seems to contradict him. Certainly no objective evidence suggests that the 'peculiarities' of any language make its native speakers poor foreign-language students as adults. In fact to learn a foreign language well is a difficult thing for anyone after puberty, and more difficult in a classroom than among native speakers. Orwell did not say what he meant by 'a German learns French in a few months', but it cannot have been fluent, colloquial, unaccented French. If Europeans learn a second language mor easily than island Britons or overseas Americans, that is because the Europeans are more accustomed to encounter second languages, not because their languages are less 'peculiar'.

Orwell's second point was sociolinguistic: because foreign-language learning is an upper-class accomplishment, the lower classes scorn it. Yet the obstacle to 'correct' pronunciation is not so much class as nation; we mispronounce 'Moscow' and 'Madrid' because we are not Russian or Spanish. Orwell had a political case against the upper classes he considered the nationalists, however, and he considered nationalism a device for the oppression of the lower classes. He did not find the lower classes guilty of complicity in their own oppression. So Orwell's comments on foreign-language ability among native English speakers were not really descriptive, not really connected, and finally not really true. Yet his underlying assumption – that his middle-class or working-class readers would not know much about languages other than English – was a constant of his contract with them. Orwell departed from it occasionally, not because he changed his assumption but because he changed his audience. Since Orwell was not usually writing for elite or 'educated' readers exclusively, however, he felt he had to translate not only from Burmese and Hindustani but from French and Spanish: 'the cafeterie of the hotel – that is, in English, the stillroom' (PL 54); 'known to everyone as the *maricón* (Nancy-boy)' (HC 18). For many present-day British readers, and for most Americans, both of Orwell's translations themselves now need translation.

Orwell's polyglottism, his experience with language contact, and his belief that English and the English class system made difficulties for English-speakers learning foreign languages, all directed his attention to artificial varieties of English as world lingua francas alongside the natural language. Through his aunt he knew Eugene Adam, a teacher of Esperanto, but in late life he told a friend that he had left their lodgings in Paris because they spoke only Esperanto, 'and it was an ideology, not just a language'.[3] Yet although Orwell had little to say in defense of Esperanto, he went out of his way to group its detractors with social obstructionists whose hypothetical objection he phrased as 'Any *made-up* language must be character-less and lifeless – look at Esperanto' and promptly dismissed as 'a long-winded way of saying that what is must be' (CE 2.7–8), not a view he shared.

Orwell's next encounter with an artificial language was with the Basic English created by C.K. Ogden and described in his 1930 book.[4] Among those who supported it for literary or other reasons were Ezra Pound and H.G. Wells, whose remarks appeared in a 1939 pamphlet that Orwell owned. During the Second World War, Basic gained popularity as a lingua franca among Allies of different nations. In 1943 Winston Churchill quoted Franklin Delano Roosevelt 'on the merits of Basic' and set up a Cabinet committee to study its potential as an international language for commerce and 'ideas'; the British government bought the rights to Basic but the project to give it official backing came to nothing. Orwell also owned the 1944 pamphlet documenting these activities.

But Orwell was more than a passive chronicler of them. He received two letters from Ogden promoting Basic, one undated and the other of December 1942; and also in late 1942, while working at the BBC, he produced a programme on the Indian Service of which he wrote 'what I am chiefly concerned with is to popularise the idea that Basic English will be particularly useful as between Indians, Chinese and other Orientals who don't know one another's language.'⁵ This role as 'pidgin' is one that he again foresaw for Basic in his 1944 essay on 'The English People' (CE 3.25, quoted above). Later in the same year he was still supporting Basic 'side by side with Standard English' because

> In Basic, I am told, you cannot make a meaningless statement without its being apparent that it is meaningless – which is quite enough to explain why so many schoolmasters, editors, politicians and literary critics object to it.
> (CE 3.210; cf. CE 2.11, 4.135)

And in an earlier column (28 January 1944) he attempted to defend Basic from some of its detractors,

> Public opinion is beginning to wake up to the need for an international language, though fantastic misconceptions still exist. For example, many people imagine that the advocates of an international language aim at suppressing the natural languages, a thing no one has ever seriously suggested.
> (CE 3.86)

In 1943 Lancelot Hogben published an alternative to Basic called Interglossa. Unlike Basic it was not simply a reduced version of a natural language; like Esperanto it was constructed out of elements common to European languages. Hogben called it 'an auxiliary for a democratic world order' (obviously not a first language) in deliberate competition with Basic which he derided as bound by 'the strait-jacket of acceptable English usage'. Orwell reviewed Hogben's book in late 1943 and, about a month later, Ogden's *Basic English versus the Artificial Languages*, so he was familiar with the conflicting claims of the two systems (and amused by the heat with which they were urged, CE 3.85–6). But he did not get directly involved with Basic after 1944, and his later references to Hogben are restricted to a slighting citation of his prose ('Politics and the English Language', CE 4.128; cf. 135) and a suggestion, a few months before the publication of *Nineteen Eighty-Four*, that his publisher approach Hogben for a blurb. His neglect is ironic. Hogben had edited and virtually co-written Frederick Bodmer's *The Loom of Language* (1944), a book that embodied much sound and, for the time, up-to-date information. Many of Orwell's language views might have been different if he had known it.

As it was, his active concern with artificial lingua francas covered only the years 1942–4, and even then it was not so intense, for example, as his life-long resistance to borrowed vocabulary. Perhaps Orwell's growing pessimism overcame his belief in a worldwide lingua franca; perhaps the last months of the war distracted him from such matters. (In January 1945, a few weeks after his last reference to Basic, Orwell went to France as a war correspondent where he collapsed and was hospitalized, only to return to England in March when his wife died.) In any event neither of the artificial international languages he knew seemed, in the long run, to hold the answer for the problems of international communication that he had observed since 1922.

Instead, Orwell turned to English:

> On its lower levels [English] is very easy to learn, in spite of its irrational spelling. It can also for international purposes be reduced to very simple pidgin dialects, ranging from Basic to the 'Bêche-de-mer' English used in the South Pacific. It is therefore well suited to be a world lingua franca, and it has in fact spread more widely than any other language. (CE 3.25; cf. 2.99)

Orwell made this claim even though in Paris French was – with etymological propriety – the 'lingua franca' (PL 71), and in Spain

> All Spaniards, we discovered, knew [only] two English expressions. One was 'O.K., baby,' the other was a word used by the Barcelona whores in their dealings with English sailors, and I am afraid the compositors would not print it. (HC 39)

It was a claim he later repeated:

> [O]ur existing spelling system is preposterous and must be a torment to foreign students. This is a pity, because English is well fitted to be the universal second language, if there ever is such a thing. It has a large start

over any natural language and an enormous start over any manufactured
one. . . .
(CE 4.305; cf. 2.58)[6]

Orwell's notion that English had 'spread more widely than any
other language' was correct in its implications though not in its
geography and demography. Other European languages such as
French and Spanish are as widespread geographically as English, and
no European language has as many native speakers as Chinese, of
which the Mandarin variety alone has well over six hundred million;
the importance of English stems from the many people on all conti-
nents who speak it as a second language, perhaps another three
hundred or three hundred and fifty million, and the uses to which
they put it.[7] English has followed British colonists, American ser-
vicemen, and multinational corporations around the world in successive waves. About forty countries, in addition to those where English
is a native language, use it as an official or semi-official language. It is
the foreign language of choice in schools and universities in, among
other places, Peru, Orwell's Spain, and the People's Republic of
China (by contrast, few non-Chinese speak Mandarin).[8] The importance of North America and Britain in communication and the mass
media makes English the language of more books, magazines, radio
and television programmes, than any other language. Three-quarters
of the world's mail is in English. Students who study abroad go
chiefly to the US, Canada, the UK or France; all but the last are
English-speaking. English is the international language of air control.

English has become the language of the large international scientific organizations. Many of the largest did not exist before the
Second World War, when international conferences often used German as their principal language. A glance through the *Yearbook of
International Organizations* shows that many have now adopted
English. Not all are scientific: English is the official language of the
Olympic Committee and the Miss Universe Pageant. But the scientific organizations are especially important, because scientific
method relies on communication: experiment and discovery are
worthless until other workers can read the result in a form they can
understand. Scientists do not need to be polyglot, but they have to
know what other scientists are doing. In 1879 thirty per cent of the
world's medical journals were in English; in 1977, it was sixty-two
per cent. Among the most often quoted journals in nuclear physics

and astrophysics, organic and physical chemistry, physiology and economics, the proportion is even higher, perhaps eighty per cent.[9]

The ascendancy of scientific English is partly accidental: scientific activity after the Second World War grew most rapidly in the countries least damaged by the war, chiefly English-speaking. The more recent growth of science and technology in other countries has only spread the use of scientific English further. English has a well-established scientific vocabulary, and a French scientist has claimed that 'the dynamic genius of the English language lends itself admirably to the expression of science'.[10] But those are really cultural, not linguistic, matters. It is not so much the inherent qualities of English as its recent history that made it the chief international scientific lingua franca in an increasingly scientific age.

Its spread is aided by governmental and semi-governmental agencies such as the United States Information Service and the British Council, and by academic enterprises such as the Departments of English as a Second Language at the University of Hawaii and the University of the Pacific, along with master's degree programmes in some twenty US universities. An instance is the New Zealand government's promotion of English in Asia and the Pacific.[11] The English Language Institute at Victoria University in Wellington has trained over a thousand students for the Diploma in the Teaching of English as a Second Language since its foundation in 1962, and a thousand more in its summer Certificate course. The government has sent advisers to Indonesia, Thailand, Singapore, the Cook Islands, the People's Republic of China, and Japan; over a thousand New Zealand teachers have worked in the Pacific islands schools alone. Government funds have provided textbooks on English for Asian and Pacific educational systems. The New Zealand Department of Education developed and published the Tate Oral English Course, now in widespread use throughout the Pacific islands. Such multifaceted official activity is bound to change language patterns throughout the region where, Orwell predicted, 'the fate of the English language in Asia is either to fade out or to survive as a pidgin language useful for business and technical purposes' (CE 2.218).

Papua New Guinea exemplifies the use of pidgin in the South Pacific that Orwell predicted.[12] The variety of languages there is so great (seven hundred by one count) and the speakers of any one so few (seldom more than a few thousand) that English is usually not the second but the third, fifth or sixth language of university students, and rarely the language of communication among them. Instead they employ one or the other of two English-based pidgins, which are beginning to become creolized – that is, spoken as first languages. Children of couples who do not share a native language often adopt neither, but speak pidgin; university students lose touch with their local language when away from it and turn to pidgin. Some writing, including government publications such as *Nius bilong Yumi*, is in pidgin. But most writing, and most education from the secondary level through the university, is in English even though it is the native language of only three per cent, as against eleven per cent for the two pidgins combined (the remaining eighty-six per cent claim one or another of 209 languages as native, but almost all also speak one of the pidgins). One observer has described English in Papua New Guinea as 'this modern Latin', thinking – apparently – of the medieval language, not the ancient. That role is scarcely what educators mean when they speak of 'the use of English'.

English has a similar role in other parts of the region that Orwell knew well. In Singapore, for example, the government supports four official languages: Malay, Tamil, Chinese, and English.[13] English is the first language of very few, but it serves as a language of 'mediation' that allows speakers of the other languages to converse. It also serves as a language of education in schools where the teacher may, for example, speak an 'unofficial' language such as Hindi; and it serves as an international language of trade. Its auxiliary role in all three spheres is supported by government policy, and that too is new.

Not every neighbour of Singapore has the same policy. Malaysia, like Singapore the ex-colony of an English-speaking country, decided to replace English with Malay in the schools and in government, although English remains the language of instruction in many university courses and bilingualism remains the declared objective of official educational policy. In India, by contrast, the 1947 Constitution recognized sixteen regional languages but provided that Hindi must progressively become the national language.[14] The clash between recognized regional languages and imposed national Hindi has been confusing and sometimes bloody. The 'national' version of Hindi on, for example, the government All India Radio, seems to some Indians an 'absurdly bombastic lingo', 'ludicrous' and – even in the Hindi-speaking areas – almost unintelligible. As a result, the government agreed in the 1960s that the regional languages would be taught within the states, and that English would be the language of communication between the states . . . a singular departure from the original patriotic support for national Hindi. The new policy and increased travel have actually resulted in a larger English-speaking population than before 1947.

But what English? Once the language of the elite and the administration, English now appears on the syllabus of village schools. The teachers are less often from Britain, more often locals for whom English is also a second language. In the eyes of some Indians themselves, the result is a decline in the quality of English. In Malaysia the worry was the high rate of failure among students of English; in India it is the drift of school English from its European origins. Yet in his time Orwell reviewed several books by Indian authors, and in our own, Indian literature in English is gaining an increasing international reputation.

Singapore retains English as one official language, Malaysia has removed it from official status, and India has reinstated it. All have suffered from a lack of well-qualified teachers. English in Orwell's Burma has a kindred but different history.[15] Nineteenth-century Burmese education was in the hands of Buddhist monks – the Burmese word for 'school' is also the word for 'monastery' – and British lay schools. Twentieth-century British schools often used Burmese as the language of instruction in the lower grades but taught English as a subject; both English and Burmese served as languages of instruction in the upper grades. Since the Second World War, Burmese has been the official national language over regional languages such as Shan, Chin, and Karen. English was banned in 1962, but reinstated in 1981 as an obligatory subject from Middle School onwards. Again the abrupt increase in the teaching of English as a second language was more than the supply of teachers could meet. A two-year teacher-training course in English was shortened by one year to meet the demand for graduates, and occasional refresher courses were held in Rangoon, Mandalay and outlying district headquarters. But political and economic troubles in Burma drained resources away from education. Burmese has replaced English as the language of instruction in higher education, and although a Burmese university graduate can look back on over five hundred hours of English classes spread over a decade or so, that is only about an hour a week – not all of it under well-trained teachers.

Similar stories could be told about Africa, South America, and eastern Europe. Orwell's vision of English as a 'universal second language', the 'world lingua franca', is widely shared, and it has come closer since his day. The number of English speakers has grown by forty per cent in the past twenty years; teaching English as a second language, teaching teachers of English as a second language, English-language textbook publishing, all have grown rapidly along with the numbers. But Orwell's vision has proven, like many a vision, elusive. Teaching English as a second language abroad is only part of the task. New Zealand is unusual because the government programme embraces not only the overseas promotion of English but its cultivation at home: teachers in schools with a high proportion of Pacific islanders can attend a twelve-week English-language course; technical institutes run courses in factories for immigrant workers. The emphasis is on training and on outreach. New Zealand has benefitted from its history. Though settled from Britain, it has always been a multilingual nation in a multilingual region.

The United States was not first settled from Britain, but by the time of the Revolution it was a British colony with a chiefly English-speaking population. Nineteenth-century and twentieth-century immigration increased the numbers of Americans who arrived without English, but acquiring the language was a priority for most of them: citizenship requirements included some mastery, so public and private schools provided English-language instruction. Because American society was in theory classless, no form of English gained status simply from its users. Instead, the target variety for native speaker and foreign student alike was the one documented in a growing store of American grammar and other textbooks. Even today, the retort 'Our forebears had to learn proper English – why can't they?' meets claims for recognition of other varieties (such as Afro-American English) or other languages (such as Spanish or Navajo).

Orwell's awareness of other languages than English in Britain was limited to Gaelic:

> Scotland is almost an occupied territory. You have an English or angli-cised upper class, and a Scottish working class which speaks with a markedly different accent, or even, part of the time, in a different language. This is a more dangerous kind of class division than any now existing in England.
> (CE 4.285)

He went on to explain his conversion to support for bilingual education; firstly, it shows respect for the culture, and

> Secondly, it is probable that the effort of being bilingual is a valuable

education in itself. The Scottish Gaelic-speaking peasants speak beautiful English, partly, I think, because English is an almost foreign language. . . . Probably they benefit intellectually by having to be aware of dictionaries and grammatical rules, as their English opposite numbers would not be.

Orwell's remarks came only after his 1946 move to the Scottish island of Jura, not as the outcome of study, so they were more than usually rooted in his subjective point of view. He used 'beautiful' to describe the English of Gaelic-speaking peasants as though it were an absolute and self-explanatory term. He assumed that peasants' English closely follows the rules of English dictionaries and grammars. And he concluded that such language is most likely to be 'beautiful English'. The assumptions form a circle, but they are individually unlikely and collectively illogical. For 'beautiful' is not a term in linguistic description; lower-class bilinguals are not usually more responsive to linguistic regulation than monolinguals; and grammars and dictionaries never guaranteed beautiful English (unless you define 'beautiful' as 'according to dictionaries and grammatical rules').

The claims for speakers of other languages than English, at any rate in America, are no longer made on these grounds. Instead they are made because of continued immigration, and increasingly because of successful litigation for language rights among the civil rights protected by law. The 1980 census found ten per cent of US households not English-speaking; some six to seven per cent of the US population is Spanish-speaking. Orwell's views on the matter got little further than the one sentence in a column 'if people feel that they have a special culture which ought to be preserved, and that the language is part of it, difficulties should not be put in their way when they want their children to learn it properly' (CE 4.285, 1947).[16] New developments in the matter would probably not have affronted the man who held that view, but their extent would certainly have astonished him.

It is the developments that are new; the matter is not. In Britain, it is true, the notion that immigrant children should receive classroom instruction in their mother tongues as well as English did not come until 1982, and then not from an official committee but in a Commission for Racial Equality report (*Ethnic Minority Community Languages*). The report argued that the linguistic diversity of Britain, hitherto either ignored or viewed as a liability, should be treated instead as a national resource. But in the United States the question of language teaching in the schools has been before courts at least since 1923, when in *Meyer* the court held unconstitutional a Nebraska law against foreign-language teaching below the ninth grade.[17] The law, passed at a high tide of American xenophobia, forbade the acquisition of a foreign language ahead of English, so that 'the English language should be and become the mother tongue of all children reared in this State.' Perhaps the Nebraska legislators were uneasy because, as the court noted, 'the foreign born population is very large', and because English did not and does not have legal status as the official language of the United States. Indeed it was not until 1981 that Senator S. I. Hayakawa, a former college president and noted semantics scholar, introduced a constitutional amendment to 'establish' English; he did not succeed with the amendment, but settled for a resolution that lacked the force of law. Notably, the proposed amendment stipulated both that 'Neither the U.S. nor any state shall make or enforce any law which requires the use of any language other than English' and that 'This article shall not prohibit educational instruction in a language other than English.' The conflict arose from legal decisions reaching back to *Meyer*, where the court held that the Fourteenth Amendment guaranteed due process and equal protection to 'all those who speak other languages as well as to those born with English on the tongue.' Subsequent cases took substantially the same view.

The right to learn a foreign language in school is not the same as the right to learn *in* a foreign language, however. It remained for *Lau* (1974) to bring the question of foreign-language speakers into the arena of civil rights legislation. The Civil Rights Act of 1964 had authorized the Department of Health, Education and Welfare to issue regulations for recipients of its aid, and the Department ruled among other things that recipients must not 'Restrict an individual in any way in the enjoyment of any advantage or privilege enjoyed by others'; in 1970 it issued clarifying guidelines which included the provision that

> Where inability to speak and understand the English language excludes national origin-minority group children from effective participation in the education program offered by a school district, the district must take affirmative steps to rectify the language deficiency in order to open its instructional program to these students.

The *Lau* decision drew on this civil rights legislation background in holding that there is no equality of treatment merely by providing students with the same facilities, textbooks, teachers, and curriculum; for students who do not understand English are effectively foreclosed from any meaningful education.

And the court pointed out that two obvious solutions, and perhaps others, were available: to teach English to the foreign-language speaking students, or to teach them in their own language. The court accepted that either solution might meet the constitutional need of a student with little or no English-language proficiency, but in practice most responses to the *Lau* decision have mixed them: the students receive some instruction in English as a second language (ESL), and some in other subjects taught in their first language. They receive bilingual education.

Lau is the basis of much subsequent regulation and litigation. In *Serna* (1974) the court ordered the Portales (NM) school board to adopt a bilingual education programme proposed by the plaintiffs, as another court also did in the New York *Aspira* case the same year. These decisions went a step further than *Lau* because they imposed a bilingual programme, and so in effect directed classroom activities, from the bench. The federal government has also implemented *Lau* through its 'Lau Remedies' so as to require school districts to provide bilingual education at the elementary school level for students who need it. The same guidelines also endorse bilingual education for older schoolchildren, but permit ESL-only programmes.

The Bilingual Education Act (Title VII, 1978) held that children learn through their linguistic and cultural heritage, and so 'children of limited English proficiency have educational needs which can be met by the use of bilingual education. . . .' The enforcement of these regulations has not always satisfied language minority groups, however; further litigation continues. As Parker put it,

> legislation, federal and state program regulations and court rulings are of increasing importance in determining the nature and extent of bilingual programs. *In combination, they outline who is to receive the services, how programs should be structured, how much can be spent and then require school districts to comply.*
> (p. 51; emphasis hers)

Of course bilingual education has its drawbacks and its critics. It is expensive because it forces the school to teach the same subjects in more than one language. It takes the children out of English-language classrooms for part of the time and hence reduces their exposure to English. It flies in the face of the time-honoured American 'melting pot' ideal by supporting 'cultural fragmentation'. The *Wall Street Journal* editorialized about the proposed Hayakawa amendment, 'This country has got to have a single culture in matters basic to citizenship. It has great assimilative powers, but even these powers will be strained to the cracking point if we let artificially supported multilingualism add to our problems' (6 May 1981, p. 26). Some think it could even damage the English language itself.

But ESL-alone also takes students out of their subject classes part of the time and exposes them to subject teaching in a strange language the rest of the time, and hence delays their acquisition of subject skills; such a delay retards both cognitive and academic development. Perhaps as a result, the dropout rate in ESL-alone programmes is far higher than in bilingual programmes, and no programme will work if the student does not stay in school. Research results are tentative and often conflicting, but it appears that bilingual education has a good effect at best, no effect at worst; students fare at least as well in bilingual as in ESL programmes. For an ESL programme leaves their native language and culture at the schoolhouse door, humiliating the students, ignoring a pedagogical opportunity, and squandering a national resource. Bilingual education will not lead to the extinction of English in America. America is not, after all, Quebec, where French is the first language of the majority, and where it is stabilized from one generation to another as languages other than English virtually never are in the US.[18] And, by contrast, America is not Wales, where nationalist fervour prompted the lament that 'only one in five speak their [sic] native language' (*Radio Times*, 31 July 1982, p. 14). English is a minority language in bilingual Quebec and a majority language in bilingual Wales; the US is multilingual. America has a constitutional guarantee of religious liberty, forbidding an 'established' church. Why shouldn't it guarantee linguistic diversity as well?

English will, to be sure, change in a bilingual environment. It has always changed, and it will continue to change no matter what happens in the schools. Change arises from speech community variety, and the allocation of speech community roles usually changes only when it benefits the community. So the question is the larger one of the role of English in the American, even the international speech community. Bilinguals, for example, will use the dominant language so long as it affords them the kind of communication they want. Hence bilingual education will not delay their acquisition of English; rather, by making them fuller participants in their own education, it will encourage them in more versatile membership of the speech community. Bilingual education appears to maximize the use of English in Hispanic and other foreign-language communities in the United States, and the spread of English abroad is probably possible only as part of the spread of bilingualism in the world, now that the population of speakers of English as a first language is no longer growing.

Some compromise with the sceptical viewpoint, all the same, is usually struck in the balance between ESL and foreign-language teaching. 'Compensatory' bilingual education emphasizes ESL. 'Transitional' bilingual education continues subject teaching in the foreign language only until the student knows enough English to learn effectively from English-language instructors; most US programmes are of this type. The Bilingual Education Act rules out use of its funds to assist English-speaking children in improving their English skills, or in learning a foreign language, so the only other version of bilingual education is 'maintenance' – instruction to improve the student's skills in the first language and English alike. For some programmes with Native Americans, 'maintenance' is really 'revitalization': they introduce the ancestral language to youngsters for whom it was lost in centuries of English-language dominance and native language suppression.

Regulations require bilingual programmes for elementary school children wherever twenty share the same language background. In some school districts, especially with students from several native American tribes, the regulations can make classroom materials a severe problem, one that becomes even more severe at the secondary school level, so that bilingual education beyond the required elementary grades is almost impossible. Textbook problems are now less severe for the better-known languages, especially Spanish; in the eyes of some speakers of other minority languages, bilingual education is too often simply Spanish-English education. (The same is true of some English-speaking educational administrators, for whom 'bilingual' can simply mean 'monolingual in Spanish'.) But research findings suggest bilingual education is not so difficult. For one thing, bilingual education involves the parents in the schools as ESL-alone never does. Lack of participation in decisions is the cause of much minority activism, so bilingual programmes can take the place of political conflict. Linguistic conflict within the education system arises when the language of the dominant group is imposed on the minority, so that the minority fails to learn the dominant language even if the system is really trying to teach it and learning is really in the interest of the minority. When minority groups have a genuine role in their education (e.g., the Amish in Pennsylvania), they have greater success.

For another thing, though teacher training is critical, teacher ethnicity is not. It may still be difficult to find good teachers who are competent speakers of a lesser-known language, but at least they do not have to be native speakers. Even the testing of their competency, however, like the testing of student language competency or programme design, can be troublesome. For while research findings have cast light on the task of bilingual education, no more than one-tenth of one per cent of expenditure in the field has been on basic research, so that much of the remainder has been spent in near-total darkness. We know, for example, that no one talks the same way all the time: that mastery of a language is not simply mastery of the words in a dictionary and the forms in a grammar, but mastery of their functional use, the appropriate variety for a specific situation. Yet second-language testing still lacks the sophistication to measure such mastery.

Language is the topic of much misinformation and much outright bias. The increasing role of courts and legislatures in directing language policy, for example in bilingual education, has wrested the decision from the biased but not backed it with significant sound information. As in so many other language topics, so in language education, many embrace preconceptions that they shelter from objective knowledge. Knowledge in language is still incomplete and often untested, but it has grown enormously in the years since the Second World War. Language regulation has grown rapidly during the same years. But they have not grown together.

Language-related decisions are continually being made in the United States, but usually without the help of dependable expertise. We adopt laws, we implement them, we revise them – but in the language area we do so almost entirely on an ad hoc basis. . . . We act without data. We act inconsistently. We act indecisively. We implement foolishly. We revise laws on the basis of as little evidence as we had when we adopted them. We evaluate poorly or in such a partisan fashion as to make a mockery of the term. We would not do so for industrial planning or for health care or other important aspects of our national life. In all these areas we have continuing agencies engaged in expert data collection, data interpretation, policy planning, policy recommending, and public information. In the language area (or areas) we have none of these. We stumble and blunder and wander aimlessly, half convinced that the country is going to the dogs linguistically and half dubious that we really do have language problems.[19]

Many bilingual education rulings have been social and constitutional, sometimes political – not primarily linguistic or even pedagogical except as a means to an end. Sporadic government funding for teaching foreign languages to English-speaking Americans has been available, usually as part of the defence effort, but no legislative and legal regulation of foreign-language education to match those for bilingual education, and no regular funding that programmes could rely on; a tentative beginning, a 1981 congressional bill that would help pay for college and school foreign-language teaching, made little headway. Yet bilingual education and foreign-language teaching are kindred. To foster bilingual education and not foreign-language education is as inconsistent as to resist bilingual education on cultural grounds and at the same time to deplore the lack of second-language competence in American business and government.

The outcome of bilingual education is bilingual students. Even maintenance bilingual education retains a component of language that is not the student's own, though such study is not at all what it was when Orwell studied French at Eton. The field now makes distinctions where once things all seemed the same, and especially the distinction between a foreign language (FL, generally limited to classroom study and use) and a second language (SL, spoken in the community outside the classroom in many social contexts – sometimes even socially required).[20] The distinction correlates to some extent with another between *learning* a language (where the study is conscious, explicit, formal) and *acquiring* a language (where it is largely unconscious, implicit, informal) – 'picking it up'. Foreign-language study is by definition foreign-language learning in this technical sense. The speaker of a native language (L^1) by definition learns another (L^2) as a foreign language, and a second language can be studied as well; but a second language is usually acquired.

Since the time when Orwell learned French a great many approaches to the goal of native-like proficiency have been tried, beginning with the grammar-translation-reading that he probably met at Eton, and including more recently the pattern-practice drills spun off from the behaviourist theory of psychology and the audio-lingual method that had spoken performance as its aim. These approaches have brought with them changes in teacher training, textbook materials, and audiovisual hardware including the language lab. All produced students more or less inadequate to communicate in a foreign language, students whose speech might suffice to see them through a day in a foreign town without insoluble problems but could hardly convey their feelings in L^2 as it did in L^1. Their speech might even be fluent ('flowing') and avoid gross errors, but real proficiency demands the social knowledge for making language choices.[21]

If such students abandon monologue for dialogue, colloquial language at normal speed swamps them. The conventional remark 'I can't speak L^2 but I can understand it' is usually a cover-up; expressive incompetence is easy to detect, but a smile can mask receptive confusion. On the Concorde project, it is said, the British engineers spoke English and the French spoke French. But they were in an L^2 acquisition environment, scientific vocabulary is largely international, and the topic of their dialogue was a narrowly limited one expressed also in mathematics, blueprints, and hard metal. Classroom models for speech, by contrast, are usually a standardized variety of L^2, not the variety that native speakers use. And native speakers do not simply 'translate' or decode discourse they hear; instead they rely on predictions developed from their experience with social language in its community roles, which they apply in parallel construction of a sentence that they check continuously with the incoming signal. That experience and application are not very easy to teach, so the emphasis of the 1950s on teaching the spoken language just made the discrepancy between FL teachers' aims and their achievements more obvious.

The emphasis on teaching also left student motivation too much out of account. Foreign-language study can be a response to any one of several motivations. A student may want the language for a narrowly practical purpose – to pass an undergraduate requirement, or to read professional literature (such as 'scientific Russian'). Another student may want the fullest possible grasp of L^2, including 'native-like' speaking proficiency. Foreign-language teachers often conduct their classes as if the latter were the model for every class, much to the burden of the scientific-Russian postulant.[22] But many an English-speaking American lacks any L^2 motivation: a nation of immigrants, America has until very recently seen disunity and worse in the spectre of multilingualism. The theoretically monolingual society renders implausible the promise of international valence to FL students, who know that English is a worldwide language. The L² such students can learn in a few years is nothing next to the ESL they encounter among people of all classes in every country of the globe. Understandably, the number of FL students among English-speaking Americans is dwindling rapidly, and the studies of those that remain are dwindling too.

Understandably, because from the start the courses they take are often misdirected: the inceptive level is 'beginning' when it should be 'basic'. Most of the students will never go on to the higher level of study that might justify the rigours of the 'beginning' course. They find a conflict between emphasis on expression and the insistence on rules that stifles it. They are sceptical about gaining native-like pronunciation when they hear the Kissingers or even the Dietrichs of international fame. They are interested in the content of language, meaning, but they study mostly form.

A basic course could feed their interest by offering materials for listening, along with sufficient vocabulary, and by delaying students' performance until they have some comprehension of what they hear. Premature performance throws the student back to problems of form. The student should strive for recognizable pronunciation, of course, because that is necessary and, unlike 'native' pronunciation, attainable. The teacher might even take a cue from 'caretaker' language, the language for example of a parent with a child: it typically concentrates on the here and now, starts with short simple sentences, repeats often, adapts speed by using pauses rather than lento tempo, and concentrates on meaning, not form; parents are quick to correct 'He my Daddy!' if the wrong man is indicated, even if they do not explicitly correct the grammar. Caretaker language does not have to be baby-talk, and it offers hints for the FL classroom although – as we saw in Chapter One – no other language learning is quite like child-language learning.

Some FL students want to read foreign literature in the original. But we need only recall our struggle to recover the sense from English literature of long ago and far away – Shakespeare, say – to realize how much mastery of an FL is requisite for us to make out the meaning of a Mann or a García Lorca. That is for the higher levels of FL study, not for a basic course. Such a course can have serious humanistic goals just the same. It can study language as language, not as backdoor linguistics but by using the FL to study the variety in which languages always manifest themselves and the functions that variation serves, to deflate language chauvinism and promote linguistic tolerance, to display 'the impressive variety of complex and delicate devices language puts at men's disposal.'[23]

If the aim is 'acculturation', social and psychological integration with the target language group, acquisition success is likely.[24] But acculturation depends a great deal on the group the students come from, the target group, and individual aptitude and personality. Although few of these are matters the school can control, the plan of study can take them into account. For example, a group of Hispanic pre-schoolers in California took part in an ESL programme that made prominent use of games and physical activities. Their culture gave the extroverted and uninhibited boys an advantage over the shy girls, as did the mixed classes – and the results. A method that adapted to the pattern even by merely separating the boys' classes from the girls' would have been more realistic about the impact of group outlook on language acquisition.[25]

A theory that relates the effects of L^2 acquistion and learning is that of the 'monitor'. It holds that performance depends chiefly on language acquisition, not learning; the learned language acts only as a monitor on the output of the acquired language when the situation demands and time permits. Learned language does not result in real proficiency, but it supplies a useful adjunct to acquired language. In fact the monitor is not restricted to second-language performance. First-language performance includes a step that initiates more possibilities than the utterance finally uses, and monitor-like functions are among those that choose the appropriate alternative for expression.[26]

Complex tasks like speech are learned 'on the job' when there is no suitable conceptual framework for verbalizing the task or where verbalization would take too much effort. Most aspects of speech are possible only if they are automatic. Language acquisition leads to automated skills, but language learning leads only to storage of individual tasks in the long-term memory; language learning yields limited proficiency in part, it seems, because retrieval of the tasks one by one from the memory uses up much of the available mental capacity. A speaker of English as a second language, Sajavaara, reports that the English article system with its definite, indefinite, and zero articles is 'one of those systems which can only be acquired', not learned; his native Finnish does without articles. The difficulty he or any ESL teacher would have in verbalizing the English system is implicit in Orwell's prescription for making 'a sophisticated title' for a novel: 'this is done by choosing a title that ought to have a "the" in it and then leaving out the "the" ' (CE 1.160), replacing the expected definite article with zero. Orwell, however, was not talking about English as a second or foreign language, but English as a literary language.

CHAPTER V

Literary Language

𝕴𝕴𝕴𝕴𝕴𝕴

GEORGE ORWELL wrote 'So long as I remain alive and well I shall continue to feel strongly about prose style' (CE 1.6), and his reputation as a stylist is high: in 1946 his friend George Woodcock called his writing 'fluent and very readable', marked by 'a colloquial ease of expression, at the same time without diminishing the quality of style'.[1] That view became the conventional wisdom, so that in 1969 the American critic Irving Howe could expand on it:

> The standard formula is that he wrote in a 'conversational' style, and he himself is partly responsible for this simplification. . . . If you compare the charged lucidity of Orwell's prose in his best essays with the merely adequate and often flat writing of his letters, you see at once that the style for which he became famous was the result of artistry and hard work. It always is.[2]

Howe's appreciation does not change the common view, but it finds a different cause for the effect. In place of a prose that is the outcome of its author's sincerity, an essayist's native woodnotes wild, we have a prose that is the outcome of its author's artistry and effort. The difference is not between sincere prose and insincere, however, as Orwell knew: 'The great enemy of clear language is insincerity' (CE 4.137), while the great shaper of clear language is commitment. A reader of Orwell's four thousand published pages will sometimes become impatient with his opinions but rarely with his commitment or his prose.

Howe links Orwell's style with his criticism of other writers: referring to Orwell's manifesto that 'Good prose is like a window pane' (CE 1.7), Howe goes on

> Part of his limitation as a literary critic is that he shows little taste for the prose of virtuosity: one can't easily imagine him enjoying Sir Thomas Browne. If some windows should be clear and transparent, why may not

others be stained and opaque? Like all critics who are also significant writers themselves, Orwell developed standards that were largely self-justifying: he liked the prose that's like a window pane because that's the kind of prose he wrote.[3]

Howe's 'Like all critics' shows that he has read Orwell closely enough to pick up some of his habits, and he seems to beg the question about window-pane prose: Orwell probably liked it in others for the same reason he wrote it himself, not *because* he wrote it himself. Howe – and Orwell – leave that reason vague. But Howe is right to imply that Orwell was no latitudinarian in prose style; he was that in nothing that mattered much to him.

In view of Orwell's declaration of strong feeling about prose style, the commitment that his prose conveys, the discipline that Howe claimed for it, Orwell's lapses were surprisingly frequent and his close studies of prose were not. He could be self-critical in general terms – he wrote of *Nineteen Eighty-Four* 'I ballsed it up rather' (CE 4.475, a phrasal verb created by conversion), and in similar terms on the completion of most of his other books – but when it came to specific self-criticism, the points he made were few, far between, and trifling. Köberl points to the index of *The Collected Essays, Journalism and Letters* for proof 'Wie sehr Orwell im Laufe seiner schriftstellerischen Tätigkeit an sprachlichen Fragen interessiert war,'[4] though in fact the index omits far more examples than it lists. 'Why I Write' (1946) is typically unspecific:

> The problem of language is subtler [than that of construction] and would take too long to discuss. I will only say that of late years I have tried to write less picturesquely and more exactly. In any case I find that by the time you have perfected any style of writing, you have always outgrown it.
> (CE 1.7)

All he said about Newspeak was 'As there are a lot of neologisms there are bound to be many printers' errors of a stupid kind' (CE 4.473).

Orwell's lack of analytical interest in the language of literature revealed itself in throw-away criticism like 'It is hard work to dredge a meaning out of such morasses of words' (CE 1.79; cf. 161, 167) which, accompanied by a brief quotation, did duty for textual analysis. More prominent writers sometimes received slightly fuller readings; he wrote of Gissing,

Certainly there is not much of what is usually called beauty, not much lyricism . . . in the texture of his writing. His prose, indeed, is often disgusting. Here are a couple of samples: . . .

> The ineptitude of uneducated English women in all that relates to their attire is a fact that it boots not to enlarge upon.

(CE 4.434)

He wrote in similar terms of Conrad in 1936 and, without much change, again in 1949 (CE 1.227; 4.489). Few would praise the sentence from Gissing, but the critic's task goes beyond mere dispraise, at least as far as show-and-tell.

Orwell was equally unspecific in praise: Edith Sitwell for the 'charm in her love of sonorous words for their own sake' (CE 1.24), Carlyle for his 'splendid words! A few passages such as this are the best justification of Carlyle's opinions' (CE 1.35), Kipling for being 'the only English writer of our time who has added phrases to the language' (CE 2.192), and Henry Miller for pages in *Tropic of Cancer* and *Black Spring* that

> give you an idea of what can still be done, even at this late date, with English prose. In them, English is treated as a spoken language, but spoken *without fear*, i.e. without fear of rhetoric or of the unusual or poetical word. The adjective has come back, after its ten years' exile. It is a flowing, swelling prose, a prose with rhythms in it, something quite different from the flat, cautious statements and snack-bar dialects that are now in fashion.

(CE 1.497, 1940)

Orwell's contrast here was with 'the typical prose of the last ten years', which had

> not got many frills or unnecessary adjectives. It's plain. It is rather questionable whether the sort of prose that has developed in this way is suitable for expressing very subtle thoughts, but it is excellent for describing action, and it is a good antidote to the over-refined type of prose which used to be fashionable – very good in its way, of course, but tending to emasculate the language altogether.

(CE 2.43, also 1940)

Those lines are quite specific, but they do not make Orwell a journeyman linguistic critic. For one thing, they are the fullest things of their kind that he ever did, far short though they fall of detailed analysis. For another, the first is the only passage about the English language in the long cultural retrospect 'Inside the Whale' (CE 1.493–527).[5] It was much the same with Orwell's admired Joyce: he praised, for example, the stylistic virtuosity of *Ulysses*, but by assertion, not demonstration (CE 1.126–8); and he held that 'For one man, or a clique, to try and make up a language, as I believe James Joyce is now doing, is . . . absurd' (CE 2.9). If so, any attempt to resist language change, a favourite proposal of Orwell's, is fruitless. A closer look at Joyce's language, however, or any writer's, would have shown Orwell that it is not the author's 'made up language' but a selection from existing language resources; a subset, not an extension.[6]

Orwell frequently listed Shakespeare among his favourite authors (e.g., CE 2.24) and twice he defended him against the animadversions of Tolstoy (CE 2.127–30 in 1941, and at greater length CE 4.287–302 in 1947). On the second occasion he claimed that Shakespeare's 'main hold on us is through language' (CE 4.300). By this Orwell turned out to mean 'the music of words' (a phrase he used twice in this passage), 'his mere skill in placing one syllable beside another' (CE 4.301; cf. 292). That is true, but it is certainly not the whole truth and it is not very specific. Yet it formed the centre of Orwell's argument: having to read Shakespeare in translation or in a language not his own, Tolstoy missed the very thing on which Shakespeare's fame rested.

Orwell also frequently invoked Shakespeare in his polemics about language, apparently to have the revered name on his side of the argument. He did so most effectively because with most compression in *Nineteen Eighty-Four*:

> 'By 2050 – earlier, probably – all real knowledge of Oldspeak will have disappeared. The whole literature of the past will have been destroyed. Chaucer, Shakespeare, Milton, Byron – they'll exist only in Newspeak versions. . . .'
> (NE 47)

Like Tolstoy's vision of Shakespeare, the Ingsoc vision is faulty because it is in the wrong language. 'Did not Hamlet say "cursing like a scullion"? No doubt Shakespeare had watched scullions at work' Orwell wrote in admiration (PL 75); under Newspeak that vision of the past, and that grasp of reality, would be lost with the loss of Shakespeare's music. After Winston Smith's counter-revolutionary erotic dream, he 'woke up with the word "Shakespeare" on his lips' (NE 29).

Literary Language

In the 1939 'Boys' Weeklies' essay, among several brief comments on the character's dialogue, Orwell included one longer analysis:

> The first thing that anyone would notice is the extraordinary amount of tautology (the first of these two passages contains a hundred and twenty-five words and could be compressed into about thirty), seemingly designed to spin out the story, but actually playing its part in creating the atmosphere. For the same reason various facetious expressions are repeated over and over again; 'wrathy', for instance, is a great favourite, and so is 'diddled, dished and done'. . . . The slang ('Go and eat coke!' 'What the thump!', 'You frabjous ass!', etc etc) has never been altered, so that the boys are now using slang which is at least thirty years out of date.
> (CE 1.464; cf. 462, 466, 471, 480; CE 3.350–1)

But that is about as far as his critical analysis went, and it was as autobiographical as it was analytical. Orwell brought close analysis only to his early criticism of literature that he disliked, highbrow and low; he did not employ it later or on literature that he liked.

Orwell's interest in the varieties of British English stemmed from his preoccupation with the class system, so his interest in literary dialects was chiefly in those of class. His long essay on Dickens makes only a few remarks about language, and then only about dialogue as a reflection of Dickens's class attitudes – the character's language, not the novelist's.

> He likes a bourgeois exterior and bourgeois (not aristocratic) accent. One curious symptom of this is that he will not allow anyone who is to play a heroic part to speak like a working man. A comic hero like Sam Weller, or a merely pathetic figure like Stephen Blackpool, can speak with a broad accent, but the *jeune premier* always speaks the then equivalent of BBC. This is so, even when it involves absurdities. Little Pip, for instance, is brought up by people speaking broad Essex, but talks upper-class English from his earliest childhood; actually he would have talked the same dialect as Joe, or at least as Mrs Gargery. So also with Biddy Wopsle, Lizzie Hexam, Sissie Jupe, Oliver Twist – one ought perhaps to add Little Dorrit. Even Rachel in *Hard Times* has barely a trace of Lancashire accent, an impossibility in her case.
> (CE 1.436–7)

Orwell's objection was not simply that Dickens misreported regional dialects, but that his class viewpoint made him inconsistent with all dialects, regional and class; so that a literary role such as 'hero' was superordinate to a social role, and the social characterization was consequently inaccurate. But the inaccuracy was one of the fictional character, not simply of the 'real world' dialect. Orwell was discussing decorum, not dialectology. It is just that his decorum was not Dickens's.[7]

Orwell's preoccupation with class is particularly clear in his remarks about Kipling where, as in his essay on Dickens, he was attempting to rehabilitate an undervalued author:

> [T]he private soldier, though lovable and romantic, has to be a comic. He is always made to speak in a sort of stylised cockney, not very broad but with all the aitches and final 'g's' carefully omitted. . . . And this accounts for the curious fact that one can often improve Kipling's poems, make them less facetious and less blatant, by simply going through them and transplanting them from cockney into standard speech. . . . Kipling ought to have known better. He ought to have . . . overridden his impulse to make fun of a working-man's accent. In the ancient ballads the lord and the peasant speak the same language. That is impossible to Kipling, who is looking down a distorting class perspective, and by a piece of poetic justice one of his best lines is spoiled – for 'follow me 'ome' is much uglier than 'follow me home'.
> (CE 2.189)

The Orwell who mocked historical revisionism in *Nineteen Eighty-Four* here found ''ome' so self-evidently 'ugly' that he proposed literary revisionism, a measure of Orwell's feelings on the class issue in literature and its priority over questions of accuracy: very few private soldiers spoke like lords.[8]

But Kipling's was not the only 'distorting perspective'. Orwell, who did not like gay people or upper-class people, found a convenient linguistic shorthand to make comic figures of both at once:

> A youth of twenty, cherry-lipped, with gilded hair, tripped Nancifully in. Moneyed, obviously. He had the golden aura of money. . . .
> 'Are you looking for any particular book?'
> 'Oh, no, not weally.' An R-less Nancy voice. 'May I just *bwowse*? I simply couldn't wesist your fwont window. I have such a tewwible weakness for bookshops! So I just floated in – tee-hee!'
> (KA 13; cf. CD 40)

Of course the shop clerk Comstock, Orwell's hero, also speaks an 'R-less' variety of English, but only where the [r] follows a vowel, not when it precedes. For Comstock, as for Orwell, that pattern was 'standard'; their spelling did not reflect it, and their outlook did not stigmatize it. The spelling and the stigma that Orwell attached to a different [r]-less pattern arose from his perspective on class and on sexuality, not from his perspective on language.

So the most-praised passage in *A Clergyman's Daughter*, the long chapter III.i (CD 167–200) that occupies over a tenth of the book without advancing its plot or the characterization of its heroine, takes place in central London, where class strata are most heavily overlaid; the divisions, consequently, are horizontal and not vertical as on a dialect map. It has been likened to the 'Nighttown' passage in Joyce's *Ulysses*,[9] and Orwell certainly admired Joyce; but it is also like passages in earlier London literature such as Jonson's *Alchemist* and Orwell's own notes on the regional and class varieties of British English. Slang figures in this Trafalgar Square night scene (' "doing a starry in the bloody Square" '), but some of it is lost in dashes (' "this ———— Square" '), and most of the chapter, though non-standard, is sparing with slang (' "It ain't the same for us as what it is for some of these others here," ' all from CD 167).

The class varieties range downwards from the highest, that of the aptly-named Mr Tallboys:

> 'Non sum qualis eram boni sub regno Edwardi! In the days of my innocence, before the Devil carried me up into a high place and dropped me into the Sunday newspapers. . . . Happy days, happy days! My ivied church under the sheltering hillside – my red-tiled Rectory slumbering among Elizabethan yews! My library, my vinery, my cook, house-parlourmaid and groom-gardener!'
> (CD 167–8)

Tallboys uses Latin, biblical allusion, landscape, and the accoutrements of the well-heeled country clergy to give his diction a social context while he explains his presence among the down-and-outs spending the night in the Square. At the other end of the social scale are lifelong outcasts like Nosy, Ginger, Charlie, and The Kike:

> 'Crooked? *Crooked*? Why, a corkscrew 'ud look like a bloody bradawl beside of him! There isn't one of them double ———— sons of whores in the Flying Squad but 'ud sell his grandmother to the knackers for two pound ten and then sit on her gravestone eating potato crisps. The geeing, narking toerag!'
> (CD 173)

Next to Tallboys's self-centred recollections of things past, Nosy's is altruistic and immediate. The Latin gives way to a reiterated rhetorical question, the pastoral image to urban, the servants to family and family foes, and, most important of all, the 'high' diction to low: obscene, mispronounced, slangy. Yet Orwell's sympathies appear to be all with Nosy and his peers. The clash of jargons reaches its appropriate conclusion with Tallboys chanting a satanic liturgy while the down-and-outs join the Square whores in a cafe and roar their breakfast orders to the proprietor.

Between the two extremes, the egocentric son of heaven and the altruistic children of earth, are ranged the rest of the crowd doing a 'starry' in the Square. Dorothy, the 'clergyman's daughter' of the title, contrasts with Tallboys: her austerity with his fleshliness, her father's debt-ridden rectory with his vinery, cook, and the rest. Her virginal diction is neither his nor Nosy's:

> 'Oh, but how can you stand it? How can you go on like this, night after night, year after year? It's not possible that people can live so! It's so absurd that one wouldn't believe it if one didn't know it was true. It's impossible!"
> (CD 189)

Dorothy's outlook is not self-centred like Tallboys's, but it is also not outgoing like Nosy's, so her diction lacks both the hauteur of the former and the colour of the latter.

Next below her are Mrs Wayne and Mrs McElligot. It is Mrs Wayne who identifies herself with Dorothy: ' "Ah, dearie, as soon as I set eyes on you I knew as you was a lady born and bred. You and me've known what it is to come down in the world, haven't we, dearie?" ' (CD 167). Mrs McElligot also recognizes Dorothy's 'difference' but does not identify herself with it (' "De poor kid, she ain't used to roughin' it de way us others are" ', CD 192), and when a policeman observes that Dorothy is ' "a cut above these others here," ' Mrs McElligot – an aging Irish ex-prostitute – takes umbrage: ' "Thank you, constable, *thank* you! 'Ear that, girls? 'A cut above us,' 'e says. Nice, ain't it? (To the policeman) Proper bloody Ascot swell yourself, ain't you?' " (CD 193). Though they are 'people clinging indiscriminately together,' their common misfortune is a society that discriminates among them and 'brands them on the tongue' to mark their differences. Despite their convergence in search of warmth, and Dorothy's decision to remain with them and reject assistance from the policeman, the hierarchy of difference is not lost, nor the outlook from each rung on the hierarchy, nor the variety of English that verbalizes that outlook.

Orwell's views on class and language often cluster in the beginning of his books and fade when he gets down to a writer's business; they were not wholly integrated with his other fictional procedures. Even in *Nineteen Eighty-Four* Newspeak is prominent only in the dialogue with Syme (NE 43–8) and the obviously unintegrated Appendix. Yet Orwell held these views until the end of his life, along with the view that a totalitarian future would harden, not erase, class boundaries. The three-tiered system of Ingsoc has an Inner Party where Newspeak is ascendant, an Outer Party where it is spreading, and a proletarian class where it is unknown and cockney remains the spoken norm. Cockney occurs in the novel *passim*; a concentrated example is Smith's pub interview with the old man who speaks standard Orwellian underclass: the missing initial aitches are spelled ' ' but the missing terminal [r]s are spelled 'r'. In the course of the conversation, the old man quotes several people from his past. One was a speaker in Hyde Park who referred to the Labour Party as " 'yenas"; another was "a young bloke on Shaftesbury Avenue. Quite a gent, 'e was – dress shirt, top 'at, black overcoat. . . . 'E says, 'I'll twist your bloody 'ead off if you get fresh with me' " (NE 77–8). It is a good touch; the old prole, consistent with a character of his class, cannot reconstruct the upper-class pattern of speech, though he can recall the upper-class garments. Orwell was not 'making fun of a working-man's accent', but he was also not really trying to reproduce it, any more than he reproduced Bozo's in lines that he claimed were 'word for word' what Bozo said. He simply used a few dropped initial aitches to creat his working-class character, much as he used dropped initial [r]s to create an upper-class gay.

Orwell's use of literary dialect, then, was parallel with his interest in natural-language dialect. In both, his overt analysis was scanty but his observations were frequent; the adequacy of his analysis was apparent not in what he said about variety but what he did with it. He recorded the natural dialect he observed and he made his observations the basis of his literary dialect, redeeming his theoretical remarks about language variety and the role of language in literature. Adequate analysis is prerequisite to accurate imitation.

But Orwell's ear was apt for more than dialect dialogue, and his literary eye was good for more than criticism. Combined, they gave him a powerful ability to don the style of other writers; in that respect Orwell was right to regard language as 'the garment of thought –

something selected from a range of possible choices, like an overcoat
in an outfitter's shop'.[10] Some of these imitations were on a small
scale: a schoolboy rhyme, headlines, news placards, a typewritten
card from one of 'those machines that tell your fortune as well as
your weight', advertisements:

> [T]he school poet (now, Flory remembered, a critic who wrote rather
> good articles in the *Nation*) came out with the couplet:
>
> New-tick Flory does look rum,
>   Got a face like a monkey's bum.
> (BD 64)

> 'PASSION DRAMA IN COUNTRY RECTORY
> PARSON'S DAUGHTER AND ELDERLY SEDUCER
> WHITE-HAIRED FATHER PROSTRATE WITH GRIEF'
> (CD 142; cf. 136)

> 'LEGS; FAMOUS SURGEON'S STATEMENT'
> 'KING ZOG'S WEDDING POSTPONED'
> (CA 31; cf. 26)

> 'You are sensitive, affectionate and always loyal to your friends. You are
> deeply attractive to the opposite sex. Your worst fault is generosity.
> Persevere, for you will rise high!
>   Weight: 14 stone 11 pounds.'
> (CA 240)

> 'Only a *penetrating* face-cream will reach that under-surface dirt. Pink
> toothbrush is *her* trouble. How to alkalise your stomach almost instantly.
> Roughage for husky kids. Are you one of the four out of five? The
> world-famed Culturequick Scrapbook. Only a drummer and yet he
> quoted Dante.'
> (KA 234–5; cf. CE 4.235)

Imitation is the sincerest form of analysis, but Orwell gave at least
some space to anaysis too:

> Another striking thing is the prose style of the advertisements, an extraor-
> dinary mixture of sheer lushness with clipped and sometimes very expres-
> sive technical jargon. Words like suave-mannered, custom-finished,
> contour-conforming, mitt-back, innersole, backdip, midriff, swoosh,
> swash, curvaceous, slenderise and pet-smooth are flung about with evi-
> dent full expectation that the reader will understand them at a glance.
> (CE 4.235)

When the hero of *Keep the Aspidistra Flying* demonstrates his mastery of advertising prose, it is with 'The vivid phrase that sticks and rankles, the neat little para. that packs a world of lies into a hundred words,' for 'He could use words with the economy that is only learned by years of effort' (KA 53, 243).

Orwell was also capable of somewhat larger effects in imitation: poetaster's verse, a jingoistic history book, a colonial newspaper editorial, a cheap magazine:

> 'Sharply the menacing wind sweeps over
> The bending poplars, newly bare,
> And the dark ribbons of the chimneys
> Veer downwards; flicked by whips of air,
> Torn posters flutter.'
> (KA 35)

'After the French Revolution was over, the self-styled Emperor Napoleon Buonaparte attempted to set up his sway, but though he won a few victories against continental troops, he soon found that in the "thin red line" he had more than met his match.'
(CD 229)

'In these happy times, when we poor blacks are being uplifted by the mighty western civilisation, with its manifold blessings such as the cinematograph, machine-guns, syphilis, etc., what subject could be more inspiring than the private lives of our European benefactors?'
(BD 9)

'David paced up and down the room, his hands pressed to his forehead. The news seemed to have stunned him. For a long time he could not believe it. Sheila untrue to him! It could not be! Suddenly realisation rushed over him, and he saw the fact in all its stark horror. It was too much. He flung himself down in a paroxysm of weeping.'
(CA 22)

Again Orwell had particular models in mind:

. . . as soon as he took a pen in his hand he became not only boring beyond measure but utterly unintelligible. His prose style was modelled upon *Peg's Paper* ('With a wild cry I sank in a stricken heap' etc), and his ineptitude with words was so great that after wading through two pages of laboured description you could not even be certain what he was attempting to describe.
(CE 1.149–50)

Orwell's literary mimicry enabled him to juxtapose several examples of one genre in one book, as he did the letters in *Burmese Days* – not only the letter of Dr Veraswami (quoted pp. 111–12), but the anonymous letter from a Burmese, the letter from a burra memsahib, the letter to members of the European club:

> 'Wherefore we are much hoping that your honour will ESCHEW same Dr Veraswami and not consort with persons who can bring nothing but evil upon your honour. . . . (Signed) A FRIEND.'
> The letter was written in the shaky round hand of the bazaar letter-writer. . . . The letter-writer, however, would never have risen to such a word as 'eschew'.
> (BD 78)

> 'I'm afraid you will find it dreadfully dull after the *delights* of Paris. But really in some ways these small stations have their advantages for a young girl. She finds herself quite a *queen* in the local society. The unmarried men are so lonely that they appreciate a girl's society in a quite wonderful way' etc., etc.
> (BD 95)

> 'In view of the cowardly insult recently offered to our Deputy Commissioner, we the undersigned wish to give it as our opinion that this is the worst possible moment to consider the election of niggers to this Club,' etc., etc.
> (BD 63; cf. 22)

The technique of juxtaposition was one that Orwell brought to bear again in *Nineteen Eighty-Four* through his literary imitations, not only in its content but in its theme: over a tenth of the book is taken up with the two long quotations from Emmanual Goldstein's *The Theory and Practice of Oligarchical Collectivism* (NE 151–64, 166–79) that mirror the style of Trotsky.

Orwell also juxtaposed spoken styles, those of official speakers and official enemies, in fictitious imitation: the radio announcer (NE 25) with Goldstein's

> rapid polysyllabic speech which was a sort of parody of the habitual style of the orators of the Party, and even contained Newspeak words; more Newspeak words, indeed, than any Party member would normally use in real life,
> (NE 14)

and the official task of Winston Smith is to compose revisionist history in the Stalinesque style of Big Brother,

> a style at once military and pedantic, and, because of a trick of asking questions and then promptly answering them ('What lessons do we learn from this fact, comrades? The lessons – which is also one of the fundamental principles of Ingsoc – that,' etc., etc.), easy to imitate. (NE 42)[11]

Orwell's own style has its 'tricks', not least the trick of ending passages 'etc., etc.'. But his stylistic self-awareness was unspecific and – like his 'ballsed up' humility formula – often sexually figurative:

> When I read a book like [*Ulysses*] and then come back to my own work, I feel like a eunuch who has taken a course in voice production and can pass himself off fairly well as a bass or a baritone, but if you listen closely you can hear the good old squeak just the same as ever. (CE 1.139)

His argument for prose 'like a window pane' was also figurative; it was, in addition, anti-style, a warning against style that obscures content. As a result, his literary imitations were masquerades where an assumed identity replaced what Orwell believed was no identity. His remarks on stylistic identity began by setting it in bad company and finished by discrediting it:

> I spent a whole afternoon trying to determine the authorship by stylistic evidence, as the literary critics employed by the Gestapo were said to do with anonymous pamphlets. Finally I decided that [the author] was a certain W———. A day or two later I met Victor Gollancz, who said to me: 'Do you know who wrote those . . . articles . . .? I've just heard. It was W———.' This made me feel very acute, but a day or two later I heard that we were both wrong. (CE 4.278; cf. 3.357)

Orwell preferred to be, if not the tramp, at any rate the Etonian in tramp's clothing; he let others play the detective, 'the geeing, narking toerag'.

The question of literary identity, of a style that marks the work, is an old one: though often subjective, it has always included some objective studies such as those of the Shakespeare attribution disputes. Linguistics, the objective study of language, has grown rapidly during the last generation, and so have linguistic approaches to literature with their attention to quantitative, even statistical, details.[12] Louis Milic wrote,

> The specific nature of these details furnishes a silent rebuke to those who, without evidence, talk about adjectives and verbs or discuss style in the vague terms of impressionistic criticism. If the exact details of style may be elicited from the texts, what can be the purpose of remaining at the general and imprecise level of description which borrows its terminology from physiology (*nervous, flabby, sinewy, muscular*), from chemistry (*limpid, crystalline*) or even from cookery (*spiced, flavored, bland*).[13]

Milic made good use of a computer in carrying out the approach he called 'quantitative', but the quantitative (or statistical or objective) approach does not absolutely require a computer so long as the data is not too lengthy and the researcher not too impatient. Ringbom knew Milic's work when he did his 'stylistic study' of Orwell, but Ringbom did not use a computer.

Ringbom encountered the same vague critical terminology that had annoyed Milic, often the same words:

> . . . there seem to be relatively few comments on [Orwell's] style, and most of those are very vague in character. The characteristic qualities of Orwell's style . . . have, for instance, been taken to be 'its firmness, its colloquial vigor, its unpretentious vividness and, above all, its limpid clarity.' Among other words used to describe his style are 'nervous, flexible and lucid,' 'spare, tough,' 'direct, active, cogent and epigrammatic,' and 'relaxed, flexible, yet balanced.' [14]

Other varieties of literary critical terminology, such as 'often', 'largely', 'mainly', 'typical', appear to embody a statistical observation but do not. Ringbom goes on, 'My aim in this study is to provide as concrete an analysis as possible of some characteristic stylistic features of Orwell's essays' (p. 11), and he notes the chief assumption and the chief problem of all such studies: 'The style of an individual presupposes a norm from which this individual style deviates' (p. 11); 'The problem is to know what to count, what features of a writer's style are significant' (p. 10).

Ringbom's study isolates only three features: Orwell's use of series, his punctuation and sentence-length, and his favourite vocabulary. Orwell's series included some of his best-known passages: 'Defenceless villages are bombarded from the air, the inhabitants driven out into the countryside, the cattle machine-gunned, the huts set on fire with incendiary bullets; this is called *pacification*' (CE 4.136). This sentence also illustrates two other features of Orwell's diction, his forward-pointing (cataphoric) structures and his frequent irony. Obviously the features of structure and tone are related, since the end of the sentence often undercuts what has gone before.

Ringbom also remarks on Orwell's use of typographical emphasis, such as quotation marks (inverted commas):

. . . then you establish 'the law'
. . . his right to enter 'decent society'
. . . the 'glamour' of public-school life
. . . an example of 'natural' death

In each case the conventional meaning of the word conflicts with its meaning as Orwell saw it. Orwell was given to other sorts of typographical emphasis, italics and dashes among them: 'Afterwards one can choose – not simply *accept* – the phrases that will best cover the meaning' (CE 4.139).

Words that a writer uses more often than the reader would expect from the context are what Ringbom calls 'pluswords', a neatly Orwellian term. Orwell's pluswords included some 'grammatical' or 'function' words, such as pronominal 'one' and negatives, that readers and critics often omit from their explicit accounts of style. Orwell's tendency to argue or illustrate by comparison also led him to use 'different', 'same', 'compare', 'resemble' relatively frequently, as his tendency to argue by example led him to frequent use of 'For example,' 'For instance,' and the preposition 'like'. His tendency to generalization accounts for the frequency of words like 'actually', 'always', 'completely', 'essentially', 'largely', 'merely', and 'probably' – the last appears 159 times against a norm of thirty-one in comparable texts.

The three categories Ringbom investigated do not exhaust the typical features of Orwell's essay prose. Even a limited investigation, such as Bailey's into the documents alleged to be by Patricia Hearst, used ten criteria in one test and six more in two others. They included the relative frequency of nominal heads and the proportion that are nouns, mean monosyllabic string length and standard deviation of the distribution of monosyllabic string lengths. Probably the features that Ringbom studied are ones that an author could cultivate or avoid; those in Bailey's study are habits that an author could scarcely change even when aware of them. Both sorts are suitable for quantitative study, but where Ringbom was attempting to give a concrete account of literary style, Bailey was trying to put 'authorship attribution in a forensic setting'.[15]

Stylistics is, at base, simply a form of variety study. It asks what the salient features of a variety are and how they contrast with the features of other kindred varieties. But stylistics assumes the text has literary rather than linguistic interest, along with substantial uniformity throughout the opus. On that basis it makes some claims in questions of attribution: if we can analyse the style of an author's known works, perhaps we can apply the analysis to a disputed work. That was one of the motivations of Milic's study, of Bailey's, and of several others. Even Ringbom, in an appendix, applies his findings to the newly-discovered essay 'The Freedom of the Press' and consequently claims it for Orwell as the intended preface to *Animal Farm*.

But Bailey points out the difficulties of this sort of procedure: the Hearst texts that he selects for comparison 'show a normal range of linguistic variability arising from subject, circumstances, and audience' (p. 4). For no one talks – or writes – the same way all the time. The salient features of an individual's style gain significance only if they correlate with Bailey's three variables, at a minimum. It is one thing to describe a style in its own terms rather than your own, objectively rather than subjectively. It is another to use the description to claim or reject a disputed work for the author. And it is another yet, by no means up to evidentiary demands, to introduce such claims in a court of law.

Any contrastive study, moreover, requires a suitable 'control' and a suitable description of it. Ringbom was hampered, as he frequently admitted, by his reliance on a group of texts not fully analyzed and not altogether comparable to Orwell's. If the document in question were crucial – an alleged confession, for example – the investigation would suffer because there is no analyzed collection of the writings of suspects, or of confessions, or of dialects, or of Modern English at large. But Ringbom was able to show, for example, that Orwell's style changed from the early essays to the late ones. His sentences became longer in later life; in accordance with his aim, his explanatory and modifying comments became more frequent and his similes and comparisons less so, while his use of series was greatest in his early essays and least in the later ones, both probably because 'of late years I have tried to write less picturesquely and more exactly' (CE 1.7, 1946). The conclusions are sound enough to support Ringbom's

attribution argument because they are based on an obviously suitable
'control' – the comparison of Orwell's earlier work with the later –
and because they arise from a careful and pertinent analysis of the
text.

T.R. Fyvel brought the hospitalized Orwell a German magazine
and 'he was pleased to learn what was new to him, that Goebbels had
systematically developed a German "Newspeak" – he had guessed
right again.' [16] The anecdote is misleading, however; Newspeak is
not Orwell's prophecy of future English, partly because *Nineteen
Eighty-Four* is not his prophecy of future England. The book is a
satire on the world he knew, not a prediction of the world he
foresaw; critics use words like 'fantasy', 'nightmare', and 'parody' to
describe it.[17] Orwell frequently made predictions, but as he wryly
observed, they almost as frequently proved to be wrong even on
subjects – such as British politics – that he knew far better than he
knew the history of English. Early in *Homage to Catalonia* he
offered a number of predictions and added 'I let the above opinions
stand, and time will show how far I am right or wrong' (HC 70);
afterwards he wrote 'Later events have proved that I was quite wrong
here' (HC 196). He could admire the accuracy of others' predictions
(e.g., Jack London's, CE 4.24), and he could catch their inaccuracies
(e.g., Burnham's, CE 4.165, 172–4; cf. 180). But he had no illusions
about his own predictions: 'All prophecies are wrong, therefore this
one will be wrong' (CE 1.275); 'Looking back through the diary I
kept in 1940 and 1941 I find that I was usually wrong when it was
possible to be wrong' (CE 3.59; cf. 293–4, 395). Orwell was well
aware that his prophecies would not suffice as the raison d'être for a
book.

Nor did he predict that Newspeak would be the evolutionary
outcome of the language he spoke and wrote. He did not have much
interest in language development as an ongoing process, though
he commented on individual phenomena. He did not claim that
Newspeak was a descendant of Oldspeak. He made it clear that
Newspeak was an artificial government creation, not an evolutionary
stage in the language. And the chronological point of view in the
Appendix on Newspeak makes it seem that the artificial creation did
not flourish. Even at the time of its employment, according to the
quotation from Goldstein's book, ' "English [was Oceania's] chief
lingua franca and Newspeak its official language" ' (NE 172). That
gives the natural language, English, a role distinct from Newspeak,
the artificial language.

The artificiality of Newspeak shows both in the origin that Orwell assigned it in his novel and in the origin it actually had. It comprised, we have already seen, the features of English vocabulary and grammar that Orwell liked least. But the idea of combining these into a language was another matter, like the idea of combining human foibles into a Gulliver and human failings into Yahoos. The connection with Swift is valid: Sheldon quotes Orwell on the Lilliputians who

> invent simplified languages. . . . [T]here is a perception that one of the aims of totalitarianism is not merely to make sure that people will think the right thoughts, but actually to make them *less conscious*.
> (CE 4.214) [18]

Unlike the features of Newspeak vocabulary and grammar, the idea for an artificial language did not appear in the English Orwell observed; that is why Newspeak is a satire and not a prediction. Instead, it appeared in dystopian books he knew, like Huxley's *Brave New World*, Wells's *The Shape of Things to Come*, and Zamiatin's *We*.[19] The differences between these books and Orwell's are important. Zamiatin's artificial language is reductionist like Newspeak, but not obscurantist; instead it is rational to the point of using equations and syllogisms for expressing emotions. Zamiatin was concerned with the encroachments of science, Orwell with the 'hybrid jargon of the Ministries' (NE 139). From Wells Orwell apparently took the idea of thought-control by a Dictionary Bureau, a small but important detail. From Huxley he apparently took the idea of official writing 'about nothing', the expunging of meaning by language, from language, and in language. So Newspeak, apart from its individual features, is as a whole a literary device with chiefly literary origins. Other sources were also written: the 'cablese' of reporters such as Orwell once was can produce ' "times 3.12.83 reporting bb dayorder doubleplusungood refs unpersons rewrite fullwise upsub antefiling" ' (NE 40).[20] The headlines that finally result can produce something similarly telegraphic: SCARSDALE DIET DOCTOR MURDER TRIAL SHOCK.

The Basic English of Ogden is, like Newspeak, an artificially simplified language based on English, and Orwell took an interest in Basic. But it is far too much to say, with Fink, that Newspeak is in origin a parody of Basic.[21] Newspeak has many attributes, including its literary history, that Basic lacks. Basic and Newspeak are somewhat similar in reduced vocabulary and regularized morphology, but not in the syntax which is normal in Basic. Moreover, Orwell never condemned Basic as he frequently condemned the forms he satirized in Newspeak. On the contrary, he praised it because 'In Basic . . . you cannot make a meaningless statement without its being apparent' (CE 3.210), the very opposite of Newspeak. The connection that Orwell made between his explicit attacks on language 'abuse' and his satirical assault on the same target is noted frequently above, especially in Chapters Two and Three. It is made also in the recurrence in *Nineteen Eighty-Four* of an image from 'Politics and the English Language':

> When one watches some tired hack on the platform mechanically repeating the familiar phrases . . . one often has a curious feeling that one is not watching a live human being but some kind of dummy: a feeling which suddenly becomes stronger at moments when the light catches the speaker's spectacles and turns them into blank discs which seem to have no eyes behind them.
> (CE 4.135–6)

> At the table on his left the man with the strident voice was still talking remorselessly away. . . . His head was thrown back a little, and because of the angle at which he was sitting, his spectacles caught the light and presented to Winston two blank discs instead of eyes.
> (NE 47–8).

Newspeak is an attack on Basic only if 'Politics and the English Language' was.

Orwell's own 'New Words' essay is a better model than Basic for Newspeak, because it has in common with other plans for language 'reform' its naive realism and its belief in 'rational design, formal control, objectivity, universality'.[22] It also illustrates inconsistencies that Orwell would never have repeated in Newspeak if he had simply taken Basic for his model. In Newspeak, euphony is the paramount consideration, but it forms 'a gabbling style of speech, at once staccato and monotonous'. Newspeak exercises control over 'exactitude of meaning' but seeks 'not so much to express meanings as to destroy them' (NE 253, 250). Words in Newspeak are without overtones – that is how limiting words can limit thoughts; yet many words are euphemisms: 'goodsex' is not the simultaneous orgasm of the marriage manuals but its opposite, sex deprived of pleasure and dedicated only to procreation.

So Orwell's Newspeak is neither a reductionist caricature of artificial Basic English and its congeners nor the evolutionary outcome of present-day natural English. Instead it is the former treatment of the latter topic, a literary satire of the language Orwell used and observed. Beauchamp persuasively argues that Newspeak is also 'a synecdoche for the totalitarian superstructure of his dystopian state',[23] although he probably errs in believing that in *Nineteen Eighty-Four* 'Newspeak is clearly formulated and emerging' and therefore 'Orwell is able to satisfy our sense that the novel of the future should have a language that reflects that future' – the Appendix just as clearly says that the emergence, if any, was temporary. These distinctions are important for Orwell and for us, because if we do not make them Newspeak will seem a very inadequate extrapolation from the present state of the language, so we will defend it by seizing everything we find distasteful in our linguistic environment and crediting Orwell with foresight he did not claim. McCormick's *Approaching 1984*, predictably, contains a chapter on 'The Horrors of "Newspeak" ' that announces the advent of Newspeak 'Long before 1984' and documents the claim with maladept phrases from psychology, bureaucracy, parliamentary speeches, Bible translations, feminist writing, and other failures to 'speak proper English', that is, whatever McCormick doesn't happen to like.[24]

The adoption of 'Newspeak' as a label for false and inept language is as common as the use of Orwell's name, and his novel's, for totalitarianism. Beauchamp quotes Marcuse adopting it, and does so himself: 'in the quarter century since his death he has proved a prophet [of] the deliberate inversion of the meaning of words and the subsequent destruction of their integrity.'[25] But since *Nineteen Eighty-Four* does not make a historical prediction, Orwell cannot have been a prophet; and since Orwell did not make Newspeak a development of English, it cannot reflect a 'historical tendency' as Beauchamp calls it. Finally, Orwell's claims for Newspeak as an organ of thought-control stemmed from his erroneous theories of language and mind.

In fact the fulfillment of Newspeak has been, like its sources, literary and not linguistic or political. Novels of the future now take more seriously the obligation to have a future language. Yet when they do, their conception of it is often different from Newspeak in a way that helps us understand the role of their language and Orwell's. The novelist-linguist Anthony Burgess's *A Clockwork Orange* (1963) has a narrator who employs a youth jargon called 'nadsat', but the variety is not official and it has no pretensions to universality; on the contrary, his elders do not understand its speaker and he does not understand the argot of those only a few years younger. Burgess is predicting nothing about the English of the future, but he is satirizing something about evanescent language fads of the present. So while the role of 'nadsat' in the action of the novel is not like that of Newspeak, its role in the satiric purpose of the author is.[26] Burgess's *1985* (1978) contains 'A Note on Workers' English (WE)' (pp. 247–53) reminiscent of Orwell's Appendix to *Nineteen Eighty-Four*; but WE is even less systematic and less integrated with the novel than either Newspeak or 'nadsat'. Quirk believes that its place in the novel is at a deeper level, because 'It is natural drift into unthinking shift-lessness that alarms Burgess. . . . In consequence, the implication of *1985* is not that we want less language engineering but more.'

Russell Hoban's *Riddley Walker* (1980) is also set in the future, uncounted millenia after a nuclear catastrophe. The author has described the language of its narrator and its characters as 'worn down, broken apart', but the English of his far-distant future seems too much like spoken English today:

> The woal thing fealt jus that littl bit stupid. Us running the boar thru that las littl scrump of woodling with the forms all roun. Cows mooing sheep baaing cocks crowing and us foraging our las boar in a thin grey girzel on the day I come a man.
> (p. 1)

The spelling is only a trifle unfamiliar, and some of the pronunciation it implies ('running', 'woodling', 'mooing', etc.) doesn't seem worn and broken enough, even for our own day. Yet this apparent failing too is like Newspeak, for it stems from a literary and not a linguistic rationale: here, the need to write dialogue that a 1980 reader can understand.

But language change involves more than entropy; Orwell was nearer the truth with his compounds like 'Newspeak' itself, building up rather than wearing down a word. And Orwell came near another truth about language in the 'headlinese' structure of Newspeak, for even headlines must derive from regular grammatical rules or fall outside grammatical intelligibility. English, said Orwell, 'is the language of lyric poetry, and also of headlines' (CE 3.25); poetry and headlines share this underlying regularity, though they reflect it in very different surface forms.[27] So both SCARSDALE DIET DOCTOR MURDER TRIAL SHOCK and CORFE BYPASS ROUTE IDEA 'INTER-

EST' CLAIM (*Swanage* [Dorset] *Times*, 7 August 1982, p. 3) begin with a proper noun (a place name, as it happens). Both have the noun 'head' as the last word and array five other noun 'modifiers' before it. As full sentences, both would use verbs and prepositions, and both would reverse their 'headline' word order: 'There has been a shock in the trial for the murder of the diet doctor from Scarsdale'; 'There has been a claim of interest in the idea of a bypass route for Corfe Castle.' The similarities argue a very stable grammar even of headlines.

Cablese too is grammatical. Mature speakers do not talk that way, omitting almost all the prepositions, linking verbs, articles, and many pronouns; but without grammaticality, the nouns, verbs, adjectives and adverbs that remain would not be worth sending because they would not be intelligible. Late in his life Orwell wrote a set of instructions for travel to his island home in Scotland:

8 am leave Glasgow Central for GOUROCK.
Join boat for Tarbert (TARBERT) at Gourock.
Abt 12 noon arrive East Tarbert. . . .
(CE 4.327–8)

This kind of utterance is like telegrams but not at all ambiguous – ambiguous telegrams, headlines and travel directions are a bad idea. And it is a good deal like Newspeak.

The 'ungrammatical' regularity of early child language also resembles Newspeak. Young children first learn forms like 'took' and 'teeth' as separate items and reproduce them. Soon, however, they begin to learn the patterns of the language, not just the items: at that point they 'correct' their earlier rote learning to conform with the regular patterns of English, and 'taked' and 'tooths' result, though not as imitations; children produce them without models as a stage of language learning.[28] The extreme 'regularity' of Newspeak inflections resembles the simplicity of its syntax: both reflect immature but normal stages in child-language learning as also, clearly, does its meagre vocabulary. So Newspeak is artificial but it is not arbitrary. The individual features are those Orwell selected for castigation in his other observations on language. The idea of a language composed of these features comes from literature he knew. And the syntax of Newspeak validly reflects the early stages of language acquisition. The fascination of Newspeak is not its prolepsis into the future of English but its atavism; it was of a piece with the world that Orwell knew, as was the political system of Ingsoc and its technology.

CHAPTER VI

Language Machines

𝕲𝕲𝕲𝕲𝕲𝕲

ORWELL took a pessimistic view of technology. His novel of the future has only machines that break (Smith's lift), snoop (the Thought Police helicopter, the telescreen), oppress (the speakwrite), or torment (the 'advanced' instruments of torture in the Ministry of Love basements).[1] His nostalgia even enabled him to say that

> the tendency of many modern inventions – in particular the film, the radio and the aeroplane – is to weaken [man's] consciousness, dull his curiosity, and, in general, drive him nearer to the animals.
> (CE 4.81)

He was as inconsistent about technical progress as about anything else: the power outage that stops Smith's lift doesn't hamper the telescreen in his building, and Orwell took for granted in his novel, as he did in his life, really intricate civil technology such as sewer systems and sky scrapers. He wrote

> There are people (Tennyson is an example) who lack the mechanical faculty but can see the social possibilities of machinery. Dickens has not this stamp of mind. . . . [P]robably he would never admit that men are only as good as their technical development allows them to be.
> (CE 1.445)

He also wrote ' "The invention of print, however, made it easier to manipulate public opinion, and the film and the radio carried the process further" ' (NE 169), and this notion that men are as evil as their technical development allows them to be is the one most characteristic of him.

Orwell gave fullest rein to that notion in *The Road to Wigan Pier* (1937) as part of his attempt to refute the objections to Socialism. 'The first thing to notice,' he said, 'is that the idea of Socialism is bound up, more or less inextricably, with the idea of machine-production,

(RW 188). The notice he took went on for twenty pages, far longer than its place in his polemic required – a measure of his absorption in the subject. He claimed

> People know that in some way or another 'progress' is a swindle, but they reach this conclusion by a kind of mental shorthand; my job here is to supply the logical steps that are usually left out.
> (RW 191)

Though worth reading without reduction, Orwell's logical steps can be reduced to ten:

1. 'Every sensitive person has moments when he is suspicious of machinery and to some extent of physical science.' (RW 190)
2. 'It is only in our own age, when mechanisation has finally triumphed, that we can actually *feel* the tendency of the machine to make a fully human life impossible.' (RW 191)
3. 'The truth is that when a human being is not eating, drinking, sleeping, making love, talking, playing games or merely lounging about – and these things will not fill up a lifetime – he needs work and usually looks for it. . . .' (RW 197)
4. 'The truth is that many of the qualities we admire in human beings can only function in opposition to some kind of disaster, pain or difficulty; but the tendency of mechanical progress is to eliminate disaster, pain and difficulty.' (RW 194)
5. '[I]n modern Western man the faculty of mechanical invention has been fed and stimulated till it has reached almost the status of an instinct.' (RW 205)
6. '[T]he future is envisaged as an ever more rapid march of mechanical progress; machines to save work, machines to save thought, machines to save pain . . . more efficiency, more organisation, more machines. . . .' (RW 193)
7. 'In a world where everything could be done by machinery, everything would be done by machinery.' (RW 200)
8. 'The process of mechanisation has itself become a machine, a huge glittering vehicle whirling us we are not certain where. . . .' (RW 208)
9. 'Mechanise the world as fully as it might be mechanised, and whichever way you turn there will be some machine cutting you off from the chance of working – that is, of living.' (RW 198)
10. 'Therefore the logical end of mechanical progress is to reduce the human being to something resembling a brain in a bottle.' (RW 201)

This reduction of the Orwellian decalogue leaves out some points – his faith in the technical perfectability of machines (RW 195); his figures of speech (mechanical progress is like heavy drinking, its goal like cirrhosis of the liver, RW 201; 'Like a drug, the machine is useful, dangerous, and habit-forming,' RW 203–4); his renewed sniping at America, here for making the English think 'an apple is a lump of highly-coloured cotton wool from America' (RW 204); and his dichotomy of the mind and body, with preference for the latter (*passim*). But the reduction retains the outline of his argument.

Orwell feared, more than the dehumanizing of life that would follow the loss of work, that 'The machine would even encroach upon the activities we now class as "art"; it is doing so already, via the camera and the radio' (RW 198); 'Mechanisation leads to the decay of taste' (RW 205). He expanded on this idea in a 1946 essay, 'The Prevention of Literature', although his concern there was not directly with technology but with totalitarianism. He speculated that 'in a rigidly totalitarian society' of the future,

> Newspapers will presumably continue until television technique reaches a higher level, but apart from newspapers it is doubtful even now whether the great mass of people in the industrialised countries feel the need for any kind of literature. . . . Probably novels and stories will be completely superseded by film and radio productions. Or perhaps some kind of low-grade sensational fiction will survive, produced by a sort of conveyor-belt process that reduces human initiative to the minimum.
>
> It would probably not be beyond human ingenuity to write books by machinery. But a sort of mechanising process can already be seen at work in the film and radio, in publicity and propaganda, and in the lower reaches of journalism.
>
> (CE 4.69)

Perhaps Orwell got this idea from his admired Swift, who described in *Gulliver's Travels* a writing machine with which 'the most ignorant person . . . may write books . . . without the least assistance from genius or study' (Pt. III, ch. v). The idea, obviously, was fulfilled in the Ministry of Truth of *Nineteen Eighty-Four*, where 'There was a whole chain of separate departments dealing with proletarian literature, music, drama, and entertainment generally.' The products are newspapers, five-cent novelettes, films, and sentimental songs 'composed entirely by mechanical means on a special kind of kaleidoscope known as a versificator' (NE 39). By contrast, the two items from the age before Ingsoc that Winston Smith surreptitiously collects are the accoutrements of an old-fashioned writer, a paper-weight and a copy-book, the restoratives for a mind numbed by the speakwrite and drained by the memory-hole.

Orwell's pessimism arose in part from his habitual nostalgia, but in part also from his dualism. He did not regard the body as a matter of interest in itself; his writings dwell often on the physically disgusting but rarely on the physically glorious, and his own body caused him constant pain, from his prep school humiliations to his sick leave from the Indian Imperial Police, to his near-fatal collapse when a teacher to his final decline and death at the apex of his literary career. Hence he thought the diminution of physical labour was certain to result in the diminution of physical prowess and its moral concomit-ants, courage and generosity.

The outcome, he believed, would be a world in which 'nothing goes wrong' – of machines that solve every problem and never break, of absolutely safe cars and airplanes (e.g., RW 195). More impor-tantly, he believed that the basic problems he observed were the only problems that could occur. He did not see that their technological solution would simply make way for new, more intricate problems. Scientific progress is a game of intellectual leap-frog: new answers always lead to new questions. When libraries were switching from manual to computer circulation in the 1960s, librarians often remarked with evident pleasure that readers were asking them more interesting questions now that machines could answer the more routine kind. Orwell was, by contrast, a naive utopian: he believed that machines would bring a world where the only problem was a lack of problems.

The nostalgic Orwell reviled mechanical progress even while he employed it, as he did linguistic progress, for his language incorpo-rated the linguistic innovations of his day and his life depended on machines: he typed well, worked for the BBC, and thought a sharp razor blade a notable comfort. His contradictory attitudes go back to the Industrial Revolution, when it was physical labour that most machines replaced, for though he mentioned 'machines to save thought' and the incursions of radio and cameras into the arts, he died too soon to see the impact of electronic machines; television alone had a place even in his nightmares. The electronic progress that he saw only in its infancy and hence overlooked has since created a 'second Industrial Revolution', a revolution of information rather than effort. So Orwell's attitudes toward technology, inconsistent about the machines of the first Industrial Revolution, are irrelevant about those of the second. Present-day sceptics of scientific innovation still maintain his double standard, but more Americans work in information services than in industry and agriculture combined, and by 1990 perhaps half of American workers will make daily use of electronic terminals. Now when new machines are invented, they are most often either parts of computer systems or controlled by computer systems, for at the heart of the new revolution are modern computers.[2] So Orwell would now find computers part of every language field that interested him: machine language as an example of language change and variety; artificial languages; translation; machines and literature; machines and thought-control.

The data-processing machines coming into use at the end of Orwell's life chiefly handled computation, so the machines got the name 'computers'. But numbers are not the only data, and computation not the only process, that computers can handle. So 'electronic data-processing machines' is more accurate than 'computers', though the latter is handy and familiar. (The French word is *ordinateur*.) The basic processes a modern digital computer can carry out are typically few:

$$2 + 3 = 5$$
$$3 - 2 = 1$$
$$3 = 3$$
$$2 < 3$$

The computer, that is, can add, subtract, or compare. Its power comes not from the sophistication of these basic processes but from its ability to do a great many very quickly. Thus it multiplies by the cumbersome method

$$3 \times 2 = 2 + 2 + 2 = 6$$

and it can divide in a similar fashion. When it comes to something demanding like $2^8 - 1$, a computer uses a far more laborious method than human mathematicians do, but because a computer is a machine it works rapidly and accurately, without fatigue or complaint.

Comparison is an important part of the computer's work. It enables the computer to stop a process at a given point; to stop writing orders for widgets when the number in stock reaches shelf capacity, for example. It also enables the computer to retrieve information; to assemble all the credit card charges that have the same card number, for another example. Of course it would be possible for workers to keep a constant eye on widgets, or to sort charge slips by hand, and for years those jobs were done that way. But it was humdrum, mechanical work. Mechanical work is best left to mechanical devices.

Computers all work in much the same way, but they differ greatly in size. The incredibly complex and expensive 'monsters' earn their keep by the amount of data they take in and the speed with which they process it. The small computers, 'microcomputers', are little larger than an old-fashioned breadbox and cost less than a good second-hand car: their use dates from their introduction, in kit form, in 1974. The smallest of all, 'pocket computers', overlap the more sophisticated pocket calculators. In between are the 'minicomputers' of small businesses and the 'mainframe' industrial and research computers. But microcomputers are in a sense more revolutionary than monster computers. The biggest machines are few and belong only to governments and the largest conglomerate industries, but microcomputers are turning up on office desks and home tables. The portable computer can easily tap the memory and speed of a mainframe by connecting over ordinary telephone lines, so the difference between them is functionally not all the difference in size and price might suggest. And today's briefcase-size microcomputers have the memory and speed of mainframe computers twenty years ago; the correlation of size to power changes almost monthly.

> If the aircraft industry had evolved as spectacularly as the computer industry over the past 25 years, a Boeing 767 would cost $500 today, and it would circle the globe in 20 minutes on five gallons of fuel.
> (Toong et al. 1982, p. 87)

The space programme and the arms race have given computer designers the money and opportunity they needed to develop the modern machines out of the early models. Many important developments, however, have been purely intellectual. Early computers accepted data from the outside but had the instructions built into the machine. It was an intellectual step to put some of the instructions, the 'program', in the input and so to make the machine simpler and more flexible.

The machine handles both data and program in a binary 'vocabulary' based on the principle of the electric switch: on or off. Where a switch has a mechanical on-or-off position, however, the basic units of machine language are on-or-off charges in minute electric cells. These units ('bits') are arranged in sets ('bytes'); the byte is the 'character' of machine language. A home computer may have bytes of eight bits, and since eight on-or-offs can be arranged in 256 combinations, such a machine can represent upper and lower case alphabets, numbers, and special characters. These characters convey the data and the program to the machine. But machine language, convenient as it is for the computer, is relatively inconvenient for the human user whose convenience the machine serves. The human user may find '00000101' awkward in comparison with the '5' it represents, but the machine would find '5' unintelligible. An important go-between is the keyboard that, though not part of the computer itself, is part of almost every computer system (it is a 'peripheral'). When the user types '5' on the keyboard, the processor forwards the digit as a series of 0's and 1's. It does the same with ABC's, and with !, ? and ( ). That method works well for the data, but not for the process. The machine only has to store data like '5' or even 'cat', but it has to act on instructions. The instructions permanently stored in the machine cater only for the most rudimentary processes. Programming languages bridge this gap; they translate instructions into directions the computer can act on. For human convenience, most programming languages – and there are several – use a vocabulary akin to natural-language words, and leave it to the program to convert them into machine language.

To instruct the computer 'Take a constant, 5; request a variable and add it to the constant; if the total is less than 10, say so; if it is 10 or more, end the program,' the programming language BASIC (Beginners All-Purpose Symbolic Instruction Code, 'born' on Mayday 1964) uses the following form:

```
10 LET c=5
20 PRINT 'Variable?'
30 INPUT v
40 LET t=c+v
50 IF t<10 THEN GOTO 60 ELSE GOTO 80
60 PRINT 'T is less than ten'
70 GOTO 20
80 END
```

When run, this program receives and remembers a constant and its symbol (line 10); it prints 'Variable?' (line 20) on the computer monitor screen, requesting a variable and suspending execution until it receives it (the variable can be positive or negative, whole or a decimal fraction), to which the user responds ('inputs') via the keyboard with a number (line 30). The computer records the variable and its symbol, then adds the constant and the variable, assigns a symbol to the sum, and tests the sum against another constant. If the number is less than 5, the sum (line 40) will be less than 10, so the program prints the message (lines 50, 60) and requests another variable number (lines 70, 20); but if the sum is 10 or more, the program simply ends (lines 50, 80). The program is laid out in numbered lines, and the line numbers form part of the program instructions: line 50, for example, directs the computer to go to line 60 on one test outcome and line 80 on the other; line 70 directs the program to begin anew from the variable prompt.

This form of the program is correct in that it will result in the desired input prompt, calculation and output message. It is also relatively easy for the reader to follow because it is very explicit and each instruction occupies a separate line. But it is very long-winded; the same prompt, calculation and message would result from a much more compact BASIC program:

```
10 c=5: INPUT 'Variable'; v
20 T=c+v: IF T<10 THEN PRINT 'T is less than ten': GOTO 10
```

This version is more automatic. It inserts the question-mark that the 'INPUT' message implicitly requires. It omits 'LET' and it leaves the logic of the 'IF . . . THEN . . . ELSE' statement implicit: a sum of ten or more does not satisfy the 'IF' condition so, instead of restarting, the program goes to the following line, finds nothing there, and quits. The shorter version is as 'correct' as the longer; it 'means' the same thing to the machine, although it has a different surface form. In English it would be equally correct to shorten the program still further by omitting the word 'THEN', but the machine would baulk and flash the message 'Syntax error'.

So 'LET', 'ELSE', and 'END' are optional terms in BASIC, but 'THEN' is not. The user's natural language also has options and obligations, although they are not quite the same ones. For example, 'look up' may mean several things, including (A) 'find' (by consulting a written source)' and (B) 'look through upwards'. We have

A1a. Look up the address (in the directory)
A1b. Look the address up
A2a. Look it up
A2b. *Look up it

of which the last is not grammatical. We also have

B1a.   Look up the chimney (while I hold the light)
B1b.   *Look the chimney up
B2a.   *Look it up
B2b.   Look up it

Because A is a phrasal verb and B is not, the pattern of noun and pronoun placement is not the same for both. Yet both offer some options of noun placement, and A offers some options of particle placement as well.

The computer-programming language BASIC is similar to the natural language English, not merely in using some English words and even phrases such as 'IF . . . THEN', but in having options that create an appropriate style, and obligations that cannot be waived. The options result from a useful redundancy in the language (often giving more than one way to 'say' the same thing), the obligations from the grammatical rules or 'syntax' of the language. BASIC is also similar to a natural language in having remote relatives. This program in the user language PL/CS carries out the same process as the BASIC programs:

```
c=5;
  Get list (v);
    Do while T<10
      T=c+v
      PUT SKIP LIST ('T is less than 10')
      END;
```

But a computer-programming language like BASIC, though based on a natural language, does not really have the properties of even such a restricted human language as a pidgin, for it is not a reciprocal language between machine and user; the computer cannot 'learn' it in a way that would result in machine contributions to the language. A programming language is made of human language, by and for humans.

Computer science has, however, contributed words to the English language, just as most other fields have, and technical discussions about computers often abound in these words. Even non-controversial observations such as 'Word processing programs and text files are easily downloaded to individual work stations, and the use of hard-disk subsystems in most networks lets the user store many large files' can seem opaque, although no single word in the sentence is unprecedented in long-established standard English. As computers begin to appear in homes they are followed by computer journals with passages like that one, and often by offspring returned from computer-science courses. The machines, journals, and offspring will all be vectors of the special language of the field. The uninitiated, and some of the newly initiated, object that the terms make the field 'sound complicated'. In an early issue of PC ('The Independent Guide to IBM Personal Computers'), for example, a reader wrote

> Please don't forget that some of your readers are not computer specialists, freaks, or even very knowledgeable in the world of RAM, ROM, DOS, BITS, BYTES *ad infinitum*. Remember that some of us are civilians and need to be patronized.

The editors' rejoinder was 'Request granted: We couldn't agree more with your comments about "computerese." '[3] Another journal reported that 'Some universities accept a course in SSPS [a statistical program] to meet language requirements for a doctorate in the humanities. Computerese, even rudimentary computerese, is considered to be a foreign language.'[4] But computerese, like any other technical vocabulary, is not a foreign language, or even just an arcane jargon that veils the mysteries of the cognoscenti. 'Byte', for example, expresses a fundamental concept more economically and unambiguously than a fuller paraphrase in lay language ever could: it is hard to be more economical than a monosyllable, and all of the PC reader's examples were monosyllables. Such resistance to technical vocabulary is not language judgment but yahooism.

Like most technical vocabularies, computerese (itself a handy short term if we don't use it judgmentally) includes new words and meanings added to the language, and established words and meanings borrowed from it. 'Byte' (also the name of a journal) appears to be the common term 'bite' in a distinctive spelling, but actually the spelling 'byte' goes back at least as far as 1499. In fact almost no computerese words are outright coinages. The following informal glossary is merely illustrative:

BOOT (vb): Short for 'bootstrap': to start up a program. The figure of speech depicts the opening lines of the program as lifting themselves by their own bootstraps.

BUG (nn): A flaw, usually in a program. The noun has produced a privative verb, 'debug', i.e. 'go through a program finding and correcting mistakes.'

CHIP (nn): A slice of silicon holding many thousands of minute electronic circuits and components: the MC68000 chip measures about a quarter of an inch on a side but contains some 70,000 transistor sites. The central processing unit of the computer is on a chip, but chips also appear in many of the peripherals like the keyboard and the printer, and in digital watches, automatic cameras, and even some kitchen toasters. One German computer journal is called *Chip*.

CURSOR (nn): Latin for 'runner' and a very old word even in English; an early Middle English poem (c. 1300) was called 'The Cursor Mundi', i.e. 'The Runner of the World'. In computers, the cursor is a small line or rectangle that appears on the monitor screen to mark the position of the current activity. If the user is writing, the cursor shows where the next character will go – usually the end of the text line.

DATABASE (nn): A collection of related data that the computer can retrieve and manipulate. If you stored your Christmas-card list on a computer disk or tape, you could retrieve it when you wanted to add or subtract names, correct addresses, append comments, and search or sort the list by name, address, or other criteria. The list would form a database.

HANDSHAKING (nn): Another figure of speech from the social world with special meaning in computerese: an exchange of data between a computer and a peripheral (such as a communications device) that establishes the interaction of the two; electronic salutations.

HARD COPY (nn): Computer printout. The computer 'prints' its output either on the monitor screen or on paper. The screen copy is instant but temporary and stationary; the hard copy on paper is delayed but permanent and portable. The implied antonym 'soft copy' for the screen text is, apparently, not used.

INTERFACE (nn and vb): An 1882 term in the sense 'A surface lying between two portions of matter or space, and forming their common boundary' (OED); now a device or program connecting two pieces of equipment that cannot be directly linked (that is, are not 'plug-compatible'). A computer may require an interface, for example, to work with certain printers.

TERMINAL (nn): Another very old word, now with the computerese sense of a device with a keyboard and a monitor screen or printer that enables the user to send input to a computer and receive output from it. Most small systems are self-contained so that the terminal is not separate from the computer, but in large systems several terminals can use a single separate computer by means of timesharing.

TIMESHARING (nn): The use of a single separate computer by several users through terminals. While 'timesharing' has been borrowed by other fields such as real estate, where it means the use of a single facility by several users taking turns – in a vacation apartment, for example – computer timesharing gives each user the impression of being alone with the computer, because it allocates the 'turns' electronically in a rota so rapid that no user. is aware of being off-line.

UP (and DOWN) (aj): A computer system in use is 'up and running'. By implication, a system out of use for any reason is 'down'. The latter term in particular has joined non-technical English, so that traffic reports can say the 'uptown lane is down' without contradiction.

-WARE (nn): The mechanics and circuitry that make up a computer system are the 'hardware', a term borrowed from standard vocabulary. The term in turn gave rise to 'software', the programs on which the hardware runs, and then 'firmware', which is software permanently installed in the hardware. Educational software is 'courseware'.

The vocabulary of computerese, in common with most other specialized vocabulary, contains very few words created from scratch. Instead it employs standard English phonology and grammar to build a small technical lexicon, borrowing some words with changed meanings, creating some new ones by compounding and acronyms, employing a genial sense of humour in figures of speech. The resulting vocabulary is more compact and precise than the loose paraphrases it replaces. Within computerese growth has continued: some words created as nouns, for example, have spawned verbs. And beyond computerese the special vocabulary is returning to the lay vocabulary, loans returned with interest. Words like 'interface', 'timesharing', 'down' and even 'database' have begun to appear in Standard English senses derived from but not identical to their computerese meanings.

So although computers have made a contribution to the vocabulary of English, it is little more than other fields or technology have done. The distinctive contribution has instead been in data processing itself, and the most straightforward of these has been word processing, 'The entry, manipulation, editing, and storage of text using a computer.' [5] A word processor, that is, uses a computer to do the job of a typewriter and many of the jobs of a file cabinet. Some word processors are 'dedicated'; word processing (WP) is all they do, just as the computer dedicated to bank cheque processing does nothing else. Like any specialized machinery they do one job very well at the cost of doing no other job at all. Multi-purpose computers from micro to monster include WP in the wide range of tasks they can accomplish, although their WP is without some of the 'bells and whistles' the dedicated machines boast.

Every computer has facilities for input and output: among the most important input devices is a keyboard with the standard QWER-TYUIOP typewriter layout, and among the output devices are a monitor screen and a printer. WP is an obvious adaptation of these devices to the creation and editing of texts. (In fact WP is a sophisticated version of the computer's facilities for writing, editing and debugging programs, of which creation and revision are the literary cousins.) As a way of creating texts, however, WP has little advantage over typewriters other than the storage capacity it offers. If every text were letter-perfect in the first draft, and if it were never needed for another purpose, WP would be just an expensive fad. But typists know that error lurks between the keys, ever ready to pounce. Small typing errors yield to erasure, but a major blunder near the end of an intricate single-spaced page is a waste of time and temper. WP treats errors with divine forgiveness: a single stroke deletes a letter, word, sentence, or paragraph, and closes up the hole electronically; another stroke inserts a letter or more, and moves the existing text to the right to make room; strikeovers displace existing text into oblivion, the perfect palimpsest.

Writers are often their own typists, especially when publishers and university departments are reducing secretarial support and when the cost of professional typing for even a short book like this one exceeds $1,000. Many writers, however, are bad typists; they have all the challenge they can handle in writing. Orwell observed

> Nowadays, when I write a review, I sit down at the typewriter and type it straight out. Till recently, indeed till six months ago, I never did this and would have said that I could not do it. Virtually all that I wrote was written at least twice, and my books as a whole three times – individual passages as many as five or ten times. . . . It is a deterioration directly due to the war. (CE 2.350, 1940)

He commented on his efforts at revision from at least 1933 (CE 1.125) onwards, and battled with typing errors into the last year of his life (CE 4.473).

Revision is the heart of the writing process, and the writer who concentrates on the process instead of the product has the best chance of success. Teachers and publishers alike, however, emphasize the product: 'I want your manuscript on [date]' focuses on the final draft and recalls the medieval illumination in which the author presents the opus to the patron, the former kneeling, the latter enthroned, the act rightly called 'submission'. Such an epiphany remains elusive if the author strives to obtain it at the first effort – to make the first draft the final product. Instead the first draft should be a wild, free thing that takes no thought of the morrow but gets it out, gets if *all* out with the concomitant hope that the author will immediately feel better. Such uninhibited episodes, however, are difficult to achieve because they carry with them the sure knowledge that the first draft will require deletions, insertions and rearrangements in successive generations of drafts, each painstakingly retyped from the previous draft and violently revised before it too is retyped. In the paper avalanche that reaches from desk to floor, each sheet is covered with self-criticisms like 'wordy', 'awkward', 'out of place here'.

The advantage of WP to the author is that revision becomes easy, removing the inhibitions on a truly free first draft along with those on small but important improvements in what seemed to be the final draft and on all revisions in between. No longer does the final draft have roots in generations of intermediate drafts. Instead, the author has only a current draft: the one on the monitor, the one in the computer's memory. The composition process takes place on a plastic medium like clay, not on an unyielding surface like stone that only replacement can correct. Writers who use WP say that they write better and faster – rare combination! – and that the composition process seems to have more mental affinities with WP than with quill, typewriter or dictating machine. Whatever the reason, much of the writing about computers is notably lucid.

WP systems can do far more than simply insert and delete: they can, for example, 'cut and paste' without scissors and tape by simply moving blocks of text from one place to another; they can, with the right software, check spelling, grammatical agreement, even sexist language; they can draw on an electronic thesaurus that automatically replaces a dull word with the user's choice from a list of livelier synonyms; they can even undelete rashly rejected material. Yet a command of wp comes readily even to the technically inept. A command of the new composition process comes more slowly, so at the outset the user will probably treat the system as an elaborate correcting typewriter. Only with experience and reflection will the new habits of composition grow.

Compared with such changes, the other advantages of wp are superficial though they are real – matters of convenience, not of essence. Because the printout is a faithful reproduction of the final authorial version, the author does not have to proofread a typists' work. Publishers report that wp manuscripts are better written, neater and more punctual. Because the final product is embodied not only in a printed output but on a magnetic disk memory, publishers can often use the author's disk to drive the typesetting machine. That way they cut out much costly effort at the printer's, and exclude errors that arise from the compositor's re-keyboarding the text; so the author does not have to proofread the compositor's work. The saving in time, effort and error is such that some publishers offer better royalty terms to authors who submit their work on magnetic disks.

The magnetic disks that record the text also enable the wp system to take over some of the functions of a file cabinet. The disks are coated with a substance like that on cassette tapes, and indeed cassette tapes can be used to record computer data. But the user must play through intervening data to find the required spot on a tape, while the contents of a disk, like those of a phonograph record, are directly accessible at any point. Like phonograph records as well, computer disks come in different sizes and capacities; this is a very fast-changing area of computer technology, but one common format is the 5.25" flexible ('floppy') double-sided disk, about the size of a 45 rpm record, which can hold the equivalent of a thousand double-spaced pages of typewritten text. This book fits on to one side of such a disk with room to spare.

The disk preserves the text in units called, appropriately, 'files'. The user can create a file, save a file, revise a file; at the beginning of a writing session, for example, the user can get the file from the last session and change it, with the alternatives of revising the file on the disk or of creating a new file with the changes while retaining the original unchanged. It as as though the user removed a document from the file, photocopied it, replaced the original, and went to work revising the copy. In the Ministry of Truth,

As soon as all the corrections which happened to be necessary in any particular number of the *Times* had been assembled and collated, that number would be re-printed, the original copy destroyed, and the corrected copy placed on the files in its stead.

(NE 36)

Orwell acknowledged that 'What happened in the unseen labyrinth to which the pneumatic tubes led, [Smith] did not know in detail,' and Orwell seems to have shared his uncertainty; but his description comes as close to computer file-handling as anything he wrote.

The computer can also 'manage' the data in its files: it can, for example, take the place of a researcher's card file. A conventional card file is limited to one physical sequence – authors' names in alphabetical order, major topics, or the like – so libraries usually have one catalogue of their collection filed by author and another by subject. But a computer can search and sort its files so quickly and thoroughly that the researcher can realistically stipulate the keywords 'sexism', 'English' and 'nouns', and the date '>1976', and the computer will assemble and display all the post-1976 records about sexism in English nouns. Microcomputer users generally make and manage their own databases, but they can also access by telephone the huge databases such as ERIC (Educational Resource and Information Center) using the same keyword-search approach.

Computers can manage form as well as content. The user can instantly vary the layout of a file, changing the margins, the line-spacing, and so forth; a file that was previously printed in single-spaced narrow columns can be double-spaced on wide lines the next time, with no retyping. The user can call up the contents of any file on the screen, print them on the printer, or both. If one file contains a list of addresses and another file contains the text of a letter, the computer will obligingly address separate 'original' copies of the letter to everyone on the list (for an illustration of this technique, called 'mail merge', just look in your mailbox). The computer will even alter the text of the letter to contain the name and address of the individual to whom it is addressed. The computer performs this function by a 'search and replace' process. The user instructs the computer to search for any examples of the string 'X' and replace it with the string 'Y'. If 'Y' is a name on a mailing list, the computer will simply insert the name wherever 'X' occurs. If you have spelled Romeo's beloved 'Julliet' throughout your term paper, you need only tell the computer that is should be 'Juliet' and the contraption will correct every instance without even grumbling 'What's in a name?'

The search-and-replace process raises another possibility. Suppose the machine searches for all examples of 'you' and replaces them with *Usted*, for example, and so on for all the words in the text; will not the output be machine translation from English to Spanish? Not necessarily. For one thing, 'you' in English is both singular and plural; *Usted* is only singular (the plural is *Ustedes*). The problem is bigger than mere search-and-replace. The machine has to know whether a given instance of 'you' is singular or plural, or how the machine can find out for itself. The difference can be more than a matter of grammatical concord. 'You [noun]' means 'You really are a [noun]' if singular, but 'You [nouns] are all [adjective]' when plural (compare 'You monster!' with 'You monsters . . .'). And the example of 'you' is not extreme; Spanish has two verbs that share the role of English 'to be', while French has two verbs that share the role of English 'to have', one of which also has the role of English 'to be'. No language is the 1 : 1 equivalent of any other, a lack of parity with consequences both inconvenient and comic. A check on machine translation from one language to another is retranslation back into the original; examples include 'Blind idiot' for 'Out of sight out of mind', 'The vodka is good but the meat is lousy' for 'The spirit is willing but the flesh is weak.' Those are perhaps apocryphal, but obviously WP is indeed straightforward compared with machine translation.[6]

In 1954, a demonstration computer with a 250-word Russian-English vocabulary did translate a few sentences, and hope was high. That was a chilly year in the cold war, so copious official funds flowed to machine translation research. But ten years later, in 1964, a linguist familiar with the field called it 'linguistics' most conspicuous and expensive failure'. In 1984, even though computers are immensely more powerful, the outlook is more like 1964 than 1954. Yet serious people remain seriously interested in the field, for serious theoretical and practical reasons. The place of linguistic theory in the opening chapter of this book illustrates the importance of theory in modern linguistics; when a descriptive grammar is completed, machine translation will be a rigorous way of testing its adequacy. For practical purposes, machine translations do not have to be impeccable. Machine translation output is useful if it is only good enough for casual perusal; the user can select interesting documents for more careful human translation.

A machine translation system includes text input and storage; a 'lookup' or dictionary program; and a grammatical program for analysing the structure of the input and retaining its meaning in the output. Present-day dictionaries underline the difference between human and machine translation, for while they are sufficient for the former they are inadequate for the latter – you cannot, that is, simply input a good English dictionary and obtain what is necessary for the dictionary part of a machine translation system. For an adjective like 'simple' a conventional dictionary may give over twenty synonyms gathered under five main headings: 'pure', 'easy', 'plain', 'naive', 'silly'. (The dictionary will also list a noun 'simple' as a different word from the adjective.) The computer's dictionary, by contrast, will list the five adjective meanings as different words to correspond with different foreign words such as Spanish *puro*, *fácil*, *sencillo*, *manso*, and *necio*.

A conventional dictionary does not include both 'friend' and 'friends', both 'care' and 'caring'; the inflectional ending changes the meaning of the simple word, but in quite regular ways. To include both forms would make the book, and any translation program, enormously more cumbersome and expensive. But what about 'grocery' and 'groceries'? The second is not just the plural of the first. And should derivational endings like '-ly' be treated like '-s' and '-ing'? Is the relationship of 'quick' and 'quickly' the same as 'fair' and 'fairly'? Finally, what about compounds, 'words' that are really two words? A 'baglady' is a woman 'living rough' (the first term is American, the second British) who keeps all her belongings in a shopping bag; but a 'bagman' is the functionary in a payoff who carries the money from one principal to the other. Despite the known relationship between 'lady' and 'man', and the common element 'bag', the two terms have no predictable meaning either in themselves or in relation to each other. In 'realtors' English', an American variety, 'home' always replaces 'house' ('I can show you a nice home on the next block'); but even for realtors, 'homework' is not the same as 'housework'. Nothing good, it seems, will come from shortcuts in this department.

Another obstacle to machine translation is the lack of a really thorough-going description of any natural language, let alone a comparative grammar of two; and conventional grammars just do not contain enough information. In English, for example, a verb like 'admire' requires an animate subject; a verb like 'astound' requires an animate object. We can equate 'I like to kiss' with 'I like kissing' but not 'Let's stop to kiss' with 'Let's stop kissing.' 'He's' differs from 'he is' only in degree of formality, but 'let's' differs totally from one meaning of 'let us': 'let us go', except in quite formal writing, is addressed to someone like a guard who will remain behind after the 'us' depart, whereas 'let's go' is addressed to those who will depart; 'let's' cannot substitute for this common meaning of 'let us' as 'he's' can substitute for 'he is'. Such differences are on the borderline between dictionary and grammar; no dictionary deals with them, and though many linguists now think they are matters of grammar, no grammar yet deals with them very thoroughly either. They are very untidy, so any translation program will have difficulty dealing with them as surface features. A program that deals with their regularities at deeper levels is hard to write and might still not produce flawless translations, but at least it tells us a great a deal about the fundamentals of language.

The grammar component has to recognize any ambiguities in the original text simply to make the translation, even if the translation does not have to be unambiguous. The English 'There are two computers you can use' may require French *Voilá* or *Il y a* depending on the meaning of the original. And how does the machine differentiate between restrictive and non-restrictive (appositive) clauses in English? Composition teachers often require the latter to begin with 'which' and have commas, the former with 'that' and no commas. If those directions were descriptions, the machine would have no trouble. Realistically, however, the machine must test the clause according to an algorithm:

1. If the clause begins with 'any', 'all', 'every' or 'no', it is restrictive ('Any computoid hominid . . .').
2. If it begins with 'The' followed by a number, it is restrictive ('The two disks you sat on . . .').
3. If it begins with a numeral and no article, it is appositive ('Sixteen programmers, which is too many . . .').
4. If it begins with a proper name, it is appositive ('Sarah, who knows FORTRAN . . .').

But the machine has to deal with many clauses that lack those helpful hints, and other problems besides.

Many of these problems would be less serious if the user would accept more than one translation of each sentence, if the machine presented all the possible translations based on the data and program it used. That might be theoretically interesting, because it would show how many different analyses of one sentence a given grammar could yield. But for practical purposes multiple translations would be intolerable. The point of machine translation is to save time and effort, not increase them. (Of course the user who had doubts about 'Blind idiot' can always ask the machine for a second opinion.)

Similar problems confront any machine processing of natural-language texts: the quantitative analysis of literary style, for example, or the preparation of concordances. Beyond superficial matters like word counts, how is the computer to analyze linguistic structures? Even concordances, alphabetical listings of the words in a text with references to or quotations of the lines in which they occur, face problems of analysis. A 1911 'manual' concordance to the 3182–line Old English poem *Beowulf* understandably did not trouble to record every instance of 'and'. The 1969 computer concordance to the same poem which did include them did not, however, distinguish between homographs (different words written the same way, comparable to Modern English 'tear' [teir] and [ti:r]) or bring together different forms of the same word (comparable to 'go' and 'went').[7]

Computers can already 'write': that is what they do when they convert the data in their memories into print on the screen or on paper. They can also 'read'. A note at the beginning of a recent book about Orwell says

Readers . . . may be interested in some of the technology used to produce this book. An automated scanner 'read' the printed novel and other material from the first edition and transferred it onto magnetic discs [sic]. The remaining portions of this edition were typed on a word processor. Then the outputs of both processes were merged onto magnetic discs that generated the printed type you see here.[8]

The development summarized in that announcement is an application of computer 'character recognition', one of several technologies that now enable machines to read, speak, hear and transcribe natural language.

At the heart of these technologies is a converter that turns digital data into analogue, and vice-versa. Digital data are any expressed in numbers, or, more generally, characters; analogue data are other kinds, such as shapes and sounds.[9] When a computer displays numbers as a graph, it is converting digital data into analogue (DA). When it processes music for a digital recording, it converts analogue data into digital (AD), 'digitizing' the music. The development of hardware and software to perform DA and AD conversions was a major step in bringing computers into the arena of human language. So a computer program can now convert shapes such as printed letters into digital information and store the text, as the scanner did with the Orwell textbook. The range of letter shapes (fonts) that the machine can 'read' is growing with the growth in computer speed and memory capacity.

The technology that enables a machine to digitize music will also enable it to encode other forms of sound, including speech. In music, however, all sound is significant, so the encoding does not have to select. In speech the language content is a small fraction of the sound input, so the machine has to 'know' something about the language to sort the linguistic wheat from the acoustical chaff. To revert to our examples of 20–90 by tens, the computer could digitize [eidi] and [naini] without trouble, but to convert the sounds to conventional spelling it would need to retrieve the <t> in those words that [siksti] retains; it would need to know something about the speech habits of every speaker who used it, and so computer recognition of speech is lagging behind computer recognition of printed characters. 'Voice prints' are not yet reliable in situations where accuracy is essential – in courts of law, for example, or where the voice is a 'key' to unlock a security device. And the computer dictating machine that will digitize speech and turn it into neat typed copy is, accordingly, not quite around the corner; but in 1982 Victor Business Products introduced an office microcomputer with a standard-equipment analogue coder and decoder aimed at digitizing the human voice, anticipating voice-to-print technology, Orwell's 'speakwrite'.

Speech synthesis by computers, on the other hand, is going forward reasonably well. Today even microcomputers have small speakers, used mostly to beep at users who need prompting (the BASIC command for a beep is 'BEEP'); the speakers are, all the same, at least up to the standard of those in pocket radios, and speech synthesis is already an experimental subject for home hobbyists. In 1982 a complete device, including a computer central processing unit, was available for under $300, able to translate keyboard input into speech output.[10] The large mainframe computers can, and at institutions like Bell Labs do, carry out much more sophisticated speech synthesis with the aid of computer models of the human vocal tract. The object of this work is not so much to prepare for a garrulous computer like HAL of the film *2001* as to gain understanding of human language, and to apply the understanding to problems of communication.

So, to one extent or another, computers can read and write, speak and listen. The most interesting devices, however, combine these abilities. They link character recognition with speech synthesis, for example, in a machine that can convert the printed page into speech for the benefit of the sightless. Such a machine, originally the invention of a lone engineer, now the product of Xerox corporation, has dwindled in size and price since its origins, and although the price is still too high for widespread private ownership, the size is not much larger than an office typewriter. The machine scans and digitizes the printed page, submitting the data to a program of several major pronunciation rules and hundreds of minor ones, and feeding the output through a speech synthesizer. It can even output the digitized characters one by one if the user, hearing an unfamiliar word, orders 'Spell that!'

A different kind of 'talking computer' is the one that seeks to apply the artificial intelligence of the machine to conversations with the user. Alan Turing once posed a test of artificial intelligence: can the user tell whether the entity on the other end of a wire is human or machine? If it is a machine and the user cannot tell, the machine has artificial intelligence. (For the Turing test, and for most attempts to pass it, the 'conversation' is written, not spoken.) Machine conversations program the computer to recognize certain input words and respond accordingly; an early one, 'Eliza' by MIT's Joseph Weizenbaum, played the role of a psychiatrist by responding to such key words as 'depressed' with remarks like 'I'm sorry that you are depressed.' 'Eliza' was followed by 'Parry', a program that played the role of a clever paranoid. Both are enjoyable games, but both get around the real problems of artificial intelligence by exploiting their fictitious roles with psychiatric mumbo-jumbo ('In what way?'; 'Tell me about your family') or psychotic irrelevancy ('I don't want to talk to you any more, buzz off'). 'Analiza II', an improved model, is described by its writer, John Holland, as 'Eliza taken to the next level of intelligence'.

More enterprising still is 'Boris', a Yale University program. It contains a list of words describing emotions and their impact on goal achievement. It can interpret input like 'Unfortunately, the news wasn't good,' and offer output like 'Richard was happy on Paul's behalf.'[11] But 'Boris' can understand only what it has been programmed to understand, specifically the vocabulary and meanings stored in it. Like other examples of artificial intelligence, it has shown no real capacity to learn by itself, and the emotions it 'conceptualizes' are simply words, not feelings. Even Carnegie-Mellon's 'Bacon', designed to take an inductive approach to physical data, can assemble concepts only as they are fed to it. It cannot strike out in a new direction, so it lacks the 'inductive leap' characteristic of true human learning and intellectual progress. An expert and up-to-date opinion is that while 'a successful program [to understand ordinary natural language] would simulate processes that seem to be close to the essence of human thought', such a program

> is one of the most difficult challenges now facing the discipline of artificial intelligence. Even the simplest programs for understanding language are large and complex, and the most powerful programs are still confined to narrow semantic domains in which they attend primarily to the most superficial meanings. . . . The best current programs for language understanding literally do not know what they are talking about; their only contact with the world is through language.[12]

The anthropomorphism displayed on buttons and bumper stickers like 'Computers are people too' and 'My computer likes me' is sentimental prolepsis.

Orwell's writing 'versificator' was like a 'special kind of kaleidoscope' presumably because it introduced random recombinations of the forms with which it was stocked. Randomization is a function that popular computer games like 'Space Invaders' already depend on for unpredictable events, and math drills use it for unprecedented problems. If Orwell was right that 'It would probably not be beyond human ingenuity to write books by machinery,' randomization will also figure in computer programs for original literary works. Among those pursuing this research are some of the best-known students of literary style, such as Louis Milic and Richard Bailey. Their goal is not, of course, to supersede the literary imagination, but to learn more about it. Some programs, such as Jim Meehan's folktale generator 'Tale-Spin', produce modest narratives that are fun to read if properly post-edited. Others, like Natalie Dehn's 'Author', are serious experiments in artificial intelligence.[13]

'Racter', the product of writer William Chamberlain and programmer Thomas Etter, 'wrote' the science-fiction short story 'Soft Ions'. But a few months later the authors were not ready to generate another story, because 'If you started the program now, the stories would be similar.'[14] The relatively small scope of a microcomputer and limitations in the program itself inhibit 'Racter' from the infinite production of randomly varying stories of which it is theoretically capable: 'It takes an immense amount of idiosyncratic knowledge to get the thing working properly,' as the writing member of the partnership put it. 'The program fools around with words based on certain formalisms we have decided upon.' The components of 'Racter', that is, are similar to those of a machine translation program: it has lists of words in dictionary files and structural routines in grammatical files. The fooling around yielded, among other passages, this apparently post-edited one:

> . . . Wendy pondered her dreams (maniacal leopards were swallowing loony oboists). Helene started brushing her braid: She was a maid, much to John's happiness, but oboists, even loony oboists, weren't in Helene's brain; she was simply commencing to comb her braid after brushing it and prepare for supper.

In any event, the program has very little creative personality of its own:

> The computer somehow seems to sound the way the person who has written the files sounds, regardless of what the computer is saying. If this is indeed the case, then this particular program in some sense captures some aspects of a living person.

The cleavage between personal style and mechanical content (how the story sounds and what it says) may explain the story's avant-garde quality. Or perhaps any output of such a program is inherently non-objective. As the author says, the computer will avoid a collocation like 'fur piano' only if the programmer tells it to, and it is hard for the programmer to anticipate all the forbidden collocations. Programming a computer is akin to instructing an amiable and immensely strong but inexperienced and somewhat dim animal (a gorilla, perhaps) to open a door: you must specify scores of things you long since internalized as unnoticed aspects of the activity. You must remind the creature to turn the knob when opening the door – but then you must also remind it not to turn the knob too far. In literature, the problem leads to rather 'unreal' fiction.

Avant-garde fictional prose is unlike the 'versificator' literature designed 'for the benefit of the proletariat', a class whose taste for the avant-garde has never been keen. But computer poetry can make the most of the same quality, and some instances border on the pleasurable. Apparently people do not expect poetry to make much sense.

The best poetry-writing programs invoke user input (like the sample BASIC program) and fit the words provided into a pattern:

THIS GAME CAN HELP YOU BECOME A POET.
PLEASE TYPE IN THE FOLLOWING KINDS OF WORDS OR PHRASES
AS THE GAME ASKS FOR THEM.
A NOUN?
User: Sky.
AN ADJECTIVE DESCRIBING THE NOUN?
Bright.
ANOTHER ADJECTIVE?
Blinding.
A PREPOSITIONAL PHRASE TELLING WHERE OR WHEN SOME-
THING CAN HAPPEN TO YOUR NOUN?
In your eyes.
A VERB?
Punishes.
AN ADVERB DESCRIBING HOW YOUR NOUN DOES IT?
Unceasingly.
ANOTHER ADVERB?
Uncaringly.
HERE IS THE POEM:

THE SKY
 BRIGHT, BLINDING
IN YOUR EYES
 UNCEASINGLY, UNCARINGLY
PUNISHES.

SATISFIED WITH YOUR POEM?
No.
WANT SOME ADVICE?
Yes.
IF YOU WANT TO TRY AGAIN, REMEMBER THAT YOU CAN USE
PHRASES _ NOT JUST WORDS _ FOR YOUR NOUN, ADJECTIVE,
ADVERB, ETC.[15]

The poem always has the structure

  NOUN (PHRASE)
  ADJECTIVE (PHRASE)
  PREPOSITIONAL PHRASE
  ADVERB(S)
  VERB OR VERBAL PHRASE

But the program does encourage improvements by the user. One user produce the poem

> The riveter,
> brawny, sweatcaked at Miller time
> carefully slouches
> bethlehembound,

adding 'The poem above is in the order I like rather than the order suggested by the program.' The user responded first to the programmed cues, then to the suggestions at the end, finally to a better idea for the poem's structure. After all, the program had promised to help the user become a poet, not to write a poem; the user's involvement is part of both the goal and the strategy of the program. The other part is its name for itself: 'a game'.

Games are among the best-known capabilities of computers. While free association with 'computer' might produce 'arcane' for older users, for younger users it would be 'arcade'. Interaction with a microcomputer or a terminal seems natural and 'fun' to student-age people, who find computers attractive, not deterrent; that alone makes them appealing for pedagogy. Add their speed, patience, adaptability, and skill at record-keeping, and you have a teaching machine – not a computer-instructor, but computer-aided instruction (CAI). In teaching English, especially prose composition, text feedback programs can report quantifiable attributes of a user's essay (average word and sentence length, word-to-preposition ratio, number of '-tion' words and parts of the verb 'be', percentage of simple and complex sentences, active and passive clauses, word repetitions and word familiarity) and render a 'Readability Score' or 'fog quotient' – usually expressed as the years of education a reader would require to grasp the essay.[16] But even text feedback programs 'cannot measure comprehensibility because the formula cannot test for sense'.[17] And, like many computer routines, they do nothing that could not be done manually – they simply do it far faster. It would be possible, but wholly impractical, for an unaided teacher to prepare a readability score for every student essay.

Computers can also take a supporting role in drill and practice. The machine easily stores a great many such problems in subject modules that the teacher or student, perhaps after a diagnostic test, can select. No two students have to work at the same module or the same pace. The University of Michigan program 'Grammar', for example, can pose the problem sentence 'EVERY CHILD WHO PASS-

ES THEIR TEST WILL BE GIVEN A PRIZE' and ask the student to correct any error. In this case the computer program expects the substitution of 'his' for 'their'; otherwise the machine will observe 'TOO BAD. "EVERY CHILD" IS SINGULAR AND ANY PRONOUN REFERRING TO "EVERY CHILD" MUST BE SINGULAR. THEREFORE, YOU MUST USE THE SINGULAR PRONOUN "HIS" IN "HIS TEST." ' Some students might wish to substitute 'her' or 'his or her' for 'their', but the program is not ready for those improvements, so it will score them 'wrong'. A drill and practice program needs to be versatile, so the programmer needs to be resourceful. At worst such programs are simply mechanized flash cards. At best they enable the student to undertake more individualized drill than teachers can supervise unaided.

Where drill and practice programs merely keep the student's score, tutorial programs act on it. Instead of going through the drill and practice lessons one after another in fixed order, tutorial CAI can branch to further supplementary or advanced drills, or skip unnecessary drills, according to student performance. Even more interactive programs for advanced writing students catechize them about their proposed subject, 'brainstorming' for ideas. Hugh Burns, of the US Air Force Academy, reports the following 'dialogue' in a program he designed:

... WOULD YOU PLEASE TYPE IN YOUR SUBJECT. (I'M LOOKING FOR ONE TO THREE WORDS, MAYBE FOUR.)
User: Dreiser's dramatic technique.
HEY, THAT'S COOL, KAREN! WE'LL HAVE A GOOD TIME BRAIN-STORMING DREISER'S DRAMATIC TECHNIQUE. ... DESCRIBE HOW DREISER'S DRAMATIC TECHNIQUE PHYSICALLY CHANGES. Please explain!
I'M LOOKING FOR YOUR NOTIONS ABOUT THE DEVELOPMENT OF DREISER'S DRAMATIC TECHNIQUE. ...
I want to show how *Sister Carrie* allowed Dreiser to grow, to confront common values. It is a mature work.
GOOD, KAREN. ADD TO YOUR RESPONSE NOW.
Hurstwood grows the other way. There are negative passages, aren't there?
YES, THAT SEEMS OKAY TO ME.
Me too.
AH, SHORT AND SWEET. PLEASE ELABORATE A LITTLE. ... [18]

The session continued for forty minutes, Burns reports, and netted

Karen eighteen pages of notes toward her paper. Other systems would have enabled her to enter her thoughts under a pen name on an electronic bulletin board, receiving the comments of her peers and further expanding the range of ideas for her essay.[19] The full range of these technologies – word processing, printout, electronic bulletin boards, information retrieval, educational games – are implemented for younger writers in a co-ordinated system by Bolt Beranek and Newman Inc., Cambridge (MA),[20] and computer-student interaction is the basis of Control Data Corporation's widely-advertised industrial and scholastic PLATO system.

The school and university teaching of English is an enormous task, involving millions of students and billions of dollars each year. If CAI can help teachers do the job better then it will soon justify itself on pedagogical grounds. Clarkson School, of Potsdam (NY), announced that

> every student who enters our program in the fall of 1983 will receive a . . . Desk Top Computer for his or her personal use during the academic year. Courses will be geared toward use of the computers in home-work.

Carnegie-Mellon University, in Pittsburgh (PA), has under development with IBM a plan to provide several thousand 'personal computer' workstations for students and faculty in their offices, laboratories and residences by 1986; the workstations will act both as independent computers and as terminals in the university's central computer system. The plan is to teach computer skills and to obtain the advantages of decentralized CAI such as individualized instruction.

But every advantage casts its own shadow, and the decentralization in CAI is only apparent; computer programs take a larger classroom role than conventional textbooks, so they make larger inroads on the teacher's role. CAI is irresistibly influential if it does not treat unresolved issues deferentially: the issue of a possessive adjective for 'every child' is an example. The more computers share human roles, the more they threaten to dehumanize. So, when Anthony Tucker described the next generation of computers as being capable of human language mastery (*Guardian*, 24 June 1982), a correspondent replied

> How splendid to know that if only we can define our words with sufficient machine-like clarity then we will be able to consult [computers] directly on our most pressing and intimate problems.

Mr Tucker might find an elaborate yet perfectly functional model on which to proceed in a novel called 1984 by G. Orwell. The Appendix on the Principles of Newspeak anticipates Mr Tucker's requirements by some 33 years.

Yours goodthinkwise,

The correspondent had in mind the semantic reduction in Newspeak, since one of Tucker's arguments had been that human affairs are in a mess because natural language is imprecise; the language of the new computers will have 'closely spaced and carefully defined meanings' akin to the language of mathematics.

The argument is not a new one – John Locke's 1690 *Essay Concerning Human Understanding* was concerned to remove the misunderstandings that arose from imprecise definitions, and the Royal Society in 1662 encouraged its members to employ 'mathematical plainness' in the language of their scientific reports.[21] But, another correspondent pointed out, 'any language where both forms and meanings are limited by definition and not susceptible to the influence of individual users is crucially distinct from "our own language".' Neither Locke's attempt nor the Royal Society's was successful, and this new attempt seems doubly likely to fail where they did – for linguistic reasons, because natural language will not stand still for such definition and limitation, and for political reasons because 'the influence of individual users' is a bulwark against language totalitarianism.

The problem of all computer-aided language activity, whether it is instruction, translation, aid for the handicapped, or any other, lies in the power it gives to the few individuals who design the machine and its programs. That power is very great, it is centralized, and it is not necessarily responsive to the user. Even non-language computer activities raise problems of privacy and the protection of individual influence. In large government and commercial offices, users connect with the big computer by terminals – sometimes very remote terminals. The hand-held terminal that enables the user to reach the firm's computer from anywhere is now available (produced in the first instance by a large brokerage firm). A home microcomputer can communicate with far-off mainframe computers by telephone, enabling it to tap their databases or employ their programs and peripherals. So users at home can receive news – business news, weather news, product and service news. If the product or service appeals, the user can order it through the computer in the family room.

The communications links among all these home computers, hand-held computers, office terminals and mainframe machines are an easy target for intruders. A telephone wiretap a decade ago might detect an indiscretion, but today it can record personal or business secrets on an enormous scale. Computer communications have brought with them a renewed interest in cryptography, but then nothing breaks a secret code so well as a computer. And where the intruder is official, an individual can do little to resist. The National Security Agency 'possesses the computerized equipment to monitor nearly all overseas telephone calls and most domestic and international printed messages – and . . . has made heavy use of its Orwellian technology.' [22] The connection is with Orwell's spirit, not his letter. Yet is seems appropriate to many, including computer scientists like Donald H. Sanders:

> In 1949, when people first read George Orwell's *1984*, with its eerie visions of a society controlled by 'Big Brother', they probably took some comfort in the fact that 1984 was a distant 35 years in the future. But those 35 years have slipped away. The fictional version of 1984 was frightening; now as we move into – and then beyond – 1984, what is likely to be the reality?
> (1981, p. 570)

This remark in a book about computers, not about language or literature, shows how Orwell's vision has become associated with a technological development he knew nothing about.

Computers themselves are innocent, even of guilt by association. They are inanimate. But they lend themselves to abuse by their animate users, and their enormous power makes those abuses unlike any others. Even mere blunders, like programming errors or flaws in gathering and inputting data, result in prolonged alarm and despondency among those who receive repeated bills for debts or library books no longer owed. When the problem is not accidental, serious ethical issues arise. Computers can amass and compare huge amounts of data. Is it ethical, say, to compare data from bank computers with those of the Internal Revenue Service? That is not exactly a question of 'computer ethics', but it arises only with the brute power of large modern computers, for without them the amassing and comparison of the data would be simply impractical on any significant scale. As Sanders goes on to say, 'the creation of superbanks with complete computer-based dossiers on individuals would give considerable power to those in charge of the banks, and this development might be the beginning of a drift towards the "Big Brother" state created by George Orwell in his book *1984*' (p. 390; cf. 399–400). Certainly a commercial name such as 'Control Data Corporation' could, though unintentionally, stand for the most totalitarian electronic state.

The pervasion of society by the computer, and the consequent vulnerability of society to computer manipulation, is the theme of Frederic Vincent Huber's *Apple Crunch* (1982), a novel about two elderly malcontents who electronically infiltrate New York City's computer system and gain control of traffic, hospitals, the payroll – everything. Its nightmare of technological New York is different from Orwell's of totalitarian London, but it shares with his the desperate vision:

> The Inquisition failed, but then the Inquisition had not the resources of the modern state. The radio, press-censorship, standardised education and the secret police have altered everything. Mass-suggestion is a science of the last twenty years, and we do not yet know how successful it will be. (CE 1.381)

CHAPTER VII

Language Abuse

𝕾𝕾𝕾𝕾𝕾𝕾

'MOST PEOPLE who bother with the matter at all would admit that the English language is in a bad way, but it is generally assumed that we cannot by conscious action do anything about it.' The generalization is equally familiar to devoted readers of Orwell and to the thousands, probably millions, of students who never get beyond the essay's first page: it is the opening sentence of the oft-anthologized 'Politics and the English Language' (1946).[1] But the essay was not especially original: Orwell said many of the same things before, and his sources had said them even earlier. He also said them again later, and his generalization remains true of 'most people who bother with the matter at all', including present-day essayists. Yet Orwell's call to 'conscious action', though it was conventional and is even now repeated, has little pertinence even to the form in which it appeared: expository prose.

One of the most striking images in 'Politics and the English Language', for example, is

> the inhabitants driven out into the countryside, the cattle machine-gunned, the huts set on fire with incendiary bullets. . . . Millions of peasants are robbed of their farms and sent trudging along the roads with no more than they can carry. . . . People are imprisoned for years without trial, or shot in the back of the neck. . . .
> (CE 4.136)

Four years earlier Orwell wrote of 'the tortures in the cellars of the Gestapo, the elderly Jewish professors flung into cesspools, the machine-gunning of refugees along the Spanish roads' (CE 2.253), a similar Orwell 'list' with similar content. The 1946 essay objected to 'pretentious diction' like 'eliminate, liquidate'; six years before, Orwell had objected to the same euphemisms (CE 1.516). Orwell's hack speech-maker, 'If the speech he is making is one that he is accustomed to make over and over again, . . . may be almost unconscious of what he is saying' (CE 4.136); eight years earlier he wrote 'These chaps can churn it out by the hour. Just like a gramophone. Turn the handle, press the button and it starts' (CA 171).

In a 1944 'As I Please' column (CE 3.108–11), Orwell pronounced 'sentence of death on the following words and expressions', including 'Achilles' heel, jackboot, iron heel, blood-stained oppressor' among those he returned to in the 1946 'Politics' essay. His 'Propaganda and Demotic Speech' piece (CE 3.135–41, 1944), like the 'Politics' essay, pillories the prose style of Harold Laski, 'abstract words habitually used by politicians', 'endlessly tacking one cliché on to another', 'ready-made phrases and . . . dead and stinking metaphors' that turn out to be those of the 'Politics' essay: 'ring the changes on, ride rough-shod over, cross swords with, take up the cudgels for'. He returned to the same phrases again in a 1945 'As I Please' column (CE 3.331–2; cf. CE 3.111).[2]

His preoccupation with euphemism and jargon grew more intense after the War, but its roots were in his earliest writing. He attacked euphemism from *Burmese Days* ('I have done so' for 'I will do so', p. 100) and 'Not Counting Niggers' ('Peace Bloc' for a warlike organization, CE 1.395) to *Animal Farm* ('readjustment' for 'reduction', p. 105) and *Nineteen Eighty-Four* ('Reclamation Centres' for 'colonies for homeless children', p. 135). He satirized jargon in *Coming Up for Air* (legal jargon, p. 20; mercantile jargon, p. 154) and 'The English Language' (professional jargons, CE 3.26), and especially political jargon: the 'horrible jargon' of socialists (RW 223), 'the base jargon of the Government offices' (BD 11) that returned fifteen years later as 'the hybrid jargon of the Ministries' (NE 139).

In 1940 Orwell wrote a prospectus for 'books . . . written in simple language without the rubber-stamp political jargon of the past'.[3] In 'The Prevention of Literature' (early 1946) he wrote 'Political writing in our time consists almost entirely of prefabricated phrases bolted together like the pieces of a child's Meccano set' (CE 4.66). The 'Politics' essay made that 'tacked together like the sections of a prefabricated hen-house' (CE 4.130; cf. 134). And 'The English Language' (written in 1944, published in 1947) protested

> against vagueness, against obscurity, against . . . the encroachment of Latin and Greek, and, above all, against the worn-out phrases and dead metaphors with which the language is cluttered up. . . .
> But probably the deadliest enemy of good English is what is called 'standard English'. This dreary dialect, the language of leading articles,

White Papers, political speeches, and BBC news bulletins, is undoubtedly spreading. . . . Its characteristic is its reliance on ready-made phrases – . . . *explore every avenue, ring the changes, take up the cudgels* . . . etc etc – which . . . have now become mere thought-saving devices, having the same relation to living English as a crutch has to a leg. Anyone preparing a broadcast or writing to *The Times* adopts this kind of language almost instinctively.
(CE 3.26–7)

This near-epitome of the 'Politics' essay distinguishes 'good English' from standard not by features of vocabulary, pronunciation and grammar, but by features of rhetoric that protect the speaker or writer from thought; 'good English' is a variety that 'has nothing to do with correct grammar and syntax, which are of no importance so long as one makes one's meaning clear' (CE 4.138).

That disclaimer conflicts with the views of many later language critics who assert their affinity with Orwell; it even seems to conflict with Orwell's praise for English 'aware of dictionaries and grammatical rules' (CE 4.285) and his minute concerns with his own 'correctness':

I notice that I have used the phrase 'a totally different person'. For the first time it occurs to me what a stupid expression this is. As though there could be such a thing as a partially different person! I shall try to cut this phrase . . . out of my vocabulary from now onwards.
(CE 4.271)

Orwell explained, if he did not resolve, the conflict when he wrote

The major problem of our time is the decay of the belief in personal immortality, and it cannot be dealt with while the average human being is either drudging like an ox or shivering in fear of the secret police. How right the working classes are in their 'materialism'!
(CE 2.265–6)

The reader may wonder why, if the prerequisite to a solution is alleviation of human suffering and fear, Orwell quibbled over 'entirely different'. His quibble was not about propriety, however, but about unthinking or obscurantist usage. As Wedgwood put it,

He was not interested in the maintenance of correct grammar as such. . . . He was interested exclusively in meaning and was profoundly disturbed by the growth of meaningless phrases and by the use of language not to convey but to conceal meaning. . . . He was arguing about something far more important than good English.[4]

That is just as well, for Orwell was very vague about his standards for prose. He first begged off 'To write or even to speak English is not a science but an art,' because

> There are no reliable rules; there is only the general principle that concrete words are better than abstract ones, and that the shortest way of saying anything is always the best. Mere correctness is no guarantee whatever of good writing.
> (CE 3.26)

At its face value, however, Orwell's 'general principle' required that writers treat only concrete topics and treat them only in telegrams. Within a few years he was more confident: 'I think the following rules will cover most cases,' he said at the end of 'Politics and the English Language':

> i. Never use a metaphor, simile or other figure of speech which you are used to seeing in print.
> ii. Never use a long word where a short one will do.
> iii. If it is possible to cut a word out, always cut it out.
> iv. Never use the passive where you can use the active.
> v. Never use a foreign phrase, a scientific word, or a jargon word if you can think of an everyday English equivalent.
> vi. Break any of these rules sooner than say anything outright barbarous.
> (CE 4.139)

But neither codification was original with Orwell. Sir Arthur Quiller-Couch had written in 1916 that 'the two main vices of Jargon' are 'it habitually chooses vague woolly abstract nouns rather than concrete ones' and 'it uses circumlocution rather than short straight speech', anticipating Orwell's double-barrelled 'general principle'. Later Quiller-Couch quoted from the Fowlers' fuller code:

> Prefer the familiar word to the far-fetched.
> Prefer the concrete word to the abstract.
> Prefer the single word to the circumlocution.
> Prefer the short word to the long.
> Prefer the Saxon word to the Romance.[5]

The Fowlers' precepts almost match Orwell's, but not quite: they say nothing about figures of speech or the passive voice, for example, and they omit his sixth rule. But Quiller-Couch wrote 'The first virtue . . . is [the] use of the active verb and the concrete noun' (p. 85), and much else in his essay recalls Orwell's: he censured unnecessary foreign words (p. 74), double negatives that merely equal a positive (p. 81), circumlocutions like 'with regard to' (p. 83); and he illustrated the chief faults of Jargon with horrible examples (pp. 79–81 and passim) and a classic passage done into Jargon (pp. 84–5). His conclusion anticipates 'Politics and the English Language':

> So long as you prefer abstract words, which express other men's summarised concepts of things, to concrete ones which lie as near as can be reached to things themselves and are the first-hand material for your thoughts, you will remain, at the best, writers at second-hand. If your language be Jargon, your intellect, if not your whole character, will almost certainly correspond. Where your mind should go straight, it will dodge: the difficulties it should approach with a fair front and grip with a firm hand it will be seeking to evade or circumvent.

That is not so far from Orwell's

> When you think of something abstract you are more inclined to use words from the start, and unless you make a conscious effort to prevent it, the existing dialect will come rushing in and do the job for you, at the expense of blurring or even changing your meaning.
> (CE 4.138)

In 1944 Orwell wrote of 'official English, or Stripetrouser, the language of White Papers, Parliamentary debates . . . and BBC news bulletins' (CE 3.109), and in the 'Politics' essay of 'the political dialects to be found in pamphlets, leading articles, manifestos, White Papers and the speeches of Under-Secretaries' (CE 4.135). But Quiller-Couch too had written, thirty years before, of 'that infirmity of speech . . . familiar to you in parliamentary debates, in newspapers, and as the staple language of Blue Books, Committees, Official Reports' (p. 74). Orwell also wrote 'you are not obliged to go to all this trouble. You can shirk it by throwing your mind open and letting the ready-made phrases come crowding in.' Quiller-Couch had written 'the writer was using Jargon to shirk prose, palming off periphrases upon us when with a little trouble he could have gone straight to the point' (p. 79). Orwell's debt to the content and method of

Quiller-Couch's essay deserved acknowledgement; but he mentioned Quiller-Couch only once, in a different piece, and then slightingly (CE 4.303).

So Orwell's standards for prose were somewhat vague and, such as they were, by no means original. In addition, his prose was not always very grammatical even by those vague standards. Near the end of 'Politics and the English Language' Orwell wrote 'Look back through this essay, and for certain you will find that I have again and again committed the very faults I am protesting against' (CE 4.137). That is disarming, of course, but it should not deter us from taking his advice. It turns out that the Orwell who stumbled over 'a totally different person' could write 'consensus of opinion' (CE 3.54);[6] and his 'two thousand internees have only eighteen latrine buckets between them' (CE 2.169) outnumber the *Guardian*'s 'Between them, the three lobbyists' and even '40 black youths, with only five CSE's between them'.

The proponent of window-pane prose could also write as through a glass, darkly. Orwell created a sentence fragment with 'And the people in the shoe-shop who were making my marching-boots.' (HC 148; cf. 9, 72, 82, and four times on 83), and his own rules barred 'It was of course distinctly possible that' (HC 119; cf. 75, 149, 196) as a 'verbal false limb' (CE 4.130), along with 'It hardly needs pointing out that' and 'This is due to the fact that' (RW 170, 205). The same rules included 'Never use the passive where you can use the active,' but Orwell used both impersonal and passive ('It was noticed that', AF 58) and piled passive on passive ('the food was thrown away from deliberate policy, rather than that it should be given to the tramps,' PL 197; cf. CE 1.183); the quotations from Orwell throughout this book illustrate the prevailing passivity of his style. Though he mocked the 'not un-' construction (CE 4.138) he wrote 'a not unfriendly grin' (HC 142) and 'it was not difficult for any person well grounded in *doublethink* to avoid doing this' (NE 255). He also wrote (in a letter) 'As for the sort of thing we shall find ourselves doing, the way I see the situation is like this' (CE 1.386).

In 'what it's all about' (CA 166) Orwell employed a common phrase that, if not actually an 'exhausted idiom' (CE 4.137), was too far gone for precision, though it endures in English, including some of the best. Aldous Huxley had written 'You can't learn a science unless you know what it's all about' (*Brave New World* [1932], ch. 2); fifty years later, *Guardian* readers could still encounter 'that is what Jabotinsky wanted and what revisionism is all about.' Yet Lord

Airedale thought the phrase a 'piece of flannel' (HL 169). The allegiance of 'all' is the issue. When the verb is transitive 'all' clearly goes with the object ('The book tells you all about grammar'). The ambiguity arises with a linking verb ('The book is all about grammar'), for the sentence may mean 'The entire book is about grammar' (though perhaps it omits some aspects of the topic) or 'The book contains everything about grammar' (and perhaps some of it is on other topics). 'That's what friendly skies are all about' may convey 'That's what the phrase "friendly skies" means,' but what is 'Lean is what pork's all about' all about? A writer who stumbles over 'a totally different person' should come to a full halt over 'all about'. 'All about' is, however, neither 'wrong' nor 'stupid' but, like 'entirely different', idiomatic in English.

None of these flaws is a rarity in Orwell. None is culpable glottocide, either. Orwell criticized others for such superficialities, however, and he felt strongly about prose style, so his own practice reasserts the realities of the writer's task and provides – not deviation from his 'rules' – but stimulating models for problem-solving. Yet he has received credit for much more. Conor Cruise O'Brien said of him that 'He was, both by precept and example, a great cleanser of the English language, and a great teacher of younger writers of English prose.' George Steiner found reason to agree that 'Political sanity, the ability of a community to view and communicate issues clearly, are closely dependent on the integrity of syntax,' commending the 'set of rules for lucid writing' and especially the sixth with which Orwell 'concludes splendidly'.[7] O'Brien and Steiner did not build their reputations on such unexamined and unexplained opinions as those.

Some doubts, all the same, accompanied the plaudits. In the year of Orwell's death E.M. Forster wrote

> He was passionate over the purity of prose, and in another essay he tears to bits some passages of contemporary writing. It is a dangerous game – the contemporaries can always retort – but it ought to be played, for if prose decays, thought decays and all the finer roads of communication are broken. . . . Many critics besides Orwell are fighting for the purity of prose and deriding officialese, but . . . [h]e is unique in being immensely serious, and in connecting good prose with liberty. Like most of us, he does not define liberty. . . . He gives six rules for clear writing, and they are not bad ones.[8]

The 'rules', however, did not prevent Forster from using a vague demonstrative pronoun as the subject of a passive verb in 'This was successfully done a few years ago' even while he praised Orwell's passion for pure prose. If the 'Politics' essay did not rescue the sympathetic and skilful Forster from such a sentence, how will it help lesser writers? Yet as recently as 1982 the *New Yorker* (16 August, p. 21) armed itself with 'Politics and the English Language' to attack the Reagan administration's 'euphemism, question-begging, and sheer cloudy vagueness' as though no one before Orwell or since had noticed such things – as though Orwell himself, or his votaries, had never employed them.

Perhaps Forster was hinting as much; his claims for Orwell were modest enough. Quirk had even stronger reservations about 'the undue reverence in which [Orwell] is held as a serious thinker on social and linguistic matters,' but he went on to allow that

It is indeed not so much the quality or originality of his writing upon language . . . as the fact that the journalist in him, the artist in him, seized upon the tenor of thought around him and articulated it into imaginatively arresting and memorable form.[9]

It remained for McNelly to show that even for tyros, however, whose need is greatest, Orwell's essays, and this one in particular, 'are prime examples . . . of how *not* to teach composition.' [10] For though Orwell is 'taught' to the very students whose cause he championed, 'working-class, minority, and even middle-class students whose training has simply not prepared them for written communication', it is these 'new students' in particular who find Orwell 'dull', 'cold', 'boring' or – worse – 'unclear' when they confront 'Politics and the English Language' in a composition class. Their reaction is valid; as Howe pointed out, Orwell's 'casual' style is neither 'natural' nor especially 'simple': its manner masks a complexity that makes him a poor model for 'plain' writing. In addition, his assumptions about language leave his success as a writer unexplained, because his assumptions are false although his success is real. Finally, the people he wrote about are not for the most part the people he wrote to, and the 'new students' do not recognize themselves in his audience. He addressed people who had learned to write badly; these students have never learned to write at all.[11]

So, for example, Orwell's assault on clichés and bureaucratic formulas ignores the utility of both for neophyte writers. His very first sentence has subtleties the beginner can hardly recognize, much less emulate: the carefully controlled point of view contrasting 'Most people' with 'we', the casual tone of 'bother . . . at all' and 'in a bad way' with the more formal (as though in stuffy reported speech) 'generally assumed', 'conscious action'. McNelly concludes that the opening sentences of the essay are less a 'windowpane' than 'a special-angle lens'. They are also, by Orwell's own six rules, apparently a failure: they contravene number 4 and, arguably, numbers 2 and 3. But they are *not* a failure. The student who overlooks that contradiction is missing the heart of the matter; the student who spots it is risking confusion.

The six rules are not for freshman composition students. McNelly tabulates their shortcomings:

1. The student is not used to 'seeing', much less identifying, figures of speech in print; and the transition from a 'live' to a 'dead' metaphor is not a simple one, the same for every audience.
2. The writing beginner rarely has the versatility to substitute a short word for a long one at will; the versatility will come, slowly, with the practice of exchanging long for short as well as short for long.
3. The first obstacle for new writing students is lack of fluency. They need to expand, not contract, their exposition.
4. 'Not a bad one', but Orwell's prose is a poor example; and 'Do as I say, not as I do,' encourages student cynicism.
5. Same drawbacks as no. 1: the status and even the legitimate use of foreign and scientific words, and many jargon words too, are not self-evident to the inexperienced writer.
6. Despite Steiner's warm endorsement of this rule, it is misleading in ways about which McNelly deserves direct quotation:

> This is charming and clever. Unfortunately, the acquisition of middle class and written codes of language is often a matter of some importance in the lives of the students we teach, as it bears directly on their ability to survive. . . . Their problem is that they do not know what sounds 'outright barbarous' especially to middle class, well-educated ears. Orwell's easy flippancy here can only offend in tone, while returning us to square one in content, since again it does not teach but simply presumes the code. (pp. 557–8)

Orwell's rule 'Never use a passive where you can use an active' is an example. Even the stringent McNelly praised it, but 'where you can use an active' assumes a sophisticated judgment. The passive voice illustrates the difference between grammatical and rhetorical features; it is perfectly grammatical, so its shortcomings are merely its wordiness and its potential 'irresponsibility' in sentences where the agent of the verb, the one responsible for its action, goes unexpressed. The Fowlers touched only on the compound passive in their discussion, and habitually used the simple passive without embarrassment. Orwell himself opened the 'Politics' essay with 'it is generally assumed', and gravely noted that 'the passive voice is wherever possible used in preference to the active.' Most readers would judge that here, of all places, he could have used an active verb, but that is only a judgment, not a rule. If the passive voice 'corrupts' the English language at all, it corrupts only the effectiveness of the English that overuses it and not the resources of English as a whole.

The same strictures apply to the somewhat different checklist earlier in the 'Politics' essay (CE 4.135): like the six rules, they address middle-class writing problems. Both guidelines ignore the realities of working-class language problems and the working-class need to solve them. McNelly concludes, 'To be "like Orwell" even for purposes of a composition, is for most students to objectify, reify and speak "down" to the very class from which they come.' The two classes, and the writing problems that enmesh them, are different. They are also real, but to follow Orwell as 'by precept and example, a great cleanser of the English language, and a great teacher of younger writers of English prose', is to venture down a tangled garden path.

Orwell's advice is frequently unrealistic even for more experienced writers. He was convinced that the euphemistic style is inflated and that simple English ensures honesty because 'when you make a stupid remark its stupidity will be obvious, even to yourself.' Much euphemism, however, is quite simple and uninflated. Advertisements that entice the reader to 'Explore [or 'discover' or 'experience'] 10,000 square feet of bargain furniture' are euphemistic; they seek to invest the commonplace with an aura of exploration, discovery, and experience. They are stupid and misleading, although, like most euphemisms, they have rapidly lost most of their intended effect. But they are not inflated; they couldn't be simpler, so simplification won't reveal anything much about their folly. The same is true of Orwell's concern over 'pretentious diction'. In present-day diction a second, abstract noun often follows a more concrete and usually self-sufficient first noun: 'cloudy conditions', 'work flow', 'safety factor', 'diet programme' replace the simpler 'clouds' or 'cloudy skies', 'work', 'safety', and 'diet'. That is a real flaw, but superficial. An attack on it, though easy, will not do much to improve writing, and it can scarcely hope to assist 'the English language', since the 'pretentious' phrases contain grammatical pairings of good English words. A grammatically sound statement like 'With all the immigration, crime is rising' misleads because it implies causality though it asserts only co-occurence. We live in the computer age when anything produced is a 'computer-age product' even if computers had no part in its design and manufacture. Even unpretentious diction can be false: 'All cats have three legs' adheres perfectly to Orwell's rules. Language is a closed system, not a reflex of the world it refers to; so falsehoods abuse the audience, not the language.

The rationale of Orwell's essay is not the pet peeves it catalogues or the rules it lays down, however, but his theories of meaning and of the connection between language and society. He said 'What is above all needed is to let the meaning choose the word.' Yet Quiller-Couch knew 'you cannot use the briefest, the humblest process of thought . . . . without forecasting it to yourself in some form of words. Words are, in fine, the only currency in which we can exchange thought even with ourselves' (p. 28).

Orwell's second important theory was that

> When the general atmosphere is bad, language must suffer. I should expect to find – this is a guess which I have not sufficient knowledge to verify – that the German, Russian and Italian languages have all deteriorated in the last ten or fifteen years, as a result of dictatorship . . . [T]he present political chaos is connected with the decay of language, and . . . one can probably bring about some improvement by starting at the verbal end. If you simplify your English, you are freed from the worst follies of orthodoxy.
> (CE 4.137, 139)

This theory enabled him to make his boldest claims for language activism:

> Silly words and expressions have often disappeared, not through any evolutionary process but owing to the conscious action of a minority. Two recent examples were *explore every avenue* and *leave no stone unturned*, which were killed by the jeers of a few journalists.
> (CE 4.138)

(News of their death, we now see, was exaggerated.) And Orwell assumed that 'suffer', 'deteriorate', 'decay' and 'silly' have constant and self-evident meaning as linguistic descriptions, and that 'stale-ness of imagery' and 'lack of precision' (CE 4.129) are attributes of 'the English language'; but neither is the case. No linguist would claim to have 'sufficient knowledge' to verify 'deterioration' in a language; and it is the writer, not the English language, that either has or lacks imagery and precision. The theoretical basis for the 'Politics' essay, like its practical advice and like the theoretical basis for Orwell's other writing on language, turns out to be specious.[12]

The 'Politics' essay, finally, does not live up to its title: 'the English language' turns out to be only writing, not speech; only prose, not poetry; only exposition, not fiction. The boundaries within which Orwell waged his struggle were not co-extensive with 'the English language'. But their real subject, expository prose, is serious enough. This book is no place for a 'chamber of horrors' to supplement Orwell's; several available books and journals collect examples, and any reader can find unintentional collections in many others. This book is particularly no place for juicy examples of bad writing by beginners, students in schools and colleges, which only show what is already obvious: that students study what they need to learn, not what they already know. But Orwell's analysis, despite its shaky theoretical basis, provides an adequate framework for illustrating the undeniable problem of skimpy verbal skills and, especially, poor expository prose among those on whom students attempt to model their prose: administrators, journalists, even the teachers themselves.

What follows, then, is the 'catalogue of swindles and perversions' (CE 4.130–3) Orwell provided, with some earlier examples from Quiller-Couch, the Fowlers, and the SPE *Tracts*, and some later examples from the available books and journals, from the 1979 House of Lords debate, and from observation. The catalogue illustrates the age and persistence of these problems.

DYING METAPHORS

[Treated at length in SPE 11 ("E. B." et al, 1923) and 12 (Smith, 1923)]

Moribund metaphors

Orwell: 'stand shoulder to shoulder with'
Fowlers: 'go hand in hand with'
Guardian: 'emerged unscathed', 'the balance could tip'

Mixed metaphors

Orwell: 'The Fascist octopus has sung its swan song'

Fowlers: 'The scourge of tyranny has breathed its last'
SPE 11: 'Let the pendulum swing back to the old rut'
Guardian: 'the cream are treated by PER with kid gloves'
'to hive off this profit-making limb'
'in the wake of the shipbuilding and motor sectors'
'the Americans are spearheading the dumping of paper'
'the economic machine is running amok'

Misunderstood metaphors

Orwell: 'tow the line' for 'toe the line'
Fowlers: 'darken the door' for 'go out'
SPE 11: 'draw our net a little wider' (for 'cast . . .')
CBS Radio News: 'A tight security blanket was thrown around the entire nuclear station'

OPERATORS, OR VERBAL FALSE LIMBS
Phrase in place of a simple verb

Orwell: 'make contact with'
Fowlers: 'make [someone] the recipient of'
Guardian: 'made renewed claims'

Passive voice

Guardian: 'A total of 13 aircraft . . . are believed to have been blown up'
'confrontations . . . are hoped to be a thing of the past'
Radio Times: 'Instead of commissioning original designs . . . actual textile patterns . . . were used'
Lawyer's letter: 'At the request of Mr. ——, I have been requested. . . .'

not un-

Orwell: 'a not unsmall rabbit'
Quiller-Couch: 'not without interest'
Fowlers: 'not unconnected therewith'
Guardian: 'Not only is it unfair that women should not be equally represented on policy-making bodies . . . it is also unsound economics to fail to exploit fully the resource of talent. . . .'
HL 128: 'I do not think the decline which I believe has begun cannot be arrested'

Language Abuse

Phrase in place of simple conjunction or preposition

Orwell: 'with respect to, having regard to'
Quiller-Couch: 'with regard to, in respect of'
Fowlers: 'in the shape of the fact that'
Lawyer's letter: 'with regard to your inquiry regarding this matter'
HL 181: 'in this connection'

Commonplace tags

Orwell: 'a conclusion to which all of us would readily assent'
Quiller-Couch: 'but such is by no means the case'
Fowlers: 'will be the result of the same'
Lawyer's letter: 'If same is not the case'
HL 186: 'as it so often is today'

PRETENTIOUS DICTION

Air of scientific impartiality

Orwell: 'categorical, liquidate'
Quiller-Couch: 'the psychological moment, antibody'
HL 181: ' "parameter" . . . used to add a spurious ring of scientific
   accuracy' [and probably influenced by 'perimeter']

Euphemism

Orwell: 'elimination of unreliable elements'; 'a certain curtailment
   of the right to political opposition is an unavoidable concomitant'
Guardian: 'Mr Mugabe said one-party Government was necessary
   to unite the people. "We are one state with one society and one
   nation: One nation, one party, one leader – that's the type of
   political concept we cherish." '
Advertisement: 'Available at participating dealers' [i.e., you can
   get it only where you can get it]

Archaic language

Orwell: 'realm, jackboot'
Fowlers: 'perchance, anent'; 'wind-flower' for 'anemone'
SPE 12: 'bounden duty, bended knee'
Guardian: 'benchmark, watchdog, workshop'

The Language of 1984

Foreign words and expressions

Orwell: 'cul de sac, mutatis mutandis, status quo, Weltan-
schauung'
Quiller-Couch: 'de die in diem, cui bono'
Fowlers: 'tête-à-tête, status quo, Schadenfreude'
SPE 5: 'canaille, noblesse'; SPE 12: 'mutatis mutandis'
Crick: 'enfant terrible, sui generis, deus ex machina'

Latin and Greek words
(especially in scientific, political, and sociological writing)
Orwell: 'expedite, extraneous'; 'antirrhinum' for 'snap-dragon'
[cf. 'wind-flower']
Quiller-Couch: 'envisage, adumbrate'
Fowlers: 'emblemed, envisaged'
An Air Force General: 'the diversion of military-training aircraft
to provide opportune airlift capacity is one method to optimize
these assists' (quoted in *Quarterly Review of Doublespeak*,
November 1981, p. 1; the aircraft had flown bowlers to a tournament)
Lawyer's letter: 'Initially, let me preface my comments by indicat-
ing to you that. . . .'
HL 126: 'many of us prefer to commence than to start, to donate
than to give'

MEANINGLESS WORDS
Point to no discoverable object, jargon

Orwell: 'plastic, values'
Quiller-Couch: 'case, instance, nature, condition'
Fowlers: 'case, question'
HL 127: 'capability'; 158 'ongoing'

Abuse of political words

Orwell: 'Fascism, democracy', etc., as value words
HL 133: 'unblushing use of jargon wherever that can assist
evasion. . . . words like "capitalism", "socialist" and "bour-
geois" '; 136 'Marxism was at one time not an abstract noun, but
now it is'

Language Abuse

Inept constructions

Orwell: 'I am not, indeed, sure whether it is not true to say that the Milton who once seemed not unlike. . . .'

Fowlers: 'I do not of course deny that in this . . . there may not be found . . . exceptional cases'

Guardian: 'How that crucial issue is handled by the islanders will provide an indicator of how harmonious relations will be with the troops'

US State Department: 'artillery that deploys a cluster concept similar to cluster bombs'

Insurance policy: 'This policy does not cover . . . operating or flying in any aircraft not owned, leased, or operated by a covered person or the policy holder except as a passenger'

Usage

Orwell: 'egregious' to mean (?) 'inept'

Fowlers: 'recrudescence' to mean (?) 'resurrection'

Furniture advertisement: 'Unparalleled uniqueness'

Guardian: 'This has acquired a totem significance'

'The society is the doyen of all the bodies interested in Scottish country dancing'

Most of these examples, including the recent ones, are unspectacular. They do not rank with the great howlers of the medium. Bad prose is not usually so far-fetched. Bad prose, inappropriate prose, is the sum of ineptitude and misjudgment about the everyday complexities of language, many of which have already occupied the attention of these pages. Shakespeare used 'perchance', now an archaism: 'To sleep, perchance to dream.' What was good enough for Shakespeare, some might argue, ought to be good enough for us (' "English is good enough for me," said the taximan. "It was the tongue of Shakespeare," said Gordon,' KA 157). But 'perhaps' has superseded 'perchance' in present-day English, even though 'perhaps' is a mixture of one French word and one English word, neither now current in English, while 'perchance' is composed of two French words, one still current as the noun 'chance'. That noun has spawned two verbs, one intransitive and one transitive; yet while the intransitive verb is suitable only for the most formal written prose ('I chanced upon a letter from the dean'), the transitive verb is distinctly colloquial ('Let's chance it'). 'Chance', in several different English words and parts of speech, some obsolete and some current, some colloquial and some quite formal, is part of the language community's repertoire. Present-day discussions of English often focus on usage and, because they deal with language one item at a time, make it seem a simple matter of right and wrong. As 'chance' shows, however, it is no such thing; instead it involves delicate judgments of medium, audience, and effect.

Orwell's examples are still with us; so are his views. As different a writer as the American James Thurber wrote of 'the smoke-screen phrases of the political terminologists' and 'My concern about the precarious state of the English language in the hands or on the tongues of politicians' (1961, pp. 119, 121–2). The politicians, he specified,

> have got through the twelve years since the war ended with only five adjectives of derogation: naive, hostile, unrealistic, complacent, and irresponsible. All these slither easily, if boggily, into bumblery, and the bumbler is spared the tedious exercising of his mental faculties.
> (1957, p. 23)

Thurber's tone here is not Orwell's, but the vast exaggeration ('only five') is like his, and so are the last eight words. Like Orwell too, Thurber resisted unwarranted neologisms: 'humature' and 'redesegregation', now harmlessly gone and forgotten, and the apparently useful and innocent 'additive' and 'automation' (1957, p. 21). One year's unwarranted neologisms, however, are another's useful terms: Thurber himself used 'automation' in 1961 (p. 43), apparently without satirical intent.

Thurber thought latinity a corrective for bad English, but he also thought that 'The present confused usage of "security" may have originated with the ancient Romans,' and he quoted *Cassell's Latin Dictionary* s.v. *securitas* to show the several distinct senses of the Latin word (1957, p. 21). Thurber did not show how he avoided the 'confused usage' other modern Americans shared with the ancient Romans. He sorrowed because Webster's Unabridged 'recognizes such mastadonisms [sic] as "psychologize" and . . . "analogize" ', and disagreed with Webster for its 'definition of "escapee" '; but elsewhere he sided with Webster, and demanded rhetorically 'who consults Webster for anything except definitions?' (1957, p. 24;

1961, pp. 46, 44). Thurber simply liked Webster when it supported his linguistic views and disliked it when it did not, a circular way of appealing to authority.

Thurber echoed Orwell when he complained that 'Sentences now run themselves, instead of being guided' (1961, p. 43), but his example was unfortunate: 'careless and reckless transition between the transitive and the intransitive . . . is a threat to meaning and clarity.' Yet such 'transitions' are common in the history of English and appear to pose no serious threat to anything. You can 'water' a horse or a lawn, for example, and you can 'milk' a cow or an audience: in the former you provide the liquid to the object of the verb, in the latter the object of the verb provides the liquid, literally or metaphorically, to you. That shade of difference leads to a more profound one: the verb 'water' can also be intransitive ('My eyes watered') but, at the moment, the verb 'milk' cannot. OED gives several examples of intransitive 'milk', but the latest is almost a century old now, and seems to have been technical usage, not common, even then; the non-technical senses are all pre-1600. On the other hand, some variations of transitivity are regional, not chronological. Even to a linguistically conservative British informant, 'It doesn't notice' (for 'It isn't noticeable') is acceptable, though Americans know 'notice' only as a transitive verb. America has a new transitive in 'a disease that deteriorates the bones' (where the formerly intransitive verb takes on the versatility of 'rot') and a new intransitive in 'the tape dispenses easily' (where the formerly transitive verb takes on the versatility of 'fold'). Because transitivity has always varied in time and space, the new versions are wholly intelligible; and they lead to even newer developments, such as printed instructions where the object of the verb is the product on which the sentence appears: 'Keep frozen until ready for use' (on frozen peas), 'Turn inside out and wash in warm water' (on a garment). No user has can possibly have misunderstood those imperatives, although a few may have had some amusement from them.

Thurber was again on Orwellian grounds when he complained

> To add to the unmeaningfulness of it all, there is the continual confusing contribution of the abbreviationists. . . . We shall have to have a special glossary, perhaps, to help us figure out 'Pea-Coex' and 'Ag-Reapp' and 'Mass-Retal.'
> (1961, p. 119)

Abbreviations like 'Inprecorr' and 'Agitprop' (NE 252) were the beginning of Newspeak, but their outcome has been nothing more sinister than, for example, a psych prof at Caltech. Thurber, who was almost blind in the last years of his life, was more sensitive than Orwell to changes in sound, for example 'opossum' in two syllables or 'evening' in three (1961, pp. 44–5). Yet both are so common in language that Greek had a word for the first, 'aphesis', and Sanskrit had a word for the second, 'svarabhakti'; familiar examples among standard English words are 'squire' (from 'esquire') and 'thunder' (from *thunr*).

Thurber's sensitivity to sounds tricked him into writing 'The conspiracy of yammer and merchandising against literate speech' (1957, p. 25). But 'literate' means 'lettered', 'able to read and write', hence 'educated'; 'literate speech' is an awkward extension at best. 'Illiterate', by the same token, means 'unlettered', 'unable to read and write'; by extension it can mean 'showing lack of culture, esp. in language and literature' (RCD). As a mere pejorative for usage, it leaves the language unequipped to name the serious and widespread inability to read and write. When a spy novel referred to 'An NKVD agent . . . surveilling Nazis', the *New Yorker*'s critic called the writing 'illiterate' (16 August 1982, p. 94), presumably for making a verb out of the noun 'surveillance'. But English 'surveillance' comes from French, where it is a noun derived from the verb *surveiller*; the English verb from either the English noun or the French verb must be 'surveille'. The novelist did not, after all, employ 'surveilling' to misprepresent the action, or in an unexampled sense, or in the wrong place, but merely in a form unprecedented in the reviewer's reading, and that surely does not make the *novelist* 'illiterate'. Sheppard announces that 'Literacy continues in its parlous state' (Thurber's 'precarious state of the English language').[13] He might enhance his own literacy, however, by study of 'parlous' itself, a version of 'perilous' that changed one sound and lost another (as did, for example, 'varsity'). The language has assigned separate but equal roles to the two versions. Yet 'parlous', though standard enough for Sheppard, embodies just the kind of sound-changes that riled Thurber.

John Simon subtitled his book on English 'Reflections on Literacy and its Decline'.[14] The word 'literacy', however, does not appear in his index, nor do 'reading' and 'writing'. The book is not about literacy, but usage. It is not a 'book', either, except as a physical object; as a literary composition it is a collection of his magazine columns. For discussions of language, the difference is important. Journalistic treatment of language, whether Orwell's or Simon's, Howard's or Safire's, is confined to the range from the trivial to the demagogic because popular assumptions about language, though strongly held, are more often wrong than right, and because a columnist does not have room to start from basics. Like the *New Yorker* reviewer, Simon gives clear examples of what he does not like but no statement of what language is, what it ought to be, how he knows or how anyone else can learn. His criticism is merely negative:

> The English language is being treated nowadays exactly as slave traders once handled the merchandise in their slave ships, or as the inmates of concentration camps were dealt with by their Nazi jailers

he opens the chapter 'Word Crimes at the *Times*' (p. 97). Doubleplusungood. Simon reifies 'the English language' as an undifferentiated physical object; he turns his (rather extreme) comparison into a (wholly insupportable) description with 'exactly'; and he botches the parallel construction by shifting from passive voice ('is being treated') to active ('slave traders once handled the merchandise') and back to passive ('inmates . . . were dealt with'). A century ago he would also have received bad marks for the progressive passive 'is being treated', but standards in such matters change.[15]

This fairly typical chapter continues for several pages of jousting at eminent targets: Robert Brustein, whom Simon calls 'the distinguished drama critic, dean of the Yale Drama School, and director of the Yale Repertory Theater', makes a blunder in 'grammar' for using 'mutual' of more than two groups, for '*Mutual* means that A is or does to B as B is or does to A; it does not mean that A is or does to C as B is or does to C.' Simon does not credit the source for his virtuoso definition, Fowler's *Modern English Usage*, which however chooses the other end of the alphabet ('x is or does to y,' etc.) and adds that 'mutual' 'was formerly used much more loosely than it now is.' Neither Simon nor Fowler says how the 'loose' usage came to tighten up – when, or by whose authority – although that might be a crucially interesting point; and Simon does not say why this is a matter of 'grammar', how Brustein can be 'distinguished' if he employs loose usage, or how the usage can be loose if distinguished people employ it.

Simon says (p. 169) that 'chair' is a 'ghastly coinage for chairman!' His 'ghastly' is on a par with Orwell's 'disgusting', which Simon elsewhere (p. 27) applies to 'chairperson': it tells us about him but not about the word. As it happens, a linguistic 'coinage' is an invention, not – as it is here – a contraction of an existing word or an extension of meaning. 'Chair' for 'chairman' is no odder than 'bench' for 'judge' or 'throne' for 'monarch', and it has wide acceptance: the McGraw-Hill Book Company guidelines (1975), for example, suggest 'presiding officer; the chair; chairperson' for 'chairman',[16] and 'The chair recognizes . . .' is good parliamentary usage. Simon's objection is not really linguistic, though his language purism camouflages what comes down to his social conservatism, a strategem Orwell long ago identified in others even though he practised it himself. Social distance, however, often gives the necessary insight: most Americans have long overlooked what the McGraw-Hill guidelines point out, that 'Logically co-ed should refer to any student at a coeducational college or university. Since it does not, it is a sexist term' (p. 69); but Americans easily place the British Chief Constable who increased minority representation on his force by adding more 'coloured boys'.

Tony Benn, in terms that Orwell would have endorsed, points out the same real but unacknowledged social bias in the language of reporters:

> Unions always 'demand' and 'threaten', management always 'offers' and 'pleads'. Pause for a moment to consider the impact of that language.
>
> Or, put it the other way round. . . . You could say that the trade unions are 'offering' to work for eight per cent when inflation is 10 per cent, and 'pleading' with their management not to cut their real wages, and management are 'demanding' they work for five per cent, and 'threatening' to sack them if they don't. Now, it does make a difference how you use the language, but we take this so naturally. . . .
> (*Guardian*, 28 July 1982, p. 14)

Simon takes such things very naturally indeed.

Simon admires some writers, however, even though the Dean of the Yale Drama School is not among them. They include Arn and Charlene Tibbetts, who 'collect horrors of this kind: nouns turned into adjectives, as when *engineering* jobs become *engineer* jobs . . .' (p. 3).[17] English adjectives regularly come from nouns (e.g., 'key'), and 'engineering' has a history that includes many conversions: Latin noun *ingenium* (kin of our 'ingenuity') > verb *ingeniare* 'to contrive' > noun *ingeniator* 'contriver' > Old French noun *engigneor* > Middle English noun 'enginer' > verb 'engineer' > noun 'engineering'; even if 'engineer' were really an adjective, nothing in the word's history would make such conversion a 'horror'. But in this example (taken from a headline) 'engineer' is not an adjective; you may hold 'a very key engineer job' but not * 'a very engineer key job'. 'Engineer' is a noun adjunct – it differs from 'engineering' only in being a concrete noun, not abstract. Therein lies a moral. Many of .the language critics boast imposing credentials as polyglots, journalists, English professors. The Tibbetts list their credits in their preface, and very impressive they are. So much, however, for credentials; a mistake from an English professor, even from two, even in print, is a mistake all the same.[18]

The Simonizers are negative, then, and inaccurate; they also argue evasively, often by comparison. They write of 'corruption of language' (*passim*); 'pollution of language' (Bush 1972, p. 238; Sheppard 1980, p. 72); 'Playing Tennis Without a Net' (title of a Simon article, pp. 163–9; cf. 'tennis requires a net,' Bush p. 239); 'cancerous grammar' (ib., p. 242); 'The carcinomenclature of our time' (Thurber 1957, p. 19); 'champions of good English' (Bush p. 239); 'holding back the tide of illiteracy' (ib., p. 240); even that 'Gresham's law operates no less in the linguistic than in the monetary sphere' (ib., p. 239); 'There is a Gresham's Law for language as well as economics' (Howard 1980, p. 140). Comparisons do not assist argument, even illustration, about language, however, because language isn't much like anything else.

The Simon-purists also like slogans. Schlesinger's essay 'Politics and the American Language' ends with several pages of almost solid slogans: 'Politics in basic aspects is a symbolic and therefore a linguistic phenomenon' is not an argument or a demonstration, it is a rather awkward slogan; 'The time is ripe to sweep the language-field of American politics,' 'But writers and teachers have, if anyone has, the custodianship of the language. Their charge is to protect the words by which they live,' 'Each venture is therefore the new beginning, the raid on the inarticulate with shabby equipment always deteriorating in the general mess of imprecision of feeling,' etc, etc.

The Simoniacs' affection for slogans extends to the adjectives they bestow on themselves and their adversaries, like 'purist' and 'permissive' respectively: 'advertising men . . . take advantage of all the slur and sloppiness, because when purists object, it simply serves to spread the news of a product advertised in lousy English' (Thurber 1961, p. 44). But 'pure' is not a good word for their criticism, and 'permissive' implies an alternative to 'permitting' users their own language. Only very rare instances – English quizzes, for example – offer any such alternative. Simon may criticize Brustein's 'mutual', but he will still have to permit it. Much the same reservations apply to 'acceptable': the bully-boy bluster of 'That diction is not acceptable' begs all the important questions.

The purists have a rich, if not pure, vocabulary of pejoration – the subject of language abuse seems to make them abusive. Sheppard's complaint that a new novel 'frequently reads as if translated from the Albanian' recalls Orwell's that 'Marxist writing . . . consists largely of words and phrases translated from Russian, German or French' (CE 4.131–2), but Sheppard goes on that the book 'is littered with grammatical outrage and wrong usage', which turn out to be misapplication of 'which' and 'that' and split infinitives. This 'decline in standards' came about because 'it was considered elitist to teach proper English', and so 'You get people coming out of top-rated schools who don't know how to put a sentence together'. Therefore Johnny can't write.[19] He can't, because 'the U.S. educational system is spawning a generation of semiliterates', 'seriously deficient when it comes to organizing their thoughts on paper' because of their 'inadequate grounding in the basics of syntax, structure and style', a favourite recipe that Sheils's article returns to in the form 'grammar, structure and style', though without saying what those basics are. It does, however, quote a prep school 'Writer's Guide' that lists 'What Not to Do'. A 'semiliterate' could doubtless use guidance about how to write before facing the niceties of how not to write.

Despite the educational failings it lists, Sheils's article retains touching faith in credentialist formal education. It complains that some aspirants to high-school English teaching go through every educational level 'without taking a single course in English composition', as though any course by that name, no matter what it contains, will enhance their professional capacity; and it reveals that half the applicants for English-teaching jobs in one county 'fail a basic test of grammar, punctuation and spelling', as though any test, no matter who defines 'basic', will be an objective and relevant measure. Yet if it contains 'chance' and 'additive', 'parlous' and 'mutual', the test will confuse what it was designed to clarify.

The issue, however, is larger than that:

> there have to be some fixed rules, however tedious, if the codes of human communication are to remain decipherable. If the written language is placed at the mercy of every new colloquialism and if every fresh dialect

demands and gets equal sway, then we will soon find ourselves back in
Babel.
(Sheils 1975, p. 65)

The tedious fixed rules of some writing teachers would censure the
weak and wordy 'there have to be', the passive 'is placed', and the
future plural 'we will' (instead of 'we shall'). But these quibbles are
not worthy of the article's grand theme. More to the point, the
English-speaking world had no real grammar book or dictionary
until Chaucer, Shakespeare, and Milton had come and gone, but it
remains the English-speaking world. The writer's prediction here is
one not even Orwell would have endorsed: it was, after all, uniformity and not variety that he feared in a future English.[20]

The language critics' view of the past is just as foggy; for them,
English – usually called 'our language' with its custodial overtones
tinged with delusions of persecution – has passed a Darwinian test:
'In the past, new words, new meanings, and new idioms had of
necessity to undergo a period of probation; if they proved useful,
they survived to enrich and refine the language' (Bush 1972, p. 245).
It will lose this evolutionary strength in a permissive environment, so
'those who care have a duty to resist. Changes that occur against such
resistance are tested changes. The language is better for them – and
for the resistance.' [21] These remarkable theories reflect no evidence
whatsoever, which may be why they adduce none. They are poetic
offshoots of the organic analogy; the Darwinian fallacy is necessary
for the defence of standard English despite the evidence of language
change, and for the attack on all other varieties as 'degenerate'. But it
does not explain the authorities' disagreement over the taxonomy of
standard, the only variety that has received careful and protracted
study. The organic analogy lends itself to doomsday diatribes about
Modern English: 'The English language is dying, because it is not
taught'; [22] 'Language is not a tough plant that always grows toward
the sun, regardless of weeds and trampling feet' (Bush 1972, p. 244);
'Language must be protected not only by poets but by the saving
remnant of people who care – even though, as the flood rises, their
role may be nearer King Canute's than Noah's' (ib., p. 247); 'They
have untuned the string, made a sop of the solid structure of English,
and encouraged the language to eat up himself' (Macdonald 1962,
repr. p. 188); 'A living language is an expanding language, to be sure,
but care should take itself that the language does not crack like a dry
stick in the process, leaving us all miserably muddling in a monstrous

miasma of mindless and meaningless mumbling' (Thurber 1961, p. 47; cf. 45, 1957 p. 19).

The henny-penny school of language critics can point to objective measures of English competency such as the Admissions Testing Program (ATP) of the College Entrance Examination Board: it includes the Verbal Aptitude Test, the Test of Standard Written English (TSWE), and the English Composition Test, among other papers. The 1981 report contained the results for about 1.4 million college-bound highschool students, as did the 1967 report; that number had not changed much. But other numbers did change: the average Verbal Aptitude Test score was down from 466 in 1967 to 424 in 1981. The TSWE, given since 1975, had declined from a mean for seniors of 43.1 to 41.5 in 1981. But other figures are as much part of the index as these. The Mathematical Aptitude Test scores had also fallen, from an average 492 to 466, during the 1967–1981 period when the Verbal scores were falling. The proportion of minority students increased eleven per cent in the decade up to 1982. Expected parental contribution to college costs correlated closely with the student's Aptitude Test average: high contribution (well-off parents) tended to go with good scores, and the reverse. The Achievement Test scores actually improved; Composition is an Achievement Test and its mean for all grades rose from 514 in 1967 to 520 in 1982 (the Mathematics Level 1 scores also rose during the same period). The Board commented,

> Because the number of students taking the Achievement Tests has declined by one-third since 1973, the increase in the average score may be attributed to the self-selected nature of this group who submit these scores for admission to the more selective colleges and universities.[23]

The Aptitude Tests, on the other hand, where the scores fell so badly, reflect student ability and general preparation rather than achievement in a specific subject. They correlate closely with financial background, and students from poor backgrounds have comprised an increasing proportion of those taking the test. Sheils finds the complicity of TV in this crime unclear, and admits that Mark Twain had similar complaints a century earlier 'when only 7 per cent of the population managed to earn high-school diplomas' (p. 59). The far larger numbers who now receive diplomas naturally do not have the elite qualifications of their forebears. So the decline in the Verbal and TSWE scores, though it appears to quantify the impression of an ailing English language, actually reflects the growing proportion of poor and minority students in the ATP. If social and racial inequality is to end, these students will have to take part in the program; but it has not yet ended, so their scores for the time being will reflect the limited opportunities in their school and family background. Those are genuine problems, problems that school and college English teachers will have to deal with, but they are not symptoms of decline in the language.

The critics' panacea for the problem of poor writing is 'grammar': 'Schools neglect the rigors of grammar, and the last generation that can parse a sentence is dying off' (Sheppard 1980, p. 72). Commercial interests have competed to peddle this cure-all. A 1982 leaflet heralded the *Dictionary of Problem Words and Expressions*,

> Speak and write with greater confidence, fewer errors, more genuine communication! This handy guide singles out and discusses 1,500 of the most common language errors – and gives you examples of both correct and incorrect usage. Also spotlighted are more than 1,000 of the most overused, inexact, trite, and slangy words and expressions you should avoid.

The copywriter seems not to have used the book, to judge by the language of the advertisement. Another ad, this one for The Newsweek Language Arts Program, promised as a bonus 'a full-color wall display which helps students identify and correct common errors in usage' with the additional incentive 'remember – you're starting off with a very big <u>motivational advantage</u>, compared to most other programs of this nature.' Such a wall-chart might, if sufficiently concerned with common errors in usage, correct 'which helps' (to 'that helps', because it is a restrictive clause), and 'compared to' (to 'compared with', because 'compare' here means 'contrast', not 'liken').

Such concern motivated *The American Heritage Dictionary of the English Language* to provide, for some selected 'problem' words, the guidance of a Usage Panel (mostly white male senior citizens).[24] But the panelists raise more problems than they solve: fifty-four per cent accept 'which' to begin a restrictive clause, but only about thirty per cent accept 'compare to' as 'contrast'. The Newsweek Language Arts Program ad loses the split decision. The student, meanwhile, or the teacher, seeking a sure command of 'correct usage', may well wonder where to find it, or whether 'greater confidence' is not after all just a confidence trick.

For 'grammar', it turns out, means very different things to different people. It can provide names for the parts of speech and 'rules' such as those for 'that' and 'compare'. Or it can describe the features of a language, including its sounds, word-formation, and sentence-structure. The first is a study; you do not automatically learn the rules for 'that', even less the name for intransitive verbs, when you acquire your native language. The second may also be a study but usually isn't. In any case you cannot study either kind of grammar until you first acquire and internalize the systematic features of your language, because otherwise you could not read the books, understand the lectures, or answer the examination questions. Critics who say a writer 'knows no grammar' always mean the first kind. Yet neither sort gives much help in writing. The first enables you to avoid breaking the rules you learn, so long as you do not forget them; but the examples show that you can easily overlook or forget the very rule your reader cares most about, and the fragmented Usage Panel shows that your next reader will probably care little about that one but deeply about some other. Since the rules are almost entirely arbitrary, rote learning (and a measure of good luck) is your only hope. As the examples also show, you can write shoddy prose even when you are writing about the rules themselves.

Grammatical terminology can help with a few writing problems: it simplifies rhetorical techniques like parallelism because sentence elements are easier to match if you can label them. But the writing of professional linguists shows that learning about language is not the same thing as learning about writing:

> Before passing on to other matters, it is significant that we note here by way of summarization that as the Old English diphthongs were smoothed into monophthongs, new diphthongs developed in Middle English.[25]

The sentence has a dangling modifier; equates 'significant' with 'important'; uses 'summarization' for 'summary'; shifts from passive to active in otherwise parallel clauses; and is too wordy by half. The same book contains 'Comparatively few which have survived can be said to show what could be called in any way a regular development' (p. 208) – the first example is not an isolated lapse. And this writer is a professional linguist; so teaching either kind of grammar, experiments have shown and observation confirms, produces at best only students who know what you taught them. It does not produce students who can write.

Considerations like those do not hamper indignant letter-writers or the editors they write to. One wrote to a mass-circulation weekly,

> I think it is of paramount importance that the proper usage of the English language be mandatory on any television broadcast. It is disheartening to note the lack of grammar skills in today's youths, the terrible example of grammar usage set by television, and the amount of time the average young person devotes to television watching. . . .
>
> Certainly your publication is in a unique position to lead a campaign to elevate the standards of the language used on television. I hope that you acknowledge the problem and are able to find means of helping solve it. . . .

The editors (of *TV Guide*, 27 December 1980), as gracious as the editors of PC, acknowledged the problem but held it too big for them to solve alone:

> until . . . society starts doing a better job of inculcating proper language skills in young people, some of those young people will, as adults, become television performers who habitually mangle the language. And their corrupted version of our mother tongue will be passed along to yet another generation of viewers. . . .
>
> Only when we as a society start watching our language more carefully will we also be able to watch television without fear of exposure to shoddy grammar and usage.

Reader and editors agreed that 'grammar usage' and 'language skills' exist as determinate entities in nature, and that failure to inculcate them would lead to a mangled language, a 'corrupted version of our mother tongue', just as failure to innoculate the young will lead to twisted limbs. None wanted to raise the question '*whose* proper usage', '*what* standards'. Yet if propriety is to become mandatory on television, in classrooms or in society at large, that question will require an answer. In fact no answer to the problems of inadequate language skills can come from an appeal to 'grammar' that is unrealistic at best and harmfully exploitive at worst, collaborating with the classroom dictator and the commercial huckster.

Equally unrealistic is the neoclassic nostrum of strange bedfellows Orwell, Thurber and Bush, that would heal English grammar with Latin studies. The differences between the two languages are so great that little from one will enlighten the dark places of the other. A common complaint against modern English writers, for example, is their propensity to split the infinitive ('to loudly sing'). Sheppard listed the split infinitive as a symptom of the 'anything-goes school of writing' (1980, p. 70); Lord Ailesbury said it caused him 'anguish', and Lord Dunleath called it an 'abuse' and 'offensive' (HL 156, 180). The Latin infinitive is in one piece (e.g., *canere* 'to sing') and is unsplittable; so was the English infinitive a thousand years ago (*singan*). Those precedents may be the reason some condemn the splitting of the English infinitive today, but at any rate the modern construction is so unlike the Latin or Old English that even Bush says to split it is no error (1972, p. 239). Modern English articles, for another example, pose as we saw an intricate obstacle to many students of English as a second language; but Latin has no articles, definite or indefinite. Like formal grammar, Latin is an interesting study in itself but an inefficient way to study English or to improve English prose composition.

That is one conclusion of modern linguistics, and not surprisingly the language critics like to blame the problems of young writers on modern linguists. Professor Mario Pei divulges the linguists' credo:

> that one form of language is as good as another; that at the age of 5 anyone who is not deaf or idiotic has gained a full mastery of his language; that we must not try to correct or improve language, but must leave it alone; that the only language activity worthy of the name is speech on the colloquial, slangy, even illiterate plane; that writing is a secondary, unimportant activity.
> (Quoted in Sheils 1975, p. 58)

Simon is more succinct: 'the structural linguists . . . contend that "language is what is spoken by the people" and . . . that "language is a living thing, not something codified by pedantic scholars" ' (1980, pp. 100–1).

No one who has reached this point in this book could believe half of those assertions; Pei, who wrote a book called *Invitation to Linguistics*, surely knows better. Every group includes a few whackos, and linguistics is no exception. But linguists as a group hold that only in itself is 'one form of language as good as another'; for any particular purpose, as even the first weeks of an introductory sociolinguistics course point out, the user must skilfully choose appropriate forms of language from the community's repertoire. No linguist thinks that such skill, or familiarity with the repertoire, is fully mastered by the age of five, or twenty-five either. No linguist thinks that the phrase 'correct or improve language' means anything if it means language in general, but of course linguists are always polishing their own use of language and, as far as they are able, helping others polish theirs. Most linguists use 'colloquial' to indicate, not to modify 'speech', and use 'illiterate' only about reading and writing; and they know, as any candid observer does, that writing is indeed a secondary language activity. But even a glance at the literature of linguistics shows that linguists know writing is important. Linguists don't think that 'language is what is spoken by the people.' The people – all of them, including John Simon – speak *parole*; language is how they do it. And most linguists would disown a figurative statement like 'Language is a living thing' – it recalls the critics' sloganeering fallacies, especially the organic analogy. These outlandish, apparently deliberate, mis-statements of what linguists believe reflect critics seriously unsure of their own language theories.

The critics are equally unreliable about linguists' practice. Linguists do not approve of verbosity, stale metaphors, confusing or misleading sentences. Any linguist worthy of the name, like any other good teacher, will help a writing student avoid such errors. The writing process is linguistic in the sense that its medium is language; linguists made the study of literary language objective by replacing the impressionism of traditional stylistic commentary with concrete description. Their training should enable them to help writing students. They know more than some of their colleagues about research in writing, and they try to put their knowledge into classroom practice. They are realistic about language even though their realism, like most, is more complicated than the simplicities of Simon.

The views common to Simon and his think-alikes falsify the demanding realities of language and usage, and they are far more imprecise than the 'sloppiness' they so readily judge. They are impractical because they lack theoretical foundations. The standard English they champion was composed by the same processes that they condemn in other varieties. The expressive superiority (precision, versatility, elegance) they claim for the standard is a myth that reflects the social role of those for whom it is the native variety, not any inherent attributes of the variety. Their statements about the standard are often factually wrong, inconsistent, or both. Yet they pronounce these statements as though they were on a par with 'water runs downhill' or '$e=mc^2$'. They are not, and those who earn their living by making them are receiving money on false pretences. Their criticism is ill-informed, indiscriminate, and above all unconstructive; it abuses the large majority of English language users, and it renders language an unattractive subject to most of them. These are important drawbacks because writing is an important problem. Yet who, reading the negative criticism by Simon or his scissors-and-paste competitors, learns anything about how to write or how to teach writing?

Linguists know that a list of errors like Orwell's 'nevers' never taught anyone to write well. Writing requires a great many skills, best learned – like the skills of any other subject – one at a time in some deliberate order. The skill a writing lesson teaches is a new one that the student will master only by trial, error, correction and retrial. So the teacher's corrections should concentrate on the subject of that lesson, note errors left over from previous lessons, and simply ignore errors that will be the subject of future lessons, no matter how 'disgusting'. The pedagogical 'knife and fork job' that corrects all the errors on every paper wastes teacher time and student confidence, precious essentials of the process.

No one can teach tyros to write, but correction and suggestion can help them learn to revise their writing. The composition teacher, however, is not the only source for correction and suggestion. The student's own peers often know what sounds vague or wooden, sometimes even how to make it clear and fluent. The conventional approach, symbolized by the class that faces in one direction while the teacher faces in the other, polarizes an effort that should be cooperative. Though conventional objections to peer tuition grumble about 'The blind leading the blind', classroom experience shows that peers can really help revision. They also free the teacher to provide the help that peers can't.

Most writing tyros have difficulty in writing enough: a task, whether a class assignment or a personal letter, evokes only a tight paragraph or two, insufficient to accomplish anything worthwhile. The early efforts of such students should all aim for fluency, and attempts to correct surface features at this stage will simply shut off the flow. So the teacher should encourage amplification and specificity, development of the theme: Orwell's 'an enjoyable time was had by all present' (CE 3.26), for example, offers colourful opportunities. Some of this development will take place in brainstorming sessions away from the writing paper and typewriter, alone or with peers; some will be in free-writing sessions, mining the ore that will undergo smelting and refining before it is cast as the final paper. A later stage demands more sophistication: organization, argument. Here a subject or paragraph outline can help, but the traditional demand for an outline at the outset defeats the dynamics of the writing process.

At the final stage the writer edits the paper to accord with expected form, usage and documentation, putting the surface features in their proper place. It is mostly because of surface features that the English department regularly receives complaints that 'You haven't taught the students to write – just look at this history paper.' If the history teacher (or chemistry, etc.) assigns papers, however, and judges the results as writing, then the history teacher too is a writing teacher, committed to a role in the writing process at every step. Only irresponsible classroom tyrants abandon students to a frantic guessing game that culminates in the final paper with its unwritten subtitle, 'Is This What You Wanted?' The teacher should aid students to develop the topic, find the sources, draft and revise the paper, prepare the final copy. Those are history skills just as much as they are English skills; time devoted to them is not time taken away from history learning, for since writing is a form that thinking takes, students learn to think about history when they learn these writing skills.

Orwell called for 'plain, vigorous writing' (CE 4.66). In those terms or others, so do most people: in the Lords debate, the terms were 'conciseness and precision' (HL 125), 'clarity and vigour' (HL 177). Like 'proper English', the terms are not entirely objective, but they label a style that almost everyone agrees is desirable: plain, vigorous prose is the staple of communication. Then why is it so hard to write or to teach? Why is plain, vigorous prose so difficult that many students write some other kind? Most effects have several causes. For one thing, plain writing avoids the abstract in favour of the specific; the writer has to organize all that detail, and the essay falls victim to the old trees-and-woods problem. The vague, abstract style has no trees, so the student who adopts it does not have this problem.

Writing is not simply a student problem, however. It is a government problem and a business problem. The Carter administration's Executive Order 'Improving Government Regulations' included the provision that '[The responsible agency official should determine that] the regulation is written in plain English and is understandable to those who must comply with it.' [26] Several of the States have similar provisions, often as part of consumer protection laws. The provisions seem admirable, and most readers will agree that the 'plain English' section is a model of its subject. Attaining its goal is another matter, however, and human weakness is not the only reason.

Lord Ardwick, a newspaperman, recalled the time that

> the family income supplement was not being taken up by many people who were entitled to benefit from it. It was thought that they had failed to apply for benefit simply because they did not understand the forms that the Ministry had made available. . . .

That sounds like typical Ingsoc, but the matter is not so simple, as Lord Ardwick went on to say:

> The difficulties that the Government departments face are very real difficulties, especially if they are talking about a pension that is available. If they put it in popular language and put a foot wrong they could receive claims from people who were not strictly entitled to make them. So it is not an easy job. However, it can be done, provided there is the will to do it and provided they are willing to put in an immense amount of work and to have it supervised by very senior officials.
> (HL 178)

We live in a complicated world, and the adjustment of the plain style to complex subjects is hard work. That is another reason many people do not write it.

Orwell wrote about 'Bad writers, and especially scientific, political and sociological writers' (CE 4.131), and social scientists have certainly had to bear a great deal of calumny for their prose. Crick took a holier-than-thou stance towards his fellow political scientists when he wrote that Orwell's 'argument that liberty and good plain style go together influenced a whole generation of journalists but not, alas, students of the social sciences' (Crick 1980, p. 495); *Time* chimed in, 'the language of academics, especially those in the social sciences, seems to lead farther and farther into forests of meaninglessness' ('Can't Anyone', p. 35). Both claims lack any real evidence. Bad writing abounds, and the writing of others makes a handy scapegoat: if the others use unfamiliar vocabulary, so much the worse for them. But social science does not of itself contaminate the prose of its adepts, many of whom write very well about their complex subjects. A popular journal such as *Psychology Today* contains many articles that are better written than some of those in 'English' journals: Glenn Collins's 'The Good News about 1984' (Jan. 1979, pp. 34–48), though not much about Orwell, is otherwise a case in point.

Writing is also a business problem: Blundell put most of his article in his title, 'Confused, Overstuffed Corporate Prose Often Costs Firms Time – and Money'. In what was left he reported the work of writing consultants who hold seminars and workshops for corporate employees. Their workshop approach is not far-fetched – some echoes of Orwell's six rules are discernible – and its results are good: adults can learn to render complex subjects in plain prose, given the incentive and the teacher. They will have to, for computers often require written input, and the litigious 'eighties demand prose that makes complicated subjects legally comprehensible to their audience. Yet the nuclear engineers who wrote up the Three Mile Island explosion called it 'energetic disassembly'. They explained, confidentially, that they knew what an explosion was but they didn't want to lose their jobs. One writing consultant pointed out the moral: plain writing can be risky. Underlings write the way they do partly out of fear. 'Little men use big words. . . . This is cover-your-ass writing.' The House of Lords debate included this quotation from Gowers's *Plain Words*:

> When the official does not know his Minister's mind or his Minister does not know his own mind, or the Minister thinks it wiser not to speak his mind, the official must sometimes cover his utterance with a mist of vagueness.[27]
> (HL 192)

The impediments to plain writing, then, are several, and they are not superficial: the writer's uncertainty, the subject's complexity, the demands and the complications of plain writing itself. Many of the language critics write well, but they cannot share their ability because they limit their 'teaching' to destructive criticism of superficialities. Writing consultants fare better but only with corporate support, financial and motivational; they hardly touch the real scope of the problem. Government plain language regulations, however, if they are to have force, will require the prose equivalents of agricultural inspectors and farm agents to assess the quality of the produce and advise producers how to improve it. The recent history of bilingual education in the United States suggests that such largescale government intervention in English composition is not out of the question. Orwell wrote 'If you say to any thinking person "Let us form a society for the invention of new and subtler words", he will first of all object that it is the idea of a crank' (CE 2.7), and his Newspeak lexicographers were figures in a literary satire. The ideas no longer sound cranky or satirical. The idea of official regulation, whether from the House of Lords or from a local school board, is alive and well and touring the English-speaking world. If computer scientists now support it, it may become irresistible.

American expressions of the same notion often come in the critics' reaction to the NCTE 'students' right to their own language' statement (Butler 1974):

> Translated into plain English, this means: Because students neither speak nor write with clarity or precision, and cannot therefore think clearly or specifically, or concretely or objectively, these lucky students are to be granted the inestimable 'right' to ultimately have some absolute authority subjectively define reality for them. 'The question is,' as Humpty Dumpty said, 'which is to be master – that's all.' And the rest is silence. (Ferguson 1975, p. 453)

Ferguson's 'plain English' proves that vigorous prose is not a trait of those who insist on rules or wish to be rulers; and his quotation shows that the 'rules' he wants are not just those in a grammar book.

The case against the 'rules' lobby is strong: the facts of language variety and change refute them, as does the history of such efforts elsewhere. Linguists would obviously object, but they are not opinion-makers, and they are not united. Among them and others who know about language, or ought to – journalists and English professors – we find disagreement about fundamental matters next to which the Usage Panel's split over 'compare to/with' is revealed for the triviality it is. Language 'changes should be inaugurated from above' according to Harvard English professor emeritus Douglas Bush (p. 244); 'its best word-makers are the uneducated' according to British poet laureate Robert Bridges (SPE 1 [1919], p. 9). 'I think that English is gradually breaking up into unintelligible varieties' says OED editor Robert Burchfield (*Newsweek*, 15 November 1982, p. 103); 'We are in fact getting closer together' says British linguistics professor Geoffrey Leech (NY *Times*, 23 November 1980, p. 9). The 'informalities of the spoken word' are blurring with the 'formalities of written language' reports journalist R.Z. Sheppard (1980, p. 72); 'The difference is growing' in the view of Harvard linguistics professor emeritus Dwight Bolinger (1981, p. 8). These contradictions concern the basic views on which any sound approach to language, including writing, must depend. Fishman said that bilingual regulations have weak theoretical foundations; these disagreements show that regulation of English would be at least as shaky. But the theoretical gap has not slowed bilingual regulation, and it will not by itself deter the plain English movement in government, the Ann Arbor decision in the courts, and the credentialist agitation of poorly-informed critics from fostering the regulation of English-language teaching.

When journalists agree with Ministers of State, it is in support of regulation. Middleton wrote

> the future of the world depends upon an infinitely greater degree of sophistication . . ., and that sophistication requires that people communicate within a well-defined set of rules. Communication is difficult under the best of circumstances. Without rules it becomes next to impossible. (Middleton 1974, p. 110)

The first statement, except in the most general terms, is not self-evident – maybe we'd all get along better with far less communication. The second statement doesn't say what 'well-defined' covers, or who is to make the definition. Like so many of Orwell's on language, the statements sound plausible but won't hold up under scrutiny.

So too in her reply to the Lords debate, the Minister of State, Department of Education and Science, said

> It is . . . important to distinguish between those usages which can properly be called 'wrong' in matters of speech and those which are merely 'different'. . . . [P]eople have far more varied social and working lives, and in addition English is now a multi-national language and we ourselves are increasingly a multi-cultural nation.
> . . . To suggest therefore that we can attain a standard pattern of usage is surely unrealistic. . . . What I think there should be is a generally accepted usage which enables us to communicate beyond our immediate community and within our own country.
> (HL 192–3)

But such communication involves intelligibility less than impression management. 'Infer' and 'imply' (HL 188) do not confuse your audience; they know what you mean, and in the light of that knowledge react unfavourably to your choice. The remedy is not 'a well-defined set of rules' or even 'generally accepted usage', but a more versatile writer and a more knowledgeable audience.

Teachers can expand their students' versatility by showing them how to use the full range of vocabulary and structures in the community's repertoire. They can even interest some students in the study of language itself by pointing out its features and some of its history. They can, finally, lead their students through the writing process to the achievement of a plain, vigorous style, 'provided they are willing to put in an immense amount of work'. For writing is hard work: essayist John McPhee, a master of the 'natural' style, said 'Writing is so difficult that if a writer is looking at words on paper . . . it's damn difficult to resist them' (quoted in Sheppard 1980, p. 71), and Princeton professor Carlos Baker, biographer of Hemingway, said 'Learning to write is the hardest, most important thing any child does' (quoted in Sheils 1975, p. 61). A responsible list of writing course objectives would reveal the course for the challenge it is, the stiffest in the curriculum.

But the language critics have nothing so difficult, or so constructive, in view. Their objective is sufficiently clear in statements like Stafford's demand 'There has got to be an official language' or Ferguson's quotation ' "The question is, which is to be master." ' It is to establish, on the pretext of its inherent clarity and precision, one variety of English as one variety of religion is established in some countries: by appeal to historical revelation. Prose will not thrive, however, under regulation by an agency, board, or commission. Language arises in the mind, and the mind is individual. Regulation is not mind-expanding and it does not regard the individual. Plain, vigorous English prose, the staple of communication, can survive anything but that, the forerunner of Newspeak.

Notes

𝕾𝕾𝕾𝕾𝕾𝕾

PREFACE
1. Waltz 1982, p. 130.
2. I also include some material published outside the collections, e.g. in Crick 1980. For what *The Collected Essays, Journalism and Letters* contains and what it omits, see Meyers 1969, repr. pp. 374–5; Crick 1980, p. 384, n.

CHAPTER ONE
1. The *Doublespeak Dictionary* is by William Lambdin (1979); the *Quarterly Review of Doublespeak* is published by the Committee on Public Double-speak of the National Council of Teachers of English. See also Hammond 1982, pp. 175–6, 183; Rawson 1982. For the influence of Orwell's language ideas, see also Pryce-Jones 1971, p. 151; Hodge et al. 1979, pp. 6–7. Senator Harrison Williams, in the US Senate defence against his 'Abscam' conviction on 4 March 1982, called the use of hidden cameras and micro-phones '1984' techniques.
2. Rosenfeld 1950, repr. p. 170.
3. Jones 1971, p. 158.
4. Barnett 1962, p. 186; Schlesinger 1974, p. 559. But Lawler 1974, though he shares with Schlesinger a title that paraphrases Orwell, does not mention him; nor does Bolinger 1980, in common with many present-day profes-sional students of language, though his subject is like Orwell's. Safire does not mention Orwell in his 1980 book, but his 1983 article has Orwellian echoes:

> Words work best when they convey specific meanings, and work worst when they are laden with ambiguities and confusions. . . .
> Certainly the meaning of a word changes, and yes, it is silly to try to freeze a living, growing language. But it is useful to defend today's meaning from the encroachments of fuzziness. . . . In a thousand years, change will win, but if we do not fight change, there will not be much left to be changed.
> (p. 9)

5. Hampshire 1946, repr. p. 210; Ringbom 1973, p. 51. See also Elliott 1957, repr. pp. 339–40: Macdonald 1942, repr. pp. 191–3.
6. Woodcock 1946, repr. pp. 242–3; Sykes 1950, repr. p. 309; Rank 1977, pp. 159, 161.
7. Crick 1980, p. 467, says 'During 1944 he wrote one hundred and ten

reviews or short articles for the *Manchester Evening News*, *Tribune*, and the *Observer*, not counting many smaller journals.' Cf. Hammond 1982, pp. 258–9.

8. Rosenfeld 1950, repr. p. 171.

9. Atkins 1971, p. 308. Noam Chomsky, one of the few modern linguists to take note of Orwell, called *Homage to Catalonia* a 'brilliant book', but only for its political observations (1967, p. 141; cf. pp. 95, 144–6, 148).

10. Hodgart 1971, p. 142; Wilson 1954, repr. p. 319. Hammond 1982, p. 209, says Orwell's 'fascination with linguistics' was 'marked by a quiet erudition'. Trilling 1952, repr. 1982, p. 349, likened Orwell's concern for the English language to that of William Cobbett, nineteenth-century author of *Rural Rides* and *An English Grammar*.

11. Crick 1980, p. 111, gives a notion of Orwell's regime as a Classical Specialist at Eton. He also mentions (p. 153) the possibility that Orwell learned Karen, a language of Burma.

12. Stansky et al. 1972, p. 166. See also Aung 1971, pp. 28–9.

13. See SPE 22 (Paget, 1925) for a scientist's account of the relationship between larynx and language.

14. For psycholinguistics, including the Whorf hypothesis, see Slobin 1979; Steinberg 1982.

15. Orwell's treatise was less practical than SPE 31 (Smith, 1929) on 'Needed Words'. In his 'Notes on Jeremy Bentham's Attitude to Word-Creation, and Other Notes on Needed Words' appended to Smith's article (pp. 333–4), Wallas quoted Bentham's call for new words to represent new objects, and his belief that 'the stock of a man's ideas is limited and determined by the stock of the words which he finds at his command for giving expression to those ideas'. Maget et al. 1982 shows, however, that most actual 'new words' apply to objects, not ideas.

16. SPE 16 (Jespersen, 1924) shows the difference between formal logical procedures and linguistic processes. SPE 6 (Graves, 1921) shows the impossibility of a constant 1 : 1 between word and meaning.

17. Orwell did not claim to know German, and Fyvel 1950, repr. p. 379, said he 'had only a sketchy knowledge' of it; but he knew and used a rather old-fashioned English construction of the same 'four-and-twenty black-birds' type when he wrote of 'a man of about five-and-thirty' (NE 185). The Hindi here and later, from McGregor 1972, is a close literary kin of the colloquial Hindustani that Orwell learned.

18. Sound, up-to-date books on phonetics are Ladefoged 1981; Wolfram et al., 1982. For the larger linguistic context, see Smith et al. 1980, Chapter Six.

19. Wicker 1962. For the background of these ideas, see Köberl 1979; Quirk 1983. I should like to thank Professor Quirk for letting me see a copy of his paper before its publication, and thus materially aiding me in the preparation of this book. Hoggart thought Orwell's 'sense of the relations between language, thought and imagination was sometimes superficial' (1965, repr. p. 47), but Strachey admired 'his brilliant linguistic insights' and wondered 'if any of the contemporary school of linguistic philosophers have made a study of' the psycholinguistic assumptions of Newspeak, since its object 'is nothing less than the destruction of human reason by linguistic means' (1962, repr. pp. 61, 56), echoing Rahv's 'Newspeak is nothing less than a plot

against human consciousness' (1949, repr. 1982 p. 311).

20. For semantics see Palmer 1981.

21. The first English dictionary, about 130 small pages of large type, appeared in 1604. See Starnes et al. 1946.

22. See Denes et al. 1973, pp. 39–41.

23. See Lepschy 1982.

24. See Aarsleff 1982.

25. Mairet 1940, repr. p. 179; Howe 1950, repr. pp. 158–9.

CHAPTER TWO

1. Crick 1980, p. 376, does not accept the equation of Orwell with Bowling, especially in the matter of nostalgia.

2. Popkin 1954, repr. p. 322. Cf. Hammond 1982, p. 152.

3. For earlier proposals for an English language committee, see Bolton 1982, pp. 239–40.

4. Elyot applied both 'corrupte' and 'abuse' to language in 1531; quoted in SPE 65 (Craigie, 1946), p. 122. Compare *The Dictionary of Diseased English* (Hudson, 1977). Steiner 1969, repr. p. 369, observed that 'Orwell arrived at the conviction that language is a sort of organism, that is has its own strength of being, that it can be damaged or destroyed.' Steiner rightly goes on to connect this conviction with the remainder of Orwell's political and literary views, but he does not find anything wrong with it.

5. The form of Orwell's quotation differs from that of modern editions which, at least since Skeat (1894), have read 'O hateful harm. . . .' Orwell's reading is the same as that of Thomas Tyrwhitt (1775–8), reprinted in 1861 and followed by several nineteenth-century editions, e.g. Routledge's (1874). Elliott 1957, repr. p. 339, thought Orwell 'displayed an abysmal ignorance of the Middle Ages, about which he often repeated the eighteenth-century clichés'. Orwell's eighteenth-century sources may be among the reasons.

6. OED s.v. 'woodwall'. (The *Shorter Oxford Dictionary* gives much the same definition without the citation.) The bird is a 'woodweele' in his source, Francis James Child, ed. *The English and Scottish Popular Ballads* (1886–98), III.91.

7. German for 'Newspeak' is *Neusprache*, not *Neuspreche*; see Weinrich 1974.

8. SPE 9 (Bridges, 1922), pp. 20–2, takes a descriptive view of 'the poverty of English accidence', that is its relative lack of distinctive grammatical endings.

9. Buddicom 1974, pp. 35–6.

10. See Meyer 1975; but his 'two-word verb' is misleading: phrasal verbs include some of three words, like 'get around to' ('We didn't get around to first names'), that differ in meaning from those of two words like 'get around' (transitive, 'How did you get around that rule?'; intransitive, 'Don't get around much any more'). SPE 12 (Smith, 1923) deals extensively with phrasal verbs pp. 16ff., 45ff., as 'English idioms'.

11. Quoted in SPE 65 (Craigie, 1946), p. 130.

12. Whitman's opinion appears, e.g., in *An American Primer* (posthumously published, 1904), especially pp. 23ff.

13. Camden in 1605 found 'the glory of our tongue before the *Norman*

Conquest'; Swift in 1712 wrote 'The Period wherein the *English* Tongue received most Improvement, I take to commence with the beginning of Queen *Elizabeth*'s Reign, and to conclude with the Great Rebellion in Forty Two' (quoted in Bolton 1966, pp. 27, 112).

14. See SPE 29, 'Shakespeare's English' (Gordon, 1928).

15. See SPE 5, 'The Englishing of French Words' (Matthews, 1921), p. 5.

16. The model of 'Newspeak' has been productive: Stephen Hilgartner and Rory O'Connor called their 1980 book *Nukespeak*; the British Air flight magazine refers to 'Radio-telephony-speak'; *Dial* (September 1982, p. 24) had a 'Criticspeak' column; *Softalk* has a 'Newspeak' feature (i.e., 'news' + 'speak'; cf. the title of the journal and its 'Marketalk' column); 'Valspeak' is the teen argot of California's San Fernando valley; and the *Guardian* described 'Left-Speak' as 'that curious jargon of Marxism that sounds only half-translated from the German. Everyone is "fighting" or "struggling" in this "arena," or that "forum," "confronting" the "contradiction" and the "violence" of the "system" ' (cf. CE 4.131–2).

17. Crowley 1980.

18. SPE 2 (Bridges, 1919) gives a reasoned account of this familiar phenomenon. Elsewhere he wrote 'Every language which is used as a practical means of oral communication has a constant tendency to degradation in sound' (quoted SPE 35 [Daryush, 1931], p. 508; cf. SPE 1 [1919], p. 10).

19. See SPE 14 (Bradley et al., 1923); cf. 19 (1925), pp. 40–1; 24 (1926), 135–6, on the source and spread of 'Britisher' and its congeners.

20. See SPE 19 (Foligno, 1925) for the antecedents of 'Fascist'.

21. *Guardian*, 4 Aug. 1982, p. 1. 'CBI' is an initialism for the Confederation of British Industry, previously the Federation of British Industry. The change of name, apparently a distinction without a difference, is actually a euphemism to avoid sharing the initialism 'FBI' with the (American) Federal Bureau of Investigation. Euphemism is another fruitful source of language change.

CHAPTER THREE

1. Such regularities are characteristic of language diversification: the descendants of Latin *octo* and *noct-* are Spanish *ocho* and *noche*, French *huit* and *nuit*.

2. Petyt 1980 contains a useful, up-to-date introduction to the study of dialect.

3. Although the OED s.v. 'good' lists other senses for 'to make good', the sense 'to succeed' is, according to the 1972 Supplement, 'orig. *U.S.*'; the attestations come from the DAE s.v. 'good'. For distinctive American forms and meanings as evidence that 'In their use of English speech, Americans have not abandoned the original tunes, but are playing them with variations,' see SPE 45 (Horwill, 1936), and cf. SPE 22 (anonymous, 1925), pp. 58–63.

4. American pronunciation received authoritative treatment in SPE 30 (Kurath, 1928).

5. Craigie's study of American English, summarizing for a British audience his years of research in the United States, appeared in SPE 27 (1927), 56–7 (1940). To say that the books were already published when Orwell wrote,

however, is not to say that they were available: the blitz made it difficult for him even to find a copy of his own works at times (CE 4.422), and in his last years he did much of his work on the inaccessible Scottish island of Jura.

6. See Meyers 1975, p. 35. But even if 'popular culture' or 'mass culture' is distinguished from the 'folk culture' that the eighteenth century so carefully studied, Orwell's writing was not in advance of, for example, Edmund Wilson's. See Coleman 1971.

7. Partridge specifies this word as 'American slang' (SPE 55 [1940], p. 195). Cf. Scott, SPE 24 (1926).

8. SPE 3 (Smith, 1920), praised 'new formations, coined in the ever-active mint of uneducated speech. . . . This process of dialectal regeneration . . . has been greatly aided in the past by men of letters, who have given a literary standing to the useful and picturesque vocabulary of their unlettered neighbours, and thus helped to reinforce with vivid terms our somewhat abstract and faded standard speech' (pp. 9–10). Davies 1933, repr. p. 44, particularly praised Orwell's record of tramp slang.

9. Partridge 1968, s.v. 'glimmer'.

10. Quoted by Crick 1980, p. 179, from his interview with Ruth Pitter.

11. But Crick 1980, p. 280, holds that 'The "diary" is not necessarily a more literal record . . . than the published book.'

12. Compare Orwell's substitutions of fictional names for similar-sounding real ones in his books: e.g., 'rue du Coq d'Or' for 'rue du Pot de Fer' (PL); 'Lackersteen' ('Latimer' in an earlier version) for 'Limouzin', his aunt's name (BD); 'Willowbed Road' for 'Willoughby Road' (KA).

13. Much the same points are made in SPE 63 (Craigie, 1944), especially pp. 48–54; e.g.,

> a purely phonetic alphabet may be adopted, with a single character for each sound. . . . [But] by what steps is it to be brought into general use? . . . [U]niversal acceptance of any scheme would certainly not be attained without much discussion and difference of opinion. It is difficult to see by what machinery this universal consent could be secured. . . .

14. Quoted by Crick 1980, p. 44.

15. The debate over the relative merits of 'educated' English and other sorts occupied the SPE throughout its history; e.g., no. 33 (Clark, 1929) thought the BBC variety 'mincing. . . . feeble and unimpressive' (pp. 415, 420), but no. 37 (Chapman, 1932) felt that standard English, though 'exposed . . . to dangers', 'deserves to play a large if not a dominating part in forming the English of the future' (pp. 562–3). No. 39 (anonymous, 1934), 'The Superiority of Received Standard English,' said 'the "best" English is most consistently heard at its best, I think, on the whole, . . . among Officers of the British Regular Army' (p. 614). See also SPE 2 (Bridges, 1919), pp. 44–6.

16. For cockney see Wright 1980.

17. As did SPE 1 (1919), pp. 9–10; e.g., 'We shall . . . encourage educated people, and, above all, teachers in country schools, to take a more sympathetic interest in the forms and usages of local speech. . . .'

18. Reprinted as SPE 32 (James, 1929); see now Burchfield 1982.

19. E.g., Butler 1974 (National Council of Teachers of English); Wolfram et al. 1979 (Center for Applied Linguistics).

20. Cf. CE 1.59, 194; PL 129, 185; KA 192; RW 150. Empson 1971, p. 96, recalls Orwell interviewing an Indian propagandist at the BBC 'in a leisurely but somehow exasperated manner, immensely carrying, and all the more officer-class for being souped up into his formalized Cockney. . . ' When Orwell met the Socialist John McNair, 'At first his accent repelled my Tyneside prejudices' (quoted in Crick 1980, p. 317).

21. For sociolinguistics see Trudgill 1974, and the first chapter in Gal 1979.

22. The background, testimony, and implications are summarized in Smitherman 1981; Whiteman 1980. For Black English in Britain, see Sutcliffe 1982.

23. Quoted in 'Can't Anyone', p. 36. Sledd 1972 uses 'doublespeak' both for the biloquial theory Stafford and others proposed and for the sinister 'Big Brother' control it implies.

24. Labov 1972, p. 222; as he makes clear in footnote 11, Labov is here contradicting not only popular opinion but the view of linguists like Chomsky who wrote that children acquire uniform grammar despite 'the degenerate quality and narrowly limited extent' of the language they hear.

CHAPTER FOUR

1. McGregor 1972, p. 13. On Indian English see SPE 41 (Goffin, 1934).

2. Crick 1980, p. 184.

3. Crick 1980, p. 190; cf. 255. For other discussion in Orwell's time, see SPE 34 (Daryush et al., 1930); for the Esperanto movement in particular, see Foster 1982.

4. 'Basic' is not the same as the computer language BASIC; see Chapter Six. The following paragraphs owe much to Fink 1971 for their information although not for their interpretation. See also SPE 62, 'Basic' (Young, 1943).

5. Crick 1980, p. 425; Fink 1971, p. 157.

6. SPE 64 (Craigie, 1944), p. 108, made the case for English as an international language on grammatical grounds:

> Those who maintain that English is prevented, or at least seriously hindered, from becoming the world language by the difficulties of its unphonetic spelling usually omit to mention that over against this, by way of compensation, can be set the great advantage of simplicity in its grammar.
> (Cf. CE 3.25.)

7. See Decker 1978; Kachru 1982; Mazrui 1975; Treen et al. 1982.

8. See, e.g., Taubitz 1978.

9. See Korff 1978.

10. See Brown 1980; Large 1982.

11. See Kennedy et al. 1979.

12. See Matane 1979; Smithies 1981; Todd 1984.

13. See Llamzon 1979, 1980; Bickley Nov. 1980.

14. See Thadani 1978; Weinstein 1982.

15. See Bickley May 1980.

16. Rayner Heppenstall seems to have been wrong to think that Orwell's view in late 1949 and early 1950, that Welsh and Gaelic deserved encourage-

ment and preservation, was a recent change of mind (quoted by Crick 1980, p. 578).

17. The sources are conveniently assembled in Gray et al. 1981; Parker 1978.

18. See Fishman 1978, 1981; Grosjean 1982.

19. Fishman 1981, p. 35.

20. The distinctions are discussed in Gingras 1978, pp. 89–96.

21. Sajavaara 1978.

22. Valdman 1978.

23. Valdman 1978, p. 84.

24. Schumann 1978.

25. Saville-Troike 1978.

26. That is, in speech; in writing things must work in a quite different way. See Krashen 1978.

27. Sajavaara 1978, p. 62.

CHAPTER FIVE

1. Woodcock 1946, repr. p. 241. Hoggart 1965, repr. pp. 48–9, describes his reservations about Orwell's 'emotional looseness' 'generalizations'. Cf. Hammond 1982, pp. 82–3.

2. Howe 1969, repr. p. 355.

3. Howe 1969, repr. p. 357; cf. O'Brien 1968, repr. pp. 347–8, and Wain 1963, repr. pp. 95–6.

4. Köberl 1979, p. 171.

5. Orwell had to recant his admiration for Miller's language when he came to review *The Cosmological Eye* in 1946, where he found that 'One of Miller's tricks is to be constantly using apocalyptic language,' so that 'what is outright meaningless can be given an air of mystery and profundity' (CE 4.107–8).

6. For a linguistic approach to Joyce's style, see Burgess 1973; compare SPE 36 (Abercrombie, 1936).

7. For a linguistic approach to Dickens, see Brook 1970.

8. For non-standard English in literature, see Blake 1981.

9. E.g., by Williams 1971, repr. p. 55. Crick 1980, p. 213, quotes Edouard Roditi's unpublished recollection that when with Orwell 'we stopped in Trafalgar Square and listened to people there. I can remember Orwell repeating phrases he had heard there so as to memorize them. I was with him when we first met the original of Mrs Wayne. . . .' The 1931 incident, however, somewhat recalls Higgins's Covent Garden 'field work' in Shaw's *Pygmalion* (1913).

10. Wicker 1962, p. 273.

11. For the equation of Goldstein and Big Brother with Trotsky and Stalin, especially stylistic, see Howe 1956, repr. 1982, p. 326; Rahv 1949, repr. 1982, pp. 311–12. Harrington 1982, p. 433, points out that 'though Orwell cleverly mimics Trotsky's style, the opinions here put into Goldstein's mouth are diametrically opposed to those of Trotsky'; cf. p. 436 and Crick 1980, p. 365.

12. On linguistic approaches to style, Traugott et al. 1980 is an up-to-date introduction with useful further references.

13. Milic 1967, p. 273.

14. Ringbom 1973, p. 9. Other impressions of Orwell's style are quoted in Crick 1980, pp. 353 n., 355, 411–12, 491.

15. Bailey 1979; cf. Farringdon et al. 1979. Senator Harrison Williams introduced a linguistic analysis of the 'Abscam' tapes by Professor Roger Shuy during his Senate defence in March of 1982.

16. Fyvel 1950, repr. p. 379.

17. See, e.g., Crick 1980, pp. 551, 565, 569. Though central to discussions of *Nineteen Eighty-Four*, the question is not a matter of critical consensus. Hodgart 1971, pp. 139–41, takes the book as a prediction; Harrington 1982, pp. 429–30, does not. Elliott 1957, repr. pp. 335–6, sees Orwell as a 'prophet' in the Old Testament sense. Wilson 1946, repr. p. 224, shows how fallible Orwell's other predictions were.

18. Sheldon 1979, p. 7.

19. See Brown 1976.

20. But Orwell called this passage 'abbreviated jargon – not actually New-speak, but consisting largely of Newspeak words', and in fact he did not give an extended example of Newspeak in *Nineteen Eighty-Four*, despite its thematic prominence. On cables and Newspeak see Steinhoff 1975, p. 169; on headlines and Newspeak see Fixler 1964, p. 51. On semiotics and New-speak, see Buczynska-Garewicz 1980.

21. Fink 1971.

22. Cf. Quirk 1983, pp. 209–17; SPE 31 (Wallis, 1929).

23. Beauchamp 1974, p. 466.

24. McCormick 1980, pp. 152–64; his 'Glossary of Newspeak' is on pp. 175–86.

25. Beauchamp 1974, pp. 468–9.

26. See Philmus 1973; Sheldon 1979.

27. The distinction between surface variety and underlying regularity is Noam Chomsky's. Chomsky's work has dominated much, if not quite all, work on language since 1957, and the present book is in his debt on almost every page: see Smith et al. 1979.

28. See Fletcher 1983. Orwell's adopted son, who would have given him the opportunity to observe these processes, may have been the inspiration for the date '1984'. He was born in 1944, and during an air-raid Orwell wrote 'in the next room the 1964 class wakes up and lets out a yell or two. Every time this happens I find myself thinking, "Is it possible that human beings can continue with this lunacy very much longer?" ' (CE 3.328). Winston Smith 'believed that he had been born in 1944 or 1945' (NE 10), the same year as Orwell's son, the '1964 class'; in Smith Orwell shows the outcome of 'this lunacy' forty years on; cf. BD 70.

CHAPTER SIX

1. For Orwell and technology, see Edelheit 1979.

2. For a general introduction see Sanders 1981 and the special issue on the mechanization of work, *Scientific American*, September 1982. For the progress and significance of microcomputers, see Toong et al., 1982.

3. PC, June-July 1982, p. 10. See the similar animadversions on the terminology of physics, SPE 48 (Darwin, 1937).

4. Heite et al., 1982. Kenner 1980 takes a pessimistic view of computers, the English language, and 'Machinespeak'.

5. *Popular Computing*, Feb. 1982, p. 111. For wp see Fluegelman et al. 1982. The vocabulary of word processing is itself a trifle unsettled. When the typewriter first appeared, the operators were called 'typewriters' briefly before 'typist' became standard. A 1982 radio advertisement likewise assured typists 'you can become a word processor.' But it is the machine that is usually so-called, so the operator awaits a suitable occupational title.

6. Parts of this discussion are drawn from the papers by Garvin, Satyanarayana and Yang in Papp et al. 1976; see also Large 1983.

7. A.S. Cook, *A Concordance to Beowulf* (Halle: Niemeyer, 1911); J.B. Bessinger, Jr., and P.H. Smith, Jr., *A Concordance to Beowulf* (Ithaca: Cornell University Press, 1969).

8. Howe 1982, p. [viii]. The present book was written on an IBM 5150 computer running the Information Unlimited Software 'EasyWriter' wp program, version 1.10, and Peter Norton's indexer.

9. The subject of computers incessantly raises the question of 'data'; though historically plural, and so used here, it is often construed as singular (the historical singular is 'datum'; 'bacteria', 'criteria', and 'phenomena' are parallel cases). The OED 1972 Supplement cites singular 'data' from WashingtonIrving in 1807. Pronunciations like [detə], [datə], or [da:tə] are all common; they reflect, like the singular 'data', uncertainty about the English status of the borrowed word.

10. See Ciarcia 1982.

11. *New York Times*, 5 September 1982, p. F19.

12. Waltz 1982, pp. 130, 133.

13. McKean 1982.

14. Chamberlain et al. 1981; Maloney 1982, p. 26.

15. Marcus 1982; cf. Schwartz 1982, pp. 145–6.

16. Angier 1982; Branchek 1980.

17. Schwartz 1982, p. 142.

18. Burns 1981.

19. Schwartz 1982, pp. 148–9; Wresch 1982.

20. Collins et al., 1982.

21. Quirk 1983 refers to Bacon's *Advancement of Learning* I.iv, Locke's *Essay* III.ii, and Jeremy Bentham's *Theory of Fictions* as examples of 'philosophic scepticism' about language.

22. *Newsweek*, 8 September 1975, p. 8.

CHAPTER SEVEN

1. McNelly 1977, p. 554, n. 5, lists some of the books that have anthologized 'Politics and the English Language', to which add Bolton et al. 1969.

2. Even after the 'Politics' essay Orwell frequently returned to its chief points, for example in his critique of the prose and policies of Bernal, CE 4.153–60; Laski, 4.471.

3. Quoted in Crick 1980, p. 402, and attributed by him to Orwell.

4. Wedgwood 1951, repr. p. 312.

5. 'Interlude: on Jargon', in Quiller-Couch 1916, pp. 76, 121; Fowler et al.

1906, p. 1. Quiller-Couch was a foundation member of the SPE; Fowler contributed often to the *Tracts*, and was the subject of a long memorial tract (43, 1935). Present-day language critics still frequently appeal to Fowler 1926, e.g. Simon 1980, p. 16 and passim; HL 129.

6. So did the scrupulous Bridges, SPE 3 (1920), p. 13; Taylor, SPE 51 (1939), p. 10, n., even had 'concensus [sic] of critical opinion'.

7. O'Brien 1968, repr. p. 348; Steiner 1969, repr. pp. 369–70.

8. Forster 1950, repr. p. 304; cf. Hammond 1982, pp. 217–19.

9. Quirk 1983, pp. 209–17. For the background of Orwell's ideas of literary propriety, see Müller-Tochtermann 1966.

10. The following paragraphs owe much to McNelly 1977.

11. On the assumptions see Chapter One, and Fixler 1964, pp. 46–50, 53–4; on the audience, Zwerdling 1974, p. 123.

12. On language and mind, see Forster, p. 194, and cf. 'language is the instrument of thought, and if we allow our usage of it to become imprecise as it changes and develops . . . we shall not be able to think clearly' (HL 130; cf. 135); 'Proper usage matters because writing is thought and clear writing is essential for clear thinking' (Sheppard 1980, p. 72), theories close to the one underlying Newspeak. For language and society, cf. 'the fads and the trends of the 1960s . . . have something to do with [why the standards of written and spoken English should have fallen so much]. . . . the rejection of traditional values and standards, the idolisation of the uncouth, the Marshall McLuhan cult, and the cult of "the white heat of technology" . . .' (HL 187). Edelman 1977 views the political connection from a professional stance.

13. Sheppard 1980, p. 72. Cf. SPE 55 (Partridge, 1945), p. 186: 'illiteracy is merely incorrectness of accidence, syntax, *pronunciation*' (emphasis mine).

14. Simon 1980 and, in more or less the same vein, Barnett 1962; Cottle 1976; Cross 1979; Howard 1980; Mitchell 1979; Safire 1980; Tibbetts et al. 1978; cf. Johnson 1980. Useful correctives include Baron 1982; Bolinger 1980; Daniels 1983; Drake 1979; Finegan 1980; Pattison 1982; Quinn 1980.

15. Baugh et al. 1978, pp. 291–93, includes quotations 1837–70 attacking the passive progressive as an 'outrage upon English idiom', a 'solecism' and 'an awkward neologism'.

16. 'What Happened', p. 70. For Orwell's sexism, see Patai 1982.

17. Tibbetts et al. 1978; he also praises Cross 1979. Tibbetts 1978 asks 'What Did Orwell Think about the English Language?' and fits the answer into five pages; Griffin 1960 managed fourteen.

18. The Tibbetts's acknowledge the influence of Orwell (p. xii; cf. 14). References to Orwell as a kind of tutelary saint are implicit or explicit in most such language criticism: 'George Orwell emphasized the close connection between disorder in language and disorder in society' (Bush 1972, p. 240); 'those wonderful examples of inflated diction that are cited in George Orwell's essay' (Howard 1980, p. 160); 'the surreal boobspeak of advertising'; 'corrupt, Orwellian gibberish' ('Can't Anyone', p. 34); 'a W.C. Fields newspeak' (ib., 35); 'George Orwell understood that "the smaller the area of choice [of words], the smaller the temptation to take thought" ' (ib., p. 36); 'We are, after all, only four years away from George Orwell's *1984*, with its ominous slogans and Newspeak' (Kanfer 1980, p. 90); 'Should We Genderspeak?' (title of a Simon article, pp. 33–8); HL 190.

19. Sheils 1975. Sheils (p. 60) is one of the many language critics who view *Webster's Third International Dictionary* (1961) as cause or result of language permissiveness because it did not omit, or even brand, words the critics held non-standard. The media reception to the new *Webster's* is now too far behind us to warrant review here, and in any event Sledd at al. 1962 reprints the most important documents (including Macdonald 1962) along with valuable discussion.

20. Thurber held the issue even more vital: 'precision of communication is important, more important than ever, in our era of hairtrigger balances, when a false, or misunderstood, word may create as much disaster as a sudden thoughtless act' (1961, p. 41). By his own theory that change of meaning is loss of meaning, however, only bad stars, not bad language, can create 'disaster'; the word is 'dis' + 'astro-'.

21. Poet John Ciardi, quoted in Bolinger 1980, p. 54.

22. College President Leon Botstein, quoted in 'Can't Anyone', p. 34.

23. College Entrance Examination Board 1982, p. 6. Although the 1982 Verbal Aptitude scores were down significantly from 1967, as the TSWE scores were down from 1975, both were up slightly from the year before: 'The long-term decline in SAT scores . . . has been halted by the 1982 seniors.' Optimists might credit stronger school response to the needs of poor students; pessimists will see only a temporary fluctuation of the figures. The long-term decline itself was open to many interpretations, as are the figures reviewed here; the 1982 reversal will take several years to reveal its real meaning, especially for the present and future of English. See Perera 1984.

24. *American Heritage* first appeared in 1961, apparently as the Houghton Mifflin 'prescriptive' response to the bad press accorded *Webster's* (1961); see note 19 above.

25. Pyles 1971, p. 163.

26. United States Government 1977. The order makes no reference to 'plain Spanish' or other languages.

27. Gowers's influential book was one of the first (1948, p. 4) to give Orwell's 1946 'Politics' essay popular notice and approval. Freedman 1981, though he spends much of his effort on unacknowledged repetition of McNelly 1977, Wicker 1962, Fixler 1964, and Rank 1977, adds a Marxist critique of the plain style because it 'necessarily discourages the posing of radical questions in a way at all commensurate to the complexity of social and ideological systems' (p. 336).

Bibliography

༄༅༄༅༄༅

See Also Abbreviations

Works About Orwell:

ATKINS, John. *George Orwell: A Literary Study*. London: Calder and Boyars, new ed., 1971.

AUNG, Maung Htin. 'George Orwell and Burma', in Gross 1971, pp. 20–30.

BEAUCHAMP, Gorman L. 'Future Words: Language and the Dystopian Novel', *Style*, 8 (1974), 462–76.

BROWN, Edward James. *Brave New World, 1984 and We: An Essay on Anti-Utopia*. Ann Arbor: Ardis, 1976.

BUCZYNSKA–GAREWICZ, Hanna. 'Semiotics and the Newspeak', *Semiosis*, 17–18 (1980), 91–9.

BUDDICOM, Jacintha. *Eric and Us: A Remembrance of George Orwell*. London: Frewin, 1974.

BURGESS, Anthony. *1985*. London: Hutchinson, 1978.

CHOMSKY, Noam. *American Power and the New Mandarins*. New York: Pantheon, 1967.

COLEMAN, John. 'The Critic of Popular Culture', in Gross 1971, pp. 102–110.

CRICK, Bernard. *George Orwell: A Life*. Harmondsworth: Penguin, 1980.

DAVIES, W.H. 'Confessions of a Down and Out', *New Statesman and Nation*, 18 March 1933, pp. 338–40. Repr. Meyers 1975, pp. 43–5.

EDELHEIT, Steven. *Dark Prophecies*. New York: Revisionist, 1979.

ELLIOTT, George. 'A Failed Prophet', *Hudson Review*, Spring 1957, pp. 149–54. Repr. Meyers 1975, pp. 334–40.

EMPSON, William. 'Orwell at the BBC', in Gross 1971, pp. 94–9.

FERGUSON, Alfred R. 'Newspeak, the First Edition: Tyranny and the Decay of Language', *Michigan Quarterly Review*, 14 (1975), 445–53.

FINK, Howard. 'Newspeak: The Epitome of Parody Techniques in *Nineteen Eighty-Four*', *Critical Survey*, 5 (1971), 155–63.

FIXLER, Michael. 'George Orwell and the Instrument of Language', *Iowa English Yearbook*, 9 (1946), 46–54.

FORSTER, E.M. 'George Orwell', *Listener*, 2 November 1950, p. 471. Repr. Meyers 1975, pp. 302–4.

FREEDMAN, Carl. 'Writing, Ideology and Politics: Orwell's "Politics and the English Language" and English Composition', *College English*, 43 (1981) 327–40.

Bibliography

FYVEL, T.R. 'A Writer's Life', *World Review*, N.S. 16, June 1950, pp. 7–20. Repr. Howe 1982, pp. 377–91.

GRIFFIN, C.W. 'Orwell and the English Language', *Audience*, 7 (1960), 63–76.

GROSS, Miriam, ed. *The World of George Orwell*. New York: Simon & Schuster; London: Weidenfeld and Nicolson, 1971.

HAMPSHIRE, Stuart. 'A Redoubtable Critic', *Spectator*, 8 March 1946, pp. 250–2. Repr. Meyers 1975, pp. 209–11.

HAMMOND, J.R. *A George Orwell Companion*. New York: St. Martin's, 1982.

HARRINGTON, Michael. '*Nineteen Eighty-Four* Revisited', in Howe 1982, pp. 429–39.

HODGART, Matthew. 'From *Animal Farm* to *Nineteen Eighty-Four*', in Gross 1971, pp. 136–42.

HODGE, Bob, and Roger Fowler. 'Orwellian Linguistics', in Roger Fower et al., eds. *Language and Control*. London: Routledge & Kegan Paul, 1979.

HOGGART, Richard. 'Introduction' to *The Road to Wigan Pier*. London: Heinemann, 1965. Repr. Williams 1974, pp. 34–51.

HOWE, Irving. 'George Orwell's Novels', *Nation*, 4 February 1950, pp. 110–11. Repr. Meyers 1975, pp. 158–61.

HOWE, Irving. 'Orwell: History as Nightmare', *American Scholar*, Spring 1956, pp. 193–207. Repr. *Politics and the Novel*. New York: Meridian, 1957; Hynes 1971, pp. 41–53; Howe 1982, pp. 320–32.

HOWE, Irving. 'George Orwell: "As the Bones Know" ', *Harper's*, January 1969, pp. 97–103. Repr. Meyers 1975, pp. 349–59.

HOWE, Irving, ed. *Orwell's Nineteen Eighty-Four: Text, Sources, Criticism*. New York: Harcourt Brace Jovanovich, 2nd ed., 1982.

HYNES, Samuel, ed. *Twentieth Century Interpretations of 1984*. Englewood Cliffs, New Jersey: Prentice-Hall, 1971.

JONES, D.A.N. 'Arguments against Orwell', in Gross 1971, pp. 154–63.

KÖBERL, Johann. 'Der Sprachphilosophische Hintergrund von Newspeak', *Arbeiten aus Anglistik und Amerikanistik*, 4 (1979), 171–83.

MAIRET, Philip ('P.M.'). 'George Orwell', *New English Weekly*, 14 March 1940, pp. 307–9. Repr. Meyers 1975, pp. 177–80.

McCORMICK, Donald. *Approaching 1984*. Newton Abbot: David & Charles, 1980.

MACDONALD, Dwight. 'The British Genius', *Partisan Review*, March-April 1942, pp. 166–9. Repr. Meyers 1975, pp. 191–3.

McNELLY, Cleo. 'On Not Teaching Orwell', *College English*, 38 (1977), 553–66.

MEYERS, Jeffrey, ed. *George Orwell: The Critical Heritage*. London: Routledge & Kegan Paul, 1975.

MEYERS, Jeffrey. 'George Orwell, the Honorary Proletarian', *Philological Quarterly*, 48 (1969), 526–49. Repr. Meyers 1975, pp. 373–81.

MÜLLER-TOCHTERMANN, Helmut. 'George Orwell und die Sprachpflege in England', *Muttersprache*, 71 (1961), 39–45.

O'BRIEN, Conor Cruise. 'Honest Men', *Listener*, 12 December 1968, pp. 797–8. Repr. Meyers 1975, pp. 344–8.

PATAI, Daphne. 'Gamesmanship and Androcentrism in Orwell's *1984*', PMLA, 97 (1982), 856–70.

PHILMUS, Robert M. 'The Language of Utopia', *Studies in the Literary Imagination*, 6 (1973), 61–78.

POPKIN, Henry. 'Orwell the Edwardian', *Kenyon Review*, Winter 1954, pp. 139–44. Repr. Meyers 1975, pp. 320–6.

PRYCE–JONES, David. 'Orwell's Reputation', in Gross 1971, pp. 144–52.

QUIRK, Randolph. 'Orwell and "Language Engineering" ', ELLAK *Journal*, 29(1) (1983), 209–17.

RAHV, Philip. 'The Unfuture of Utopia', *Partisan Review*, July 1949, pp. 743–9. Repr. Meyers 1975, pp. 267–73; Howe 1982, 310–16.

RANK, Hugh. 'Mr. Orwell, Mr. Schlesinger, and the Language', *College Composition and Communication*, 28 (1977), 159–65.

RINGBOM, Håkan. *George Orwell as Essayist: A Stylistic Study*. Acta Academiae Aboensis, Ser. A., Humaniora, 44.2, 1973.

ROSENFELD, Isaac. 'Decency and Death', *Partisan Review*, May 1950, pp. 514–18. Repr. Meyers 1975, pp. 169–74; Howe 1982, pp. 316–20.

SCHLESINGER, Arthur, Jr. 'Politics and the American Language', *American Scholar*, 43 (1974), 553–62.

SHELDON, Leslie E. 'Newspeak and Nadsat: The Disintegration of Language in *1984* and *A Clockwork Orange*', *Studies in Contemporary Satire*, 6 (1979), 7–13.

STANSKY, Peter, and William Abrahams. *The Unknown Orwell. Orwell: The Transformation*. New York: Knopf, 1972, 1980.

STEINER, George. 'True to Life', *New Yorker*, 29 March 1969, pp. 139–51. Repr. Meyers 1975, pp. 363–73.

STEINHOFF, William. *George Orwell and the Origins of 1984*. Ann Arbor: University of Michigan Press, 1975.

STRACHEY, John. 'England', *The Strangled Cry*. London: Bodley Head, 1962. Repr. Hynes 1971, pp. 54–61.

SYKES, Christopher. 'An Enigmatical Genius', *New Republic*, 4 December 1950, p. 30. Repr. Meyers 1975, pp. 308–9.

TIBBETTS, A.M. 'What Did Orwell Think about the English Language?', *College Composition and Communication*, 29 (1978), 162–6.

TRILLING, Lionel. 'Introduction' to *Homage to Catalonia*. New York: Harcourt Brace Jovanovich, 1952. Repr. Williams 1974, pp. 62–79; Howe 1982, pp. 343–57.

WAIN, John. 'George Orwell', *Essays on Literature and Ideas*. London: Macmillan, 1963. Repr. Williams 1974, pp. 89–102; Howe 1982, pp. 357–67.

WEDGWOOD, C.V. 'George Orwell', *Time and Tide*, 10 February 1951, p. 120. Repr. Meyers 1975, pp. 311–12.

WEINRICH, Harald. 'Warnung vor der Neusprache', *Merkur*, 28 (1974), 997–1000.

WICKER, Brian. 'An Analysis of Newspeak', *Blackfriars*, 43 (1962), 272–85.

WILLIAMS, Raymond, ed., *George Orwell: A Collection of Critical Essays*. Englewood Cliffs, New Jersey: Prentice-Hall, 1974.

WILLIAMS, Raymond. 'Observation and Imagination', *Orwell*. New York: Viking, 1971. Repr. Williams 1974, pp. 52–61.

Bibliography

WILSON, Angus. 'Orwell and the Intellectuals', *Observer*, 24 January 1954, p. 8. Repr. Meyers 1975, 318–20.

WILSON, Edmund. 'George Orwell's Cricketing Burglar', *New Yorker*, 25 May 1946, pp. 86–90. Repr. Meyers 1975, pp. 224–6.

WOODCOCK, George. 'Prose Like a Window Pane', *The Crystal Spirit: A Study of George Orwell*. Boston: Little Brown, 1966. Repr. Williams 1974, pp. 161–76.

WOODCOCK, George. 'George Orwell, 19th Century Liberal', *Politics*, December 1946, pp. 384–8. Repr. Meyers 1975, pp. 235–46.

ZWERDLING, Alex. *Orwell and the Left*. New Haven: Yale University Press, 1974.

Other Works:

AARSLEFF, Hans. *From Locke to Saussure: Essays on the Study of Language and Intellectual History*. Minneapolis: University of Minnesota Press, 1982.

AGER, D.E., et al., eds., *Advances in Computer-Aided Literary and Linguistic Research*. Birmingham: University of Aston, 1979.

ANGIER, Natalie. 'Bell's Letters', *Discover*, July 1981, pp. 78–9.

BAILEY, Richard W. 'Authorship Attribution in a Forensic Setting', in Ager et al. 1979, pp. 1–20.

BARON, Dennis E. *Grammar and Good Taste: Reforming the American Language*. New Haven: Yale University Press, 1982.

BARNETT, Lincoln. *The Treasure of Our Tongue*. New York: Knopf, 1962.

BAUGH, Albert C., and Thomas Cable. *A History of the English Language*. Englewood Cliffs, New Jersey: Prentice-Hall. 3rd ed., 1978.

BICKLEY, Verner. 'English as a Language of Mediation', *English Around the World*, 23 (November 1980), pp. 1–5.

BICKLEY, Verner. 'English Teaching in Burma', *English Around the World*, 22 (May 1980), pp. 1–3.

BLAKE, N.F. *Non-Standard Language in English Literature*. London: Deutsch, 1981.

BLUNDELL, William E. 'Confused, Overstuffed Corporate Prose Often Costs Firms Time – and Money', *Wall Street Journal*, 28 August 1980, p. 21.

BODMER, Frederick. *The Loom of Language*. New York: Norton, 1944.

BOLINGER, Dwight. *Language, the Loaded Weapon: The Use and Abuse of Language Today*. London: Longman, 1980.

BOLINGER, Dwight. 'Voice Imprints', *New York Times*, 26 July 1981, sect. 6, pp. 7–8.

BOLTON, W.F. *A Living Language: The History and Structure of English*. New York: Random House, 1982.

BOLTON, W.F., ed. *The English Language: Essays by English and American Men of Letters, 1490–1839*. Cambridge University Press, 1966.

BOLTON, W.F., and D. Crystal, eds. *The English Language: Essays by Linguists and Men of Letters, 1858–1964*. Cambridge University Press, 1969.

BRANCHEK, Robert. 'Computer Mechanisms for Man-Machine Dialogues', *Creative Computing*, July 1980, pp. 42–7.

BROOK, G.L. *A History of the English Language*. London: Deutsch, 1958.

BROOK, G.L., *The Language of Dickens*. London: Deutsch, 1970.

BROWN, Arnold L., 'Another Look at English as the Language of Science', *English Around the World*, 23 (November 1980), pp. 1–3.

BURCHFIELD, Robert. *The Spoken Word : A BBC Guide*. Oxford University Press, 1982.

BURGESS, Anthony. *A Clockwork Orange*. New York: Norton, 1963; London: Heinemann, 1962.

BURGESS, Anthony. *Joysprick: An Introduction to the Language of James Joyce*. London: Deutsch, 1973.

BURNS, Hugh. 'Computing as a Way of Brainstorming in English Composition', *Proceedings* of NECC 1981 National Educational Computing Conference. Ed. Diana Harris, 1981, pp. 105–8.

BUSH, Douglas. 'Polluting Our Language', *American Scholar*, 4 (Spring, 1972), pp. 238–47.

BUTLER, Melvin A., et al. *Students' Right to their Own Language*. Special edition of *College Composition and Communication*, Fall 1974.

'Can't Anyone Here Speak English?' *Time*, 25 August 1975, pp. 34–6.

CHAMBERLAIN, William, and Thomas Etter. 'Soft Ions', *Omni*, Dec. 1981, pp. 79–91.

CIARCIA, Steve. 'Build the Microvox Text-to-Speech Synthesizer, Part 2: Software', *Byte*, October 1982, pp. 40–64.

College Entrance Examination Board. *College-Bound Seniors, 1981, 1982*. Princeton, New Jersey: 1981, 1982.

COLLINS, Allan, et al. 'Microcomputer-Based Writing Activities for the Upper Elementary Grades', *Proceedings* of the Fourth International Congress and Exposition of the Society for Applied Learning Technology. Orlando, Florida: 1982.

Commission for Racial Equality. *Ethnic Minority Community Languages: A Statement*. London: 1982.

COTTLE, Basil. *The Plight of English*. New York: Arlington, 1976.

CROSS, Donna Woolfolk. *Word Abuse: How the Words We Use, Use Us*. New York: Coward, McCann and Geoghegan, 1979.

CROWLEY, Ellen T. *Acronyms, Initialisms, & Abbreviations Dictionary*. Detroit: 3 vols., Gale, 7th ed., 1980–2.

DANIELS, Harvey A. *Famous Last Words: The American Language Crisis Reconsidered*. Carbondale: Southern Illinois University Press, 1983.

DECKER, Donald M. 'The Importance of the English Language in Today's World', *English Around the World*, 19 (November 1978), pp. 1–7.

DENES, Peter B., and Elliott N. Pinson. *The Speech Chain: The Physics and Biology of Spoken English*. Garden City, New York: Doubleday, 1973.

DILLARD, J.L. *Black English: Its History and Usage in the United States*. New York: Random House, 1972.

DRAKE, Glendon F. *The Role of Prescriptivism in American Linguistics*. Atlantic Highlands, New Jersey: Humanities, 1979.

EDELMAN, Murray. *Political Language: Words that Succeed and Policies that Fail*. New York: Academic, 1977.

FARRINGDON, Michael, and Jill Farringdon. 'A Computer-Aided

Study of the Prose Style of Henry Fielding and its Support for his Translation of the Military History of Charles XII', in Ager et al. 1979, pp. 95–105.

FINEGAN, Edward. *Attitudes Toward English Usage*. New York: Teachers College Press, 1980.

FISHMAN, Joshua A. 'In Defense of Learning English and Maintaining Other Languages (in the United States and Elsewhere Too), *English Around the World*, 25 (November 1978), pp. 1–3.

FISHMAN, Joshua A. 'The Need for Language Planning in the United States', *Profession*, 81 (1981), 34–5.

FLETCHER, Paul, *The Child's Learning of English*. Oxford: Blackwell, 1985.

FLUEGELMAN, Andrew, and Jeremy Hewes. *Writing in the Computer Age: A Guide to Skills and Styles for Word Processing*. Garden City, New York: Doubleday, 1982.

FOSDICK, Raymond B. 'We Need New Words and New Faith', *New York Times*, 19 December 1948, sect. 6, pp. 7–35.

FOSTER, Peter G. *The Esperanto Movement*. Hague: Mouton, 1982.

FOWLER, F.G., and H.W. Fowler, *The King's English*. Oxford: Clarendon, 1906.

FOWLER, H.W. *Modern English Usage*. Oxford University Press, 1926.

GAL, Susan. *Language Shift: Social Determinants of Linguistic Change in Bilingual Austria*. New York: Academic, 1979.

GARVIN, P.L. 'Machine Translation in the Seventies', in Papp et al. 1976, pp. 445–59.

GINGRAS, Rosario C., ed. *Second-Language Acquisition & Foreign Language Teaching*. Washington, DC: Center for Applied Linguistics, 1978.

GRAY, Tracy C., et al., comp. *The Current Status of Bilingual Education Legislation: An Update*. Washington, DC: Center for Applied Linguistics, 1981.

GROSJEAN, François. *Life with Two Languages: An Introduction to Bilingualism*. Cambridge, MA: Harvard University Press, 1982.

HEITE, Ned, and Lou Heite. 'Breaking the Jargon Barrier: Designing Programs for Humanists', *Byte*, July 1982, pp. 76–104.

HOBAN, Russell. *Riddley Walker*. New York: Summit Books, 1980; London: Jonathan Cape, 1980.

HOGBEN, Lancelot. *Interglossa*. Harmondsworth: Penguin, 1943.

HOWARD, Philip. *Words Fail Me*. London: Hamish Hamilton, 1980.

HUBER, Frederic Vincent. *Apple Crunch*. New York: Seaview Books, 1981.

HUDSON, Kenneth. *The Dictionary of Diseased English*. New York: Harper & Row, 1977.

HUXLEY, Aldous. *Brave New World*. London: Chatto & Windus, 1932.

JOHNSON, Flora. 'Making the Mother Tongue Safe from Democracy', *TWA Ambassador*, June 1980, pp. 53–9.

KACHRU, Braj B. *The Other Tongue: English across Cultures*. Champaign, IL: University of Illinois Press, 1982.

KANFER, Stefan. ' '80s-Babble: Untidy Treasure', *Time*, 28 January 1980, p. 90.

KENNEDY, T.F., and N.D. Peat. 'How New Zealand Promotes English in Asia and the Pacific', *English Around the World*, 21 (November 1979), pp. 3–7.

KENNER, Hugh. 'Machinespeak', in Leonard Michaels and Christopher Ricks, eds. *The State of the Language*. Berkeley: University of California Press, 1980, pp. 467–77.

KORFF, Serge A. 'The Use of English as the Language of Science', *English Around the World*, 19 (November 1978), pp. 4–7.

KRASHEN, Stephen. 'The Monitor Model for Second-Language Acquisition', in Gingras 1978, pp. 1–26.

LABOV, William. *Language in the Inner City: Studies in the Black English Vernacular*. Philadelphia: University of Pennsylvania Press, 1972.

LADEFOGED, Peter. *A Course in Phonetics*. New York: Harcourt Brace Jovanovich, 2nd ed., 1981.

LAMBDIN, William. *Doublespeak Dictionary*. Los Angeles: Pinnacle, 1979.

LARGE, J.A. *The Foreign-Language Barrier: Problems in Scientific Communication*. London: Deutsch, 1983.

LAWLER, Justus George. 'Politics and the American Language', *College English*, 35 (1974), 750–5.

LEPSCHY, G.C. *A Survey of Structural Linguistics*. London: Deutsch, new ed., 1982.

LLAMZON, Teodoro. 'English in Malaysia, Singapore and the Philippines', *English Around the World*, 21 (November 1979), pp. 4–6; 22 (May 1980), pp. 1–7.

MACDONALD, Dwight. 'The String Untuned', *New Yorker*, 10 March 1962, pp. 130–60. Repr. Sledd et al. 1962, pp. 166–88.

McGREGOR, Ronald Stuart. *Outline of Hindi Grammar*. Oxford: Clarendon, 1972.

McKEAN, Kevin. 'Computers, Fiction, and Poetry', *Byte*, July 1982, pp. 50–3.

MAGER, N.H., and S.K. Mager. *The Morrow Book of New Words*. New York: Quill, 1982.

MALONEY, Eric. 'Professors Take Plunge', *Microcomputing*, March 1982, pp. 24–6.

MARCUS, Stephen. 'Compupoem: A Computer-Assisted Writing Activity', *English Journal*, February 1982, pp. 96–9.

MATANE, Paulias. 'English as a Tool for Development in Papua New Guinea', *English Around the World*, 21 (November 1979), pp. 3–7.

MAZRUI, Ali A. *The Political Sociology of the English Language: An African Perspective*. Hague: Mouton, 1975.

The Mechanization of Work. Special edition of *Scientific American*, September 1982.

MENCKEN, H.L. *The American Language*. New York: Knopf, 4th ed., 1936; supplements 1945, 1948.

MEYER, George A. *The Two-Word Verb: A Dictionary of the Verb-Preposition Phrases in American English*. Hague: Mouton, 1975.

MIDDLETON, Thomas H. 'Language and Survival', *Saturday Review/World*, 10 August 1974, p. 110.

MILIC, Louis Tonko. *A Quantitative Approach to the Style of Jonathan Swift*. Hague: Mouton, 1967.

MITCHELL, Richard. *Less Than Words Can Say*. Boston: Little, Brown, 1979.

Bibliography

OGDEN, C.K. *Basic English*. London: K. Paul, Trench, Trubner, 1930.

OGDEN, C.K. *Basic English versus the Artificial Languages*. London: K. Paul, Trench, Trubner, 1935.

PALMER, F.R. *Semantics: A New Outline*. Cambridge University Press, 2nd ed., 1981.

PAPP, Ferenc, and György Szépe, eds. *Papers in Computational Linguistics*. The Hague: Mouton, 1976.

PARKER, L. Leann. 'Current Perspectives', *Bilingual Education: Current Perspectives*. Vol 5: Synthesis. Arlington, Virginia: Center for Applied Linguistics, 1978, pp. 1–62.

PARTRIDGE, Eric. *A Dictionary of Slang and Unconventional English*. London: Routledge and Kegan Paul, 7th ed., 1970.

PARTRIDGE, Eric. *A Dictionary of the Underworld, British and American*. London: Routledge and Kegan Paul, 3rd ed., 1968.

PATTISON, Robert. *On Literacy: The Politics of the Word from Homer to the Age of Rock*. New York: Oxford, 1982.

PERERA, Katherine. *Written Language in the Classroom*. Oxford: Blackwell, in association with Deutsch, 1984.

PETYT, K.M. *The Study of Dialect: An Introduction to Dialectology*. London: Deutsch, 1980.

PYLES, Thomas. *The Origins and Development of the English Language*. New York: Harcourt Brace Jovanovich, 2nd ed., 1971.

QUILLER–COUCH, Arthur. *On the Art of Writing*. Cambridge University Press, 1916.

QUINN, Jim. *American Tongue and Cheek: A Populist Guide to Our Language*. New York: Pantheon, 1980.

RAWSON, Hugh. *A Dictionary of Euphemisms & Other Doubletalk*. New York: Crown, 1982.

SAFIRE, William. *On Language*. New York: Times Books, 1980.
'Ay, There's The Rub', *New York Times*, 30 January 1983, sect. 6, pp. 8–9.

SAJAVAARA, Kari. 'The Monitor Model & Monitoring in Foreign Language Speech Communication', in Gingras 1978, pp. 51–67.

SANDERS, Donald H. *Computers in Society*. New York: McGraw-Hill, 3rd ed., 1981.

SATYANARAYANA, P. 'A Semantics-Oriented Syntax Analyzer of Natural English', in Papp et al. 1976, pp. 245–57.

SAUSSURE, Ferdinand de. *Course in General Linguistics*. New York: Philosophical Library, 1959.

SAVILLE–TROIKE, Muriel. 'Implications of Research on Adult Second-Language Acquisition for Teaching Foreign Languages to Children', in Gingras 1978, pp. 68–77.

SCHUMANN, John H. 'The Acculturation Model for Second-Language Acquisition.', in Gingras 1978, pp. 27–50.

SCHWARTZ, Helen J. 'Monsters and Mentors: Computer Applications for Humanistic Education', *College English*, 44 (1982), 141–52.

SHEILS, Merrill. 'Why Johnny Can't Write', *Newsweek*, 8 December 1975, pp. 58–65.

SHEPPARD, R.Z., et al. 'The Decline of Editing', *Time*, 1 September 1980, pp. 70–2.

SIMON, John. *Paradigms Lost: Reflections on Literacy and Its Decline*. New York: C.N. Potter, 1980.

SLEDD, James. 'Doublespeak: Dialectology in the Service of Big Brother', *College English*, 33 (1972), 439–56.

SLEDD, James, and Wilma R. Ebbitt, eds. *Dictionaries and That Dictionary*. Chicago: Scott, Foresman, 1962.

SLOBIN, Dan. *Psycholinguistics*. Glenview, Illinois: Scott, Foresman, 2nd ed., 1979.

SMITH, Neil, and Deirdre Wilson. *Modern Linguistics: The Results of Chomsky's Revolution*. Bloomington: Indiana University Press, 1980.

SMITHERMAN, Geneva, ed. *Black English and the Education of Black Children and Youth*. Detroit, Michigan: Center for Black Studies, Wayne State University, 1981.

SMITHIES, Michael. 'English as a University Language: The Case of the Papua New Guinea University of Technology', *English Around the World*, 25 (November 1981), pp. 6–8.

STARNES, De Witt T., and Gertrude Noyes. *The Dictionary from Cawdrey to Johnson, 1604–1755*. Chapel Hill: University of North Carolina Press, 1946.

STEINBERG, Danny D. *Psycholinguistics*. London: Longman, 1982.

SUTCLIFFE, David. *British Black English*. Oxford: Blackwell, 1982.

TAUBITZ, Ronald. 'English Teaching in Spain', *English Around the World*, 19 (November 1978), p. 5.

THADANI, Jaya. 'The Role of English in India', *English Around the World*, 18 (May 1978), pp. 1–8.

THURBER, James. *Alarms and Diversions*. New York: Harper, 1957.

THURBER, James. *Lances and Lanterns*. New York: Harper, 1961.

TIBBETTS, Arn, and Charlene Tibbetts. *What's Happening to American English?* New York: Scribner's, 1978.

TODD, Loreto. *Modern Englishes: Pidgins and Creoles*. Oxford: Blackwell, in association with Deutsch, 1984.

TOONG, Hoo-Min D., and Amar Gupta. 'Personal Computers', *Scientific American*, December 1982, pp. 86–107.

TRAUGOTT, Elizabeth Closs, and Mary Louise Pratt. *Linguistics for Students of Literature*. New York: Harcourt Brace Jovanovich, 1980.

TREEN, Joseph, et al. 'English, English Everywhere', *Newsweek*, 15 November 1982, pp. 98–103.

TRUDGILL, Peter. *Sociolinguistics*. Harmondsworth: Penguin, 1974.

United States Government, Executive Order 12044 (18 November 1977). *Federal Register* 1978, pp. 12661–5.

VALDMAN, Albert. 'Implications of Current Research on Second-Language Acquisition for the Teaching of Foreign Languages in the United States', in Gingras 1978, pp. 78–87.

WALTZ, David L. 'Artificial Intelligence', *Scientific American*, October 1982, pp. 118–33.

WEINSTEIN, Brian. *The Civic Tongue: Political Consequences of Language Choices*. London: Longman, 1982.

WELLS, H.G. *The Shape of Things to Come*. London: Hutchinson, 1933.

'What Happened to the Good Guys? Or, Desexing the Language', *The*

Bibliography

Personnel Administrator, December 1979, pp. 68–76.

WHITEMAN, Marcia Farr. *Reactions to Ann Arbor: Vernacular Black English and Education*. Arlington, Virginia: Center for Applied Linguistics, 1980.

WHITMAN, Walt. *American Primer*. Boston: Small, Maynard, 1904.

WOLFRAM, Walt, and Donna Christian. *Dialogue on Dialects*. Arlington, Virginia: Center for Applied Linguistics, 1979.

WOLFRAM, Walt, and Robert Johnson. *Phonological Analysis: Focus on American English*. Washington, DC: Center for Applied Linguistics, 1982.

WRESCH, William. 'Computers in English Class: Finally beyond Grammar and Spelling Drills', *College English*, 44 (1982), 483–90.

WRIGHT, Peter. *Cockney Dialect and Slang*. London: Batsford, 1980.

YANG, S.C. 'Interactive Language Learning through a Private Computer Tutor', in Papp et al. 1976, pp. 565–81.

ZAMIATIN, E.I. *We*. New York: E.P. Dutton, 1925.

Subject and Name Index

Index